The Foreign Policy
of North Korea

PRAEGER SPECIAL STUDIES IN
INTERNATIONAL POLITICS AND PUBLIC AFFAIRS

The Foreign Policy of North Korea

Byung Chul Koh

FREDERICK A. PRAEGER, Publishers
New York · Washington · London

The purpose of the Praeger Special Studies is to make specialized re-search monographs in U.S. and international economics and politics available to the academic, business, and government communities. For further information, write to the Special Projects Division, Frederick A. Praeger, Publishers, 111 Fourth Avenue, New York, N.Y. 10003.

FREDERICK A. PRAEGER, PUBLISHERS
111 Fourth Avenue, New York, N.Y. 10003, U.S.A.
5, Cromwell Place, London S.W.7, England

Published in the United States of America in 1969
by Frederick A. Praeger, Inc., Publishers

Library of Congress Catalog Card Number: 68-55009

Printed in the United States of America

To Hae Chung

PREFACE

Twice in its two decades of existence, the tiny Asian Communist nation of North Korea has catapulted itself into the center of the world stage, precipitating grave international crises and raising the specter of an all-out East-West showdown. If its first confrontation with American power in the costly Korean War of 1950-53 was a grossly miscalculated venture inspired and directed by Moscow, its second challenge to Washington, embodied in the forcible seizure of the U.S.S. Pueblo with eighty-three men aboard in the Wŏnsan Bay on January 23, 1968, probably originated solely in P'yŏngyang. Not only did the Pueblo incident dramatically underline the extent to which the North Korean regime had changed, but it also raised a host of puzzling questions regarding P'yŏngyang's strategic aims and tactical considerations.

It was precisely to examine the evolving nature of the P'yŏngyang regime and its patterns of response to the stimuli of world politics that this study was begun in the summer of 1965--long before the Pueblo incident. For three consecutive summers, I leafed through most of the huge North Korean collection in the Library of Congress in Washington, D.C. As the following pages show, I relied most heavily, perhaps too heavily, on the North Korean party newspaper, Nodong Sinmum. I am under no illusion that the picture of North Korea's external behavior and internal dynamics sketched here resembles the reality. At best, it is a patchwork of hunches and educated guesses. At worst, it is an idle exercise in the as yet underdeveloped art of North Korea-watching.

Although I approached my task with an open mind, viewing North Korea in as detached and clinical a manner as was humanly possible, the study is not completely objective. I am painfully aware that my own values and biases may have unwittingly crept in, thus slanting my narrative and coloring

my analysis. I feel, therefore, constrained to
articulate at least a part of my normative predilec-
tions at the outset. Of primary relevance is a
wholehearted commitment to the values of human
dignity. I am persuaded that the ideal political
system, be it national or global in scope, is one
in which man's free choice and opportunity to pursue
happiness with a minimum of external constraints
are maximized. To the extent that democratic
political systems and their variants approximate
this goal, they enjoy a preferred position on my
scale of values. To the extent that Communist
political systems diverge from this goal, they
generate little enthusiasm in me. Cynicism toward
much of North Korea's domestic and international
behavior over the past twenty years, then, does
not necessarily imply endorsement of the direction
in which the successive regimes in South Korea have
moved during the same period. I believe, however,
that the Government of the Republic of Korea, notwithstanding its disturbingly numerous failings and
shortcomings, offers the best hope there is for a
brighter Korea--a Korea which is genuinely free,
democratic, independent, and unified.

The modest outcome of this study belies the
extent of my intellectual debt to a number of
singularly competent persons. Key P. Yang and
Young Hyun Yoo, Korean reference librarians at the
Library of Congress, not only guided me through
the maze of North Korean publications there for three
long summers but also went far beyond the call of
duty by sharing with me their expert knowledge of
North Korea. By calling my attention to Kim
Il-sŏng's obsession with Korean national pride,
epitomized in North Korea's national slogan chuch'e
("autonomy" or "self-identity"), Mr. Yang has
significantly increased my insight into North
Korean behavior. From Mr. Yoo I have learned the
usage of the McCune-Reischauer system of romanizing
Korean--an indispensable tool of every student of
Korea in the United States. Professor Dae-Sook Suh
of the University of Houston and Professor Chong-Sik
Lee of the University of Pennsylvania, both pioneers
in the study of Korean Communism, were kind enough
to read the first draft of the study and to offer
valuable criticisms. Although their incisive
counsel was far from heeded, it nevertheless sharp-
ened my awareness of the limitations of this study,
appreciably influencing the reorganization and
revision of the present draft.

Although my debt to numerous other scholars
is documented in the footnotes and bibliography, I
wish to single out three more persons whose works
have proved to be of particular value. Professor
Jan F. Triska of Stanford University contributed
the basic analytical framework of the study. Professor Triska's conceptual scheme for analysis of
Soviet foreign policy, although not rigorously
followed, has guided my quest for the sources of
North Korean conduct. Professor Glenn D. Paige of
the University of Hawaii and Professor Soon Sung
Cho of the University of Nebraska provided pene-
trating analyses of the enigmatic North Korean
regime. I am also grateful to the Graduate College
of the University of Illinois for a Faculty Research
Fellowship, which sponsored a sojourn in Washington
in the summer of 1966.

Finally, I would like to express my heartfelt
thanks to my wife, Hae Chung, to whom this work is
affectionately dedicated. She not only gracefully
put up with a husband glued to his typewriter
throughout their first year of married life but
valiantly spurred him on. Whatever merit this study
may possess is due to the previously mentioned persons and all other scholars whose works have been
drawn upon. For errors of fact and judgment, however, I alone bear responsibility.

CONTENTS

LIST OF ABBREVIATIONS

CCP	Chinese Communist Party
CPSU	Communist Party of the Soviet Union
D.P.R.K.	Democratic People's Republic of Korea (North Korea)
JCP	Japanese Communist Party
KCNA	Korean Central New Agency
KWP	Korean Workers Party (North Korean Communist Party)
NKWP	North Korean Workers Party
P.R.C.	People's Republic of China (Communist China)
NLF	National Liberation Front (South Korea)
R.O.K.	Republic of Korea (South Korea)
SKWP	South Korean Workers Party
UNCURK	United Nations Commission on the Unification and Rehabilitation of Korea
UNKRA	United Nations Korean Reconstruction Agency

LIST OF CHARTS

INTRODUCTION

With the growing fragmentation of the Communist world, analysis of the behavior patterns of
individual Communist nations has taken on added
significance. Such analysis is useful not only
for the light it may throw on the nature and dynamics of divergent Communist political systems, but
also for elucidating the dynamic interplay of the
two powerful ideological currents of the contemporary world--Communism and nationalism.

Once the focal point of the East-West conflict
and still a potential tinderbox of a major international conflagration, North Korea stands today as
a striking example of the metamorphosis of international Communist politics. Created as an apparent
Soviet satellite, the P'yŏngyang regime has grown,
in the space of two decades, sufficiently independent-minded to defy both Moscow and Peking. Its
domestic and international behavior vividly exem-
plifies the blending of Marxist-Leninist ideology
and modernizing nationalism.[1]

This book is a modest attempt to describe,
analyze, and interpret North Korea's foreign policy
over the past two decades. Foreign policy is
viewed in this study as "the complex and dynamic
political course that a nation follows in relation
to other states."[2] Although it has not been rigorously followed, an analytical scheme developed
by Jan F. Triska provides a basic frame of reference
for the study. Originally formulated for the
analysis of Soviet foreign policy, the scheme
postulates that a foreign policy consists of five
component parts: (1) ideology, (2) strategy, (3)
operational direction, (4) tactics, and (5) propaganda. In the words of Jan F. Triska:

> Ideology is the essence of the
> matter, the eschatological key
> to the past, present, and future;
> it is the rigid frame of reference

and basis for action and a permanent component. It stands
uncompromisingly for revolutionary
conquest....

   Strategy concerns the
direction of Soviet security,
the sine qua non of world conquest; it attempts to achieve
the greatest possible results
in the foreseeable future under
foreseeable circumstances. It
is subordinate to ideology, by
which it is guided. Although a
long-range concept, it does
change with the passage of time
from one stage to another....

   Operational direction is
subordinate to strategy and concerns the direction and unification of tactical episodes. It
is more flexible than strategy,
but less so than tactics. Its
range of duration is shorter than
strategy: it changes with new
clusters of tactics, which it
funnels along the lines established by strategy....

   Tactics are individual
episodes of Soviet foreign
policy in different parts of
the world; they consist of
choices of particular actions
or responses best fitted to
existing exigencies. Tactics
are subordinate to operational
direction and to goals determined
by strategy; tactics require
initiative and discipline. A
tactical victory which endangers
ideology is viewed entirely as
temporary and meaningless in the
long run. It may be necessitated
by propaganda considerations,
expedience, etc....

> Propaganda serves as a tool
> of these four components of policy.
> It may have content as well, how-
> ever, especially when tactics are
> being utilized primarily for prop-
> aganda purposes.... Propaganda
> plays a prominent part in the execu-
> tion of Soviet foreign policy. It
> often contradicts ideology and
> strategy and supports tactics. It
> is an economical, convenient, and
> expedient instrument for both
> ideology and strategy.[3]

It is further recognized that a foreign policy
is in a state of continuous and dynamic interaction
with a multitude of factors, internal and external,
material and nonmaterial. They include geography,
natural resources, industrial capacity, cultural
patterns, political institutions, military preparedness, historical traditions, and human elements.
Ideology is both a component part and an influencing factor of foreign policy.[4]

The practical utility of the preceding analytical considerations, however, is drastically reduced
by the closed nature of the North Korean regime,
with the consequent inaccessibility of reliable
data. Decision-making in P'yŏngyang is surrounded
by such an impenetrable wall of secrecy that it is
impossible to ascertain what decisions have been
made, let alone how and why they have been made.
The major sources of information concerning North
Korea are its newspapers, ideological journals,
Party documents, and government publications, all
of which, as is well known, are thoroughly manipulated by its ruling elites to maximize their
internal and external propaganda effects. If carefully scrutinized, however, the above sources may
yield some insights into the problems, processes,
and behavior patterns of the North Korean regime.
Supplemented by the growing body of secondary
analyses of North Korea in the Korean, Japanese,
and English languages, furthermore, they enable
an alert observer to speculate on P'yŏngyang's
probable aims and motivations in undertaking a
given course of action.

The approach taken here, then, is a combination of a historical narrative and an interpretative analysis. The primary aim of the study is to delineate North Korea's over-all posture in the world arena on the basis of its verbal and physical responses to the shifting currents of international politics. Secondarily, an effort is made to identify and assay the complex, interacting forces that underlie the surface manifestations of North Korea's foreign policy. If the book has a thesis, it is that North Korea's foreign policy, underpinned by the ideologies of Marxism-Leninism and nationalism alike, has vigorously pursued the strategic objectives of modernizing North Korea and Communizing South Korea. Its operational directions and tactics have been carefully tailored to promote these national objectives. Its fluctuating behavior in intrabloc politics, psychological and guerrilla campaigns against South Korea, and multifaceted relations with the rest of the world become more clearly intelligible in terms of their intended and actual impact on its overriding national goals.

The book begins by delineating the internal setting of North Korea's foreign policy--that is, its political and economic evolution over the past two decades. It then examines P'yŏngyang's delicate position in the ever-widening rift between Moscow and Peking. P'yŏngyang's initially ambivalent posture, subsequent ideological alliance with Communist China, and recent rapprochement with the Soviet Union are described and analyzed. Next, North Korea's reunification policy is probed. The manifest and latent goals of its tactical maneuvers are scrutinized, and their effectiveness is assayed. The book then focuses on P'yŏngyang's expanding relations with the Third World, examining its vigorous campaign to win friends, allies, and trading partners in Asia, Africa, and Latin America. Particular attention is paid to its relations with North Vietnam and Japan. Then follows a brief discussion of P'yŏngyang's attitude toward and relations with the Western nations. Finally, a composite picture of North Korea's foreign policy is drawn, and its implications are explored.

NOTES TO INTRODUCTION

1. On the meaning and significance of "modernizing nationalism," see Paul E. Sigmund, Jr. (ed.), The Ideologies of the Developing Nations (New York: Frederick A. Praeger, 1963), pp. 3-40.

2. Feliks Gross, Foreign Policy Analysis (New York: Philosophical Library, 1954), pp. 54-55.

3. Jan F. Triska, "A Model for Study of Soviet Foreign Policy," American Political Science Review, LII (March, 1958), pp. 64-83. The quoted portion is from pp. 67-69. Reproduced with the permission of the author and the American Political Science Association.

4. See Gross, op. cit., pp. 48-49; Kenneth W. Thompson and Roy C. Macridis, "The Comparative Study of Foreign Policy," in Roy C. Macridis (ed.), Foreign Policy in World Politics (2d ed.; Englewood Cliffs, N.J.: Prentice-Hall, Inc., 1962), pp. 1-28; Richard C. Snyder and Glenn D. Paige, "The United States Decision to Resist Aggression in Korea: The Application of an Analytical Scheme," Administrative Science Quarterly, III (1958), pp. 342-78.

The Foreign Policy
of North Korea

CHAPTER **1** THE INTERNAL SETTING
OF NORTH KOREA'S
FOREIGN POLICY

This chapter sketches in broad strokes the
political and economic characteristics of North
Korea. It traces the process through which Kim
Il-sŏng has consolidated his political power,
appraises P'yŏngyang's economic growth, and
describes the nature of North Korea's party and
governmental apparatus.

The Democratic People's Republic of Korea
(D.P.R.K.) made its debut on the world scene on
September 9, 1948, trailing the birth of the
Republic of Korea (R.O.K.), its southern rival,
by more than three weeks. Although the occasion
was celebrated as marking the establishment of a
new regime, its real significance was that it lent
the aura of legitimacy to an already functioning
political apparatus. All the available evidence
indicates that the apparatus was, if not a creature
of the Soviet occupation authorities, closely controlled by the Soviet Union.[1] It may even be
asserted that the Soviets succeeded in installing
in the northern half of the Korean peninsula a
political regime thoroughly subservient to their
dictates and interests--that is, a satellite. The
unqualified success with which the Soviets accomplished their goal in North Korea is due not so
much to Soviet ingenuity as to fortuitous circumstances.*

---

*The Soviet success was relatively short-lived,
as subsequent events were to show. Yet the
initial Soviet objective of creating a Soviet-
oriented regime in North Korea was amply realized.
More on this later.

1

When the Russian troops marched into P'yŏngyang in late August, 1945, they found the most ideal situation imaginable for the implementation of their scheme of forming a satellite. Not only did North Korea lack indigenous political groupings of any significant strength,* it was also devoid of any cultural or religious tradition strong enough to act as a rallying point for the elated but confused Korean people. Further, the Koreans readily accepted the Soviet claim to the decisive role in the "liberation" of North Korea from the yoke of Japanese colonial rule.[2]

Posing as benevolent liberators of the Korean people and facing little or no indigenous opposition, the Soviets proceeded to carry out their blueprint for the Sovietization of North Korea. Unlike the American occupation authorities in South Korea, who experimented with military government, they eschewed direct overt involvement in the management of North Korean affairs from the very beginning. Instead, they chose to establish an ostensibly autonomous political apparatus consisting solely of Koreans and to pull the strings from behind the scenes. Such an indirect form of control was facilitated, if not prompted, by the availability of a legion of Koreans owing primary loyalty to the Soviet Union. These were the so-called Soviet-Koreans, who had either migrated to or been born in Korean colonies in the Soviet Far East.[3] The Soviet-Koreans, presumably instructed by Moscow to retain both their Soviet citizenship and membership in the Communist Party of the Soviet Union (CPSU), filled an estimated 200 critical positions in the North Korean political machinery. Practically all major government agencies counted at least one Soviet-Korean, who, although not necessarily occupying the top position, was nonetheless unsurpassed in terms of actual power. Key party posts and other nongovernmental positions of power were similarly held by Soviet-Koreans.[4]

To underline the crucial role played by the Soviet-Koreans in the formative stage of the North Korean regime, however, is not to imply that they

---

*This, of course, is not to imply that there were no political groupings whatever. The point is that none of them was strong enough to pose any serious barriers to the Soviet scheme.

monopolized political power. Two points need to
be stressed. First, strictly speaking, the Soviet-
Koreans enjoyed the form but not the substance of
power. For, although they were accorded substantial
prerogatives as well as some leeway in decision-
making, they were under close control and surveil-
lance of the Soviet Union. They were but the last
link in the Soviet chain of command in North Korean
operations, which included the Kremlin, the Soviet
Mission in P'yŏngyang, and Soviet advisers attached
to North Korean government ministries.[5] Second,
there were other Korean groups of varying political
strength in North Korea, of which at least four
may be identified. First of all, there were those
presumed returnees from the Soviet Union whose
ties to that country were considerably weaker than
the Soviet-Koreans. Most of them had engaged in
anti-Japanese guerrilla activities in Manchuria
but had apparently spent the last few years of
World War II in the Soviet Union. This group was
led by Kim Il-sŏng, a thirty-three-year-old former
partisan leader and the Kremlin's apparent choice
for North Korean leadership. Although Kim reportedly
wore a Red Army uniform with the rank of major upon
his arrival in North Korea with Soviet troops,[6]
there is no documentary evidence to verify his
alleged service in the Russian Army.[7] This group,
labeled the "partisan group" by Dae-Sook Suh,
eventually rose to the pinnacle of political power
in North Korea.[8]

    Next, returnees from China made up the so-called
Yenan faction, Koreans who had been active in the
anti-Japanese struggle on the side of the Chinese
Communists. They included such prominent leaders
as Kim Tu-bong, Ch'oe Ch'ang-ik, and Mu Chŏng. This
group had the unique advantage of being both politically organized and militarily trained--an advantage
which, as it turned out, they were unable to exploit
fully. Politically, they belonged to the North
China Korean Independence League (Hwapuk Chosŏn
Tongnip Tongmaeng), an organization formed in main-
land China in 1942.[9] Militarily, the Yenan group
boasted of a well-trained and battle-tested army
known as the Korean Volunteer Corps (Chosŏn Ŭiyongdae).
Led by Mu Chŏng, the Korean military unit had established a reputation for bravery and efficiency in
northern China.[10]

Still another group vying for power in post-Liberation North Korea was the domestic Communist faction. The ruthlessly efficient suppression by the Japanese police notwithstanding, Communism continued its clandestine existence in Korea, and when the Liberation came it promptly entered Korea's chaotic political arena. Full of hopes for a legitimate and, hopefully, a leading role in the political life of an independent Korea, the Korean Communists set about the task of organizing themselves. When the Korean Communist Party was formally re-established on September 12, 1945, Pak Hŏn-yŏng, a veteran of the Korean Communist movement, was elected Chairman of the Party. The center of the domestic Communist faction's political activity was in Seoul, but there were some veteran Communists with primarily domestic roots in North Korea as well. They included O Ki-sŏp, Chŏng Tal-hŏn, Yi Pong-su, Chu Yŏng-ha, Yi Chu-ha, Kim Yŏng-bŏm, Pak Chŏng-ae, and Hyŏn Chun-hyŏk.[11]

Finally, there were Korean nationalists with no Communist ties or sympathies. According to Chong-Sik Lee, this "non-Communist nationalist group" was potentially the most powerful group in North Korea at the time of the arrival of Russian troops. This, Lee reasons, is indicated by two related facts: Not only did the Japanese governor of the province of South P'yŏngan (P'yŏngan Namdo) transfer his authority to the leader of the group, Cho Man-sik, but the Soviet military authorities subsequently ratified the Japanese decision by appointing Cho as the chief of the Provisional Political Committee and later of the Five Provinces Administration Bureau.[12] An important factor in the distribution of political influence, both potential and actual, in North Korea in this period was the concentration of most prominent "old Communists" in the American-occupied South Korea where there was little chance of successful Communist take-over. As Dae-Sook Suh points out, this enabled relatively obscure Communists to rise to positions of prominence in the North. Cho's influence was no doubt related as much to the absence of any nationally known Communists in the North as to his own fame and popularity.[13]

If the Soviet plan of creating a satellite, or at least a Moscow-oriented regime, in North Korea was to succeed, it was imperative that all rival

groups to the Soviet faction (including Kim Il-sŏng's
"partisan group") be either eliminated or neutralized. Although there is no conclusive proof regarding the extent of Soviet control, it can be surmised
that Kim Il-sŏng could not have carried out his
purge of political rivals without the blessing and
support of the Russian occupation authorities.

The most striking element in Kim's path to
power is the mystery surrounding his true origins.
The official biographies which have long become
required reading in North Korean schools and factories proudly depict him as the "father of the
Korean revolution." Born on April 15, 1912, in
what is now P'yŏngyang, Kim grew up "personally
experiencing the misfortune of his fatherland and
the sufferings of his people," these sources claim.
Both of his parents were of poor peasant origin,
they add. His father, Kim Hyŏng-jik, was a fervent
patriot who died in 1926 of "revolutionary struggles
and the torture and imprisonment by the Japanese
police." He allegedly left a will in which he
urged his son to carry on the torch of revolutionary
struggle. Kim's mother is said to have died in
1932. Imbued with revolutionary spirit and Marxism-
Leninism, Kim went to Manchuria at the age of fourteen. While attending a middle school in Kirin,
Kim joined the Young Communist League.[14]

It was during this period that Kim "studiously
absorbed" the principles of Marxism-Leninism and
pondered their relevance for the task of Korean
liberation. He was arrested by the "reactionary
military cliques of China" and was in jail from
1927 to 1928.* Graduating from middle school in
1929, Kim continued to be active in the Communist
Youth League, serving as a secretary for its Special
District of Eastern Manchuria. In 1931, he joined
the Korean Communist Party, formed in 1925. He
also organized anti-Japanese partisan forces,
rallying under his leadership progressive factory
workers, peasants, and students. Because of his
exceptional leadership abilities, Kim began to be
called "General Kim Il-sŏng" by the "entire Korean
people," who took "enormous national pride" in his

---

*The two sources cited above do not agree on the
 date of Kim's alleged imprisonment. According to
 Yun, Kim was arrested and imprisoned in 1929,
 being freed the following year.

heroic campaigns against the Japanese. The North Korean sources lay special emphasis on Kim's intimate links with the masses. In 1934, Kim merged all Korean guerrilla forces operating in Manchuria into the Korean People's Revolutionary Army. The following year, Kim organized the Fatherland Restoration Society (Choguk Kwangbok Hoe) and was elected its president. The society, whose charter fully embraced the principles of Marxism-Leninism, consisted of some 200,000 toiling masses. Among Kim's notable accomplishments was the Battle of Poch'ŏnbo in June, 1937, in which Kim led a unit of the Korean People's Revolutionary Army across the Yalu River to deal a mighty blow to the Japanese imperialists. The battle was waged in close cooperation with Kim's followers in Kapsan, a Korean town near the Manchurian border. Kim is alleged to have continued his anti-Japanese guerrilla activities until the Japanese were defeated by the Russian Army in August, 1945.

The foregoing version of Kim's "revolutionary struggle" bears the obvious marks of fabrication. The least credible part of the Kim Il-sŏng legend is the allegation that Kim became a "general" at the age of nineteen. Although the true origins of the North Korean dictator remain to be uncovered, considerable light has been thrown on his probable past by Dae-Sook Suh's painstakingly meticulous study of the Korean Communist movement. Relying mainly on Japanese intelligence reports, Suh has persuasively demonstrated that Kim Il-sŏng did have "a revolutionary past, not as splendid as he claims and perhaps not devoted solely to the spread of communism in Korea or to the independence of Korea, but still a revolutionary record of some repute, of which any man thirty-three years old could be proud."[15]

According to Suh, there were many Korean revolutionaries, Communist and nationalist alike, who assumed the name of Kim Il-sŏng, of whom the present North Korean Premier was but one.[16] He was probably born Kim Sŏng-ju, the oldest of three sons of a poor peasant. Suh points out that Kim received most of his academic training in Chinese schools, apparently by choice. The claim that Kim began to organize revolutionary and Communist activities in school days is not borne out by the available evidence. Kim allegedly joined the Communist Party in October,

1931, but there was no Korean Communist Party at
that time in Manchuria, Suh reveals. Kim probably
joined the Chinese Communist Party (CCP). However,
Kim did participate in an attempt to organize a
Communist youth group and was imprisoned by the
Japanese for a brief period. Despite Kim's claim
that he began his guerrilla fighting against the
Japanese in late 1931, the earliest record of his
military activities in Japanese intelligence files
is in early 1935.

His association, however, was not with any
Korean groups but with a Chinese military group
known as Tung-pei K'ang-Jih Lien-chun /Northeast
Anti-Japanese United Army (NEAJUA)7. NEAJUA was
controlled by the Chinese Communists. When it
expanded and was reorganized in 1936, Kim Il-sŏng
was named the Sixth Division Commander of the First
Route Army. He apparently scored some significant
victories against the Japanese, for they made a
determined effort to curb his activities. The
Battle of Poch-ŏnbo, in which Kim allegedly scored
a major victory against the Japanese, did actually
take place, according to Suh. Even though Kim
maintains that he fought against the Japanese in
Manchuria until August, 1945, it is most likely
that he and his forces left Manchuria in early 1941.
He probably spent the interval in the Soviet Union.
If Kim actually joined the Russian Army, as is
claimed by some sources, there is no verifiable
record of the fact. Suh further points out that
Kim was not known to the Russians until the early
1940's. If there is any truth in the hypothesis
that Kim was handpicked and groomed for the top
leadership position in North Korea by the Kremlin,
then the Soviets surely did not err in their assess-
ment of Kim's Machiavellian talents. For he has
shown a remarkable capacity for political survival
and aggrandizement.[17]

One of the first steps Kim Il-sŏng took to
consolidate his power was to emasculate the leadership of the domestic Communist faction in North
Korea. This objective was pursued in a most cold-
blooded fashion: One of the most articulate, capable, and popular domestic Communists, Hyŏn Chŭn-hyŏk,
was assassinated in broad daylight in P'yŏngyang.
A graduate of the prestigious Keijo Imperial University (the forerunner of Seoul National University),
Hyŏn had been rated as a first-rate intellectual

who had advocated the need for a "bourgeois-democrat
revolution" in Korea. In his view, the most urgent
task facing post-Liberation Korea was not the establishment of the dictatorship of the proletariat as
such, but the healing of the wound of national
humiliation as well as the shedding of the stigma
of backwardness. This, he had argued, required a
joint effort by all political forces regardless of
class origins, and hence the politically naive and
inexperienced proletarians and peasants should
refrain from dogmatically insisting on leading the
Korean revolution. True to his convictions, Hyŏn
had tried to form a nonpartisan united front, with
the revered nationalist Cho Man-sik as its symbolic
leader. As one of the most popular personages in
P'yŏngyang in the days immediately following the
Japanese surrender, Hyon had come into close contact
with the Soviet military authorities, meeting leading members of the Soviet faction, including Kim
Il-sŏng. He reportedly had become most enraged
when he learned of the Soviet scheme to enthrone
Kim Il-sŏng as the leader of the Korean Communists.
On September 28, 1945, Hyŏn was cut down by an
assassin's bullet in front of the P'yŏngyang City
Hall. The circumstances surrounding the murder
strongly suggested that it may have been committed
by Kim Il-sŏng's followers with Soviet approval.18
Hyŏn's violent death was not only a severe blow to
the domestic Communist faction, but it also served
as an effective warning to all would-be challengers
to Kim Il-sŏng.

It should be pointed out that the preceding
account of Hyŏn's death, furnished by Kim Ch'ang-sun
is by no means authoritative. As Dae-Sook Suh notes
Kim Il-sŏng did not emerge as the formal leader of
the North Korean Communists on the heels of Hyŏn's
assassination. When the North Korean Branch Bureau
of the Korean Communist Party was formed on October
13, 1945, it was not Kim Il-sŏng, but Kim Yŏng-bŏm,
his close collaborator, who was elected as its first
secretary. Mu Chŏng, a powerful member of the Yenan
group, was elected second secretary. On December
17, 1945, however, Kim Il-sŏng took over the leadership of the North Korean Branch Bureau, now renamed
the North Korean Communist Party, from Kim Yŏng-bŏm.

That the non-Communist nationalist faction woul
not be allowed to gather strength was a foregone con
clusion. As noted, its leader, Cho Man-sik, had

initially been co-opted by the Soviet authorities,
but he soon began to clash openly with Soviet occupation policies. Particularly embarrassing to the
Soviets was his outspoken opposition to their policy
of collecting grains from the impoverished Korean
peasants. When Cho adamantly opposed the decision
of the Moscow foreign ministers' conference to
impose a five-year trusteeship on Korea, the Soviets
let it be known that Cho's criticisms could no longer
be tolerated. Cho is said to have been told flatly
that as long as he persisted in his opposition to
the Moscow decision his safety could not be guaranteed. On January 4, 1946, the Five Provinces
Administration Bureau held a meeting to discuss the
trusteeship controversy and passed a resolution
endorsing the Soviet position, whereupon Cho resigned
as its head. The following day Cho was arrested by
Soviet troops, and he has not been heard of since.[20]

The Yenan faction, after operating under the
banner of the Korean Independence League for a
while, organized itself into the New People's Party
(Sinmindang) with Kim Tu-bong as chairman on March
30, 1946. The party attracted mainly petty bourgeois citizens and intellectuals. Its wide popularity, as demonstrated by its growing membership, was
viewed with a keen sense of alarm and jealousy by
the North Korean Communist Party. Five months later,
the two parties merged to form the North Korean
Workers' Party (NKWP).[21]

Because of an unexpected turn of events at the
joint party congress working out the merger, chair-
manship of the new party fell not to Kim Il-sŏng
but to Kim Tu-bong, leader of the Yenan faction.
According to Kim Ch'ang-sun, who was an eyewitness
to the events, the Soviet faction at first made a
vain attempt to win hegemony. When one of its
spokesmen publicly suggested that Kim Il-sŏng was
the only logical choice for the top post in the new
apparatus, delegates from the New People's Party
were visibly stirred. Fearing an impasse, a Soviet
adviser present at the meeting discreetly ordered
a recess. As soon as the meeting reconvened, North
Korean Communist Party leaders had O Ki-sŏp, a
domestic Communist who enjoyed popularity among the
members of the New People's Party, declare that
there was no reason why only Kim Il-sŏng and no
one else should be elected chairman. O's speech
instantaneously drew thunderous applause, Kim

Ch'ang-sun recalls. Kim Il-sŏng later personally
nominated Kim Tu-bong to the post and settled for
vice-chairmanship. Since the second vice-chairmansh.
went to Chu Yŏng-ha, a leader of the domestic factio
the newly created NKWP also managed to present the
façade of a coalition.[22]

A further assault on the already-enfeebled
domestic faction was made at the Second Congress of
NKWP, held in P'yŏngyang from March 27 to March 30,
1948. The chief target of the Soviet-faction-led
assault was O Ki-sŏp, Chairman of the Committee on
Labor and a member of the Central Committee. In a
speech to the Congress, Kim Il-sŏng singled out O
as a "representative example" of "some inexperienced
party members" who had manifested a penchant for
"hero worship" and "sectarianism." O's vigorous
opposition to the establishment of an independent
Communist Party in North Korea and his "arbitrary
behavior" while directing land-reform programs in
the province of North P'yongan in March, 1946, were
cited as part of his sins. O's previous advocacy
of the right of labor unions to protect the interest
of their members vis-à-vis the nationalized industrial organizations was also condemned. Even though
O made an impassioned defense of himself, with a
copy of the Japanese translation of The Selected
Works of Lenin in his hand, by demonstrating the
consistency of his expressed views with those of
Lenin, Kim Il-sŏng and his followers remained
unimpressed. O was eventually stripped of his party
posts but was assigned the relatively obscure post
of the vice-presidency of the Soviet-Korean Sea
Transport Share Company (Chosso Haeun Kongsa), also
known as Mortran. In the aftermath of the Twentieth
CPSU Congress in 1956, O made a brief comeback to
North Korea's political scene but was purged again
toward the end of 1958.[23]

The emergence of the NKWP in North Korea was
followed by the founding of its southern counterpart,
the South Korean Workers' Party (SKWP) in November,
1946. Like the NKWP, the SKWP was the product of
a merger: Pak Hŏn-yŏng's Korean Communist Party
joined hands with both the New People's Party (South
Korean version) and the People's Party. At its peak
in 1947, the SKWP claimed a membership of 370,000.
Subsequent suppression of leftist activities in
South Korea, however, forced it to go underground,
drastically curtailing its political effectiveness.

Many party leaders fled north. Its complete dis-integration as a viable political force was signaled in June, 1949, when it was formally annexed with the NKWP. With the birth of the unified Korean Workers Party (KWP), Kim Il-sŏng assumed the formal leadership of the Korean Communists. He was elected Chairman, and Pak was chosen as Vice-Chairman.[24]

The events that led to the creation of two Korean governments in 1948, each of which claimed to be the sole legitimate government of all of Korea, are described later in the book. Briefly, the Soviet boycott of the United Nations Temporary Commission on Korea led to the holding of U.N.-supervised elections in the southern half of the Korean penin-sula only. The offshoot was the formation of the Korean National Assembly, which in turn mapped out the nation's basic charter and elected Syngman Rhee, a then popular Korean national hero, the first President of the Republic of Korea (R.O.K.). The R.O.K. was shortly accorded international recogni-tion both by the United Nations and by the United States and its allies. Charging that South Korean elections were a complete sham and, further, that the R.O.K. was a mere puppet of United States imperialism, the North Koreans proceeded to hold elections on their own in August, 1948. According to North Korean sources, "free" elections were held throughout Korea, North and South, with 99.97 per cent of eligible voters in the North and 77.52 per cent of qualified voters in the South participating, respectively.[25] With the proclamation of the Dem-ocratic People's Republic of Korea (D.P.R.K.) on September 9, 1948, with Kim Il-sŏng as its Premier, the partition of Korea took a more rigid form.

By the time North Korea launched its unprovoked attack on South Korea on June 25, 1950, Kim Il-sŏng must have established a firm control over the North Korean political system. No less certain, perhaps, was the Soviet Union's grip on that fledgling Asian satellite. While the painfully one-sided power struggle was being won by Moscow-oriented Korean Communists in the political arena, the Soviets were busy spreading an intricate net of economic exploi-tation and cultural penetration over North Korea. Simultaneously, they helped to organize, train, and supply the North Korean Army in preparation for the impending invasion. Not only did Soviet military advisers carefully guide and direct the whole

operation, but they also took pains to assign to
key military posts only those Koreans "who were
completely responsive to Soviet direction," that
is, mostly Soviet-Koreans. On the eve of the
invasion, each North Korean Army division had
three to eight Red Army advisers, who typically
held the rank of major and gave "suggestions" on
all aspects of the division's operations--military,
political, and logistic. Their suggestions in
actual practice had the weight of orders. The
North Korean Army's subservience to the Soviet
Union was further ensured by the former's dependence
on the latter for both training and supplies. According to information obtained in North Korea by a U.S.
State Department study mission in 1950:

> ...pilots, aircraft mechanics, and
> experts in tank warfare and mainte-
> nance were trained in the U.S.S.R.
> during the years 1946 to 1949. Their
> training included a complete polit-
> ical orientation to the U.S.S.R. and
> they were returned to Korea in 1949
> to serve as cadres in the mechanized
> units of the North Korean Army. The
> Russians armed the North Korean forces
> only gradually; in 1946 they gave them
> Japanese rifles; subsequently they
> replaced this Japanese equipment with
> limited quantities of Russian arms;
> but they did not supply the trucks
> required to make the army mobile or
> the tanks and heavy guns calculated to
> give it an edge over South Korea in
> fire-power until April and May 1950.
> Finally, the U.S.S.R. was able to keep
> close check over the movement of the
> North Korean army by allocating gaso-
> line to the army on a monthly basis.[26]

Although the origins of the Korean War have yet to
be illuminated,[27] what little is known about the
nature and extent of Soviet control in North Korea
in 1950 makes it highly improbable that the decision
of the Kim Il-sŏng regime to attack South Korea
could have been taken without "Soviet approval if
not inspiration."[28]

In any event, the North Korean venture ended
in a disaster. Not only did North Korea fail to
"liberate" South Korea and unify the peninsula, but

it was all but devastated. Indeed, North Korea
came perilously close to annihilation as a political entity when the sixteen-member United Nations
forces under General MacArthur's command crossed
the 38th Parallel, rapidly advancing toward the
Yalu in the months of September and October, 1950.
The massive intervention by the "Chinese People's
Volunteers" in October, however, turned the tide
of the war, thus saving North Korea from a humiliating defeat. North Korea had been spared a defeat,
but it had not won a victory. In the midst of the
war, Kim Il-sŏng tried to shift the blame for the
fiasco to his subordinates. Prominent among his
scapegoats was Mu Chŏng, who had commanded North
Korea's Second Corps in the early stage of the war
and who had later been entrusted with the impossible
task of defending P'yŏngyang against the United
Nations offensive. At the Third Plenum of the
Central Committee of the KWP held at Pyŏlŏri (a
Korean town near the northwestern border of Manchuria) in December, 1950, Kim Il-sŏng personally
accused Mu Chŏng of "insubordination," "the propaga-
tion of a defeatist mood," and "wanton killings."
As Kim Ch'ang-sun points out, this was an extraordinarily bold, but perhaps necessary, move on the
part of the North Korean ruler. For to challenge
and humiliate a man of Mu Chŏng's stature at that
particular moment was to risk offending Communist
China, a country that had just come to the rescue
of North Korea. Mu Chŏng was not only credited
with having founded the artillery of the famed
Communist Chinese Eighth Route Army, but he was
also a veteran of the Long March. Yet, as Kim
Ch'ang-sun reasons, it may have been precisely this
background of Mu Chŏng that led Kim Il-sŏng to take
the move. If he was to remain in power, Kim had to
eliminate any and all potential challengers. Mu
Chŏng was subsequently imprisoned, but was later
released and taken to Communist China at the request
of the Chinese Communist authorities. He is rumored
to have died of illness there a few years later.
Others who shared the blame for North Korea's failure to win the war included Kim Il, Deputy Minister
of National Defense, and Kim Han-jung and Ch'oe
Kang, both division commanders. A host of lesser
figures were also penalized.[29]

The Fourth Plenum of the KWP Central Committee,
which was held in November, 1951, also witnessed a
witch-hunting. This time the victim was a prominent

Soviet-Korean, Hŏ Ka-i. Ho had held numerous high-
ranking party and government posts, including membership in the all-powerful seven-man War Committee and
vice-premiership. Foremost among Hŏ's alleged
wrong-doings was his "indiscriminate" admission into
the KWP of South Korean Communists whose behavior
during the Korean War proved them to have been
utterly unworthy of KWP membership. Hŏ's growing
influence within the KWP appears to have been the
real motive of the attack. Pressed to vindicate
himself, Hŏ committed suicide.[30]

     The shooting phase of the war came to an end
with the signing of the Armistice Agreement on July
27, 1953, at P'anmunjŏm.[31] Although it hailed the
Armistice as a "historic victory for the Korean
people,"[32] North Korea faced the painfully grim
prospect of a long and arduous journey to national
recovery. No less urgent than the reconstruction
of the war-shattered economy, from Kim Il-sŏng's
standpoint, however, was the further consolidation
of his political control. This, he must have
reasoned, called for the liquidation of South
Korean Communists, that is, former SKWP members.
Twelve leading members of the group were thus tried
on trumped-up charges, nine of them being sentenced
to death. The latter group included Yi Sŭng-yŏp,
Secretary of the Central Committee of the KWP and
Chairman of the People's Inspection Committee
(Inmin Kŏmnyol Wiwŏnhoe) of the North Korean Cabinet; Cho Il-myŏng, Vice-Minister of Culture and
Propaganda; Im Hwa, Vice-Chairman of the Central
Committee of the Soviet-Korean Cultural Association;
and Yi Kang-guk, a ranking official of the Ministry
of International Trade. The undisputed leader of
the SKWP group, as already noted, was Pak Hŏn-yŏng,
but he was spared in the 1953 purge. Two years
later, however, the North Korean regime disclosed
that Pak had been convicted of treason and espionage
by North Korea's highest military tribunal and had
been executed.[33]

     Kim Il-sŏng's purges thus far had been largely
precautionary in nature. At no time did he allow
the situation to get out of hand; on the contrary,
he invariably moved to eliminate his potential
rivals before they had grown powerful enough to
challenge him. In August, 1956, however, Kim was
confronted with the first and only serious challenge
to his leadership. Yet so invincible had he become

that he routinely crushed the revolt. The abortive
rebellion was staged against the backdrop of the
famous Twentieth Congress of the CPSU, in which
Premier Khrushchev initiated the de-Stalinization
and antipersonality cult campaigns. The leading
actors in the tension-packed drama were Ch'oe
Ch'ang-ik, Pak Ch'ang-ok, and Yun Kong-hŭm. Ch'oe
was known as the chief theoretician of the Yenan
faction, and Pak enjoyed the same reputation among
members of the Soviet faction. Yun was a veteran
member of the Yenan faction. While Kim Il-sŏng was
on a two-month tour of the Soviet Union and Eastern
Europe in search of "the cooperation and assistance
of the Socialist bloc" for North Korea's developmental efforts, Ch'oe and Pak published a series of
articles in various journals and periodicals boldly
suggesting that the KWP had been guilty of practicing personality cult and that, in keeping with
the decision of the Twentieth CPSU Congress, it
must substitute democratic party management and
collective leadership for one-man dictatorship.
Simultaneously, they tried to organize an anti-Kim
Il-sŏng coalition comprising discontented members
of both the Yenan and Soviet factions. The revolt
was climaxed at the August, 1956, plenum of the KWP
Central Committee, called to hear Kim Il-sŏng's
report on his European tour.[34]

Speaking for the rebellious group, Yun bluntly
pointed out that Kim's style of leadership was not
merely dictatorial, but his policies ran counter to
the interests of the people. Yun pointed to the
stark contrast between the distressingly low wages
and incomes of workers and peasants, on one side,
and the disproportionately high salaries of North
Korean army officers, on the other, adding that
such a condition had made Kim extremely unpopular
among the masses. Yun's charges were echoed by both
Pak and Ch'oe. But the anti-Kim faction was out-
numbered by those loyal to the Premier, and the
revolt was quenched. Predictably, a wholesale purge
was quickly set in motion, but its severity was
tempered somewhat by the intervention of both the
Soviet Union and Communist China. Anastas I.
Mikoyan, then First Deputy Premier of the U.S.S.R.,
and P'eng Te-huai, then Defense Minister of the
People's Republic of China (P.R.C.), allegedly
came to P'yŏngyang to urge moderation to Kim Il-
sŏng. The principal casualty of the ill-fated
revolt proved to be Kim Tu-bong, leader of the

Yenan faction and Chairman of the Presidium of the
Supreme People's Assembly. He was stripped of his
post in August, 1957, and expelled from the Party
in March, 1958. Kim Tu-bong's ouster symbolized
the demise of the Yenan faction. All anti-Kim Il-
sŏng elements in the Soviet faction were also eliminated from positions of authority. Thus was
ushered in the period of the absolute ascendancy
of the partisan group led by Kim Il-sŏng.[35] At the
leadership conference (taep'yoja hoeŭi) of the KWP
held in P'yŏngyang during October 5-12, 1966, the
hegemony of the partisan group became crystal clear.
The overwhelming majority of key party positions
went to members of this group.[36]

    While all this was taking place on the polit-
ical front, North Korea was frantically engaged in
the ambitious task of economic reconstruction and
modernization. During the five-year period between
the Liberation and the outbreak of the Korean War,
North Korea had taken some basic steps toward the
socialization of its economy. Most significant,
perhaps, was the adoption by the Provisional People's
Committee, then North Korea's governing body, of a
law on August 10, 1946, which had the effect of
nationalizing more than 1,000 industrial enterprises, accounting for 90 per cent of all the industry north of the 38th Parallel. A decree promulgated two months later, however, sought to "preserve
the right of private property in plants and factories
which belong to Korean citizens, and also to encourag
the private initiative of manufacturers and traders
for the development of industry and trade."[37] Con-
sumers' cooperatives made their first appearance
in 1946. A rudimentary form of economic planning
was also introduced in 1947. In short, North Korea
moved cautiously but unmistakably toward a socialized
economy. By 1949, the state and cooperative sector
accounted for 90.7 per cent of total industrial
production.[38]

    What was the status of the North Korean economy
during the prewar period in terms of structure,
output, and potential? A generalization frequently
made about the Korean economy is that the northern
half of the country is industrial and its southern
half primarily agricultural. Such a neat dichotomy,
however, turns out, upon close inspection, to be
somewhat misleading. For, as of 1940, in some
industrial sectors the South had a definite lead

over the North. Thus, although North Korea led in
such heavy industries as chemical and metal industries, it lagged behind South Korea in consumer-
goods industries, notably textiles. More important,
the South enjoyed a comfortable edge over the North
in the machine-making industry. As Joseph S. Chung
shows, however, the North also had many blessings.
Not only was it the "chief supplier of electricity,
providing 80 per cent of the electricity generated
in 1940," it was also "favorably endowed with minerals strategic to industrial development." Thus,
in 1940, North Korea "produced 79 per cent of the
coal, 63 per cent of the gold, 97 per cent of the
iron ore, 96 per cent of the limestone, 100 per
cent of the magnesite and apatite, 71 per cent of
the nickel, and 75 per cent of the zinc" produced
in the entire Korea.[39]

Not to be overlooked also is the fact that the
Japanese had left behind "a basis for industrialization" in North Korea. Among other things, they
introduced modern mining methods and built chemical
and hydroelectric plants as well as a superb rail-
road system. Yet all this was done with their own,
not Korean, interests in view. Thus the Korean
economy became heavily dependent on Japan for final
processing and finished products. The paucity of
machine-building plants in Korea was the result of
a carefully calculated Japanese colonial policy.[40]

It is clear, then, that North Korea did not
start from scratch when it embarked upon the socialist path of economic modernization. Building upon
the groundwork laid by the Japanese, North Korean
economic planners could benefit from the experience
of the Soviet Union and later from that of Communist
China. North Korea's economic plans, of which there
have been five thus far--the two One-Year Plans of
1947 and 1948, the first Two-Year Plan of 1949-50,
the Three-Year Plan of 1954-56, the first Five-Year
Plan of 1957-61, and the Seven-Year Plan of 1961-67,
which has been extended for three more years--have
emphasized the need to correct the structural
imbalance and to create a fully self-reliant economy. After completing its two One-Year Plans, North
Korea claimed that its total industrial output[41]
had increased 3.4 times that of 1946. Means of
production allegedly had increased 3.8 times that
of 1946, and the growth figure for consumer goods
was 2.9 times.[42] In the realm of agriculture,

North Korea's claims were less spectacular: The
gross output of farm and animal products was said
to have increased 1.4 times between 1944 and 1949.[43]

Whatever North Korea may actually have accomplished, it was heavily destroyed during three
years of the Korean War. North Korea reported that
its total industrial output suffered a 34 per cent
decline, and agricultural output decreased by 12
per cent. More than 8,700 industrial plants were
allegedly destroyed, and some 370,000 chŏngbo (one
chŏngbo is 2.45 acres) of farm land damaged. Also
demolished were 600,000 homes, 5,000 schools, 1,000
hospitals and clinics, and 260 theaters. All told,
the war inflicted an estimated damage of 4,200
million (old) won (approximately $1,700 million)
to North Korea.[44]

North Korea's most pressing task after the
Armistice was to recover from the shattering effects
of the war. Determined to restore its economy to
the prewar level, North Korea gave top priority to
heavy industry, while paying moderate attention to
light industry and agriculture. Its Three-Year
Plan was aimed primarily at economic rehabilitation.
North Korea did not, and obviously could not, pursue this goal single-handedly. Generous offers of
assistance were forthcoming from all Socialist
countries. The Soviet Union pledged a two-year
grant of 1,000 million rubles (approximately $250
million), and agreed to cut North Korea's debt to
that country by half. Furthermore, it consented to
a deferred payment of North Korea's outstanding
debt. Communist China not only promised a four-
year grant of 800 million yuan in People's Currency
(approximately $324 million), but also decided to
regard all the expenses incurred by Chinese participation in the Korean War as a gift to North Korea.
Both countries additionally pledged technical
assistance in various fields. The grant from China,
however, was to be delivered in the form of materials such as coal, textiles, grain, lumber, agricultural implements, machinery, ships, and so on.
Albania, Bulgaria, Czechoslovakia, East Germany,
Hungary, Mongolia, Poland, and Romania also offered
material and technical assistance.[45]

The Three-Year Plan, according to North Korean
claims, was fulfilled four months ahead of schedule,
compiling impressive records. Total industrial

output allegedly rose 2.8 times that of 1953.
Irrigation, mechanization, and cooperativization
combined to raise North Korea's agricultural output enormously, it was claimed. Thus the farm
output for 1956 exceeded the highest ever achieved
under the Japanese by 8 per cent. In that year,
80.9 per cent of North Korean farm households
belonged to agricultural cooperatives.[46]

The first Five-Year Plan of 1957-61 sought to
solidify the base of a socialist economy and to
provide the people with the basic necessities of
life. The aim, in different words, was to completely do away with the colonial lopsidedness of
the economic structure and to firmly establish the
foundation for an independent economy. By August,
1958, North Korea was proudly asserting that the
socialistic form of economy had been fully adopted
by that country. The apparent basis for this bold
assertion was the successful completion of agricultural collectivization: The entire farm population had joined, or, more accurately, been forced
to join, the so-called cooperatives, of which there
were 13,309 with an average of eighty households
each. The number was presently reduced to 3,843
in an integration drive closely resembling China's
commune movement.[47]

The second year of the Five-Year Plan also
saw the appearance of a new slogan on the North
Korean scene--a slogan that was to serve as a symbolic rallying point for a stepped-up campaign
for economic modernization. The slogan was
"Ch'ŏllima," literally meaning "the Thousand ri
Horse" (1 Korean ri is approximately 0.25 miles),
but commonly translated as "the Flying Horse." A
legendary horse in a Chinese classical novel,
Ch'ŏllima is known to be able practically to fly,
running a thousand ri in a day. North Koreans in all
walks of life were exhorted to "gallop like the
legendary Flying Horse on the path of building
socialism." North Korean claims to originality
notwithstanding, the timing of the Ch'ŏllima Movement strongly suggests that it was heavily influenced by, if not patterned after, China's Great
Leap Forward.[48] The goals of the Five-Year Plan
were allegedly fulfilled in two and a half years.
As a result, a "strong machine-building industry"
was constructed, providing a nucleus for an independent economy encompassing both heavy and light

industries. Because of a change in the ratio between industry and agriculture, North Korea became
more nearly an industrial nation.[49] In the agricultural field, the problems of irrigation and
electrification were "fundamentally solved," while
mechanization was being pursued vigorously. North
Korean planners designated 1960 as the year of
"shock absorption," in which the necessary tidying-
up and adjustments would be made in preparation for
the more ambitious Seven-Year Plan of 1961-67.[50]

The fundamental objective of the Seven-Year
Plan is said to be an all-encompassing technical
revolution, accompanied by a corresponding "cultural revolution." The phenomenal achievements of
the first Five-Year Plan provide a solid foundation
for the preceding goal, it is argued. If success-
fully implemented, the Plan would make North Korea
not merely a self-sufficient country but an affluent
one. The total industrial output would grow at the
average rate of 18 per cent a year; thus, at the
end of 1967, it would have grown 3.2 times that of
1960. This would mean that North Korea's industrial
output will have expanded 20 times that of the
prewar period.[51] As North Korea entered the ter-
minal year of the Seven-Year Plan, however, there
was growing evidence that the overly ambitious
goals of the Plan were not being accomplished in
full. As opposed to the projected growth rate of
18 per cent a year, the actual growth-rate figures
as reported by North Korea are: 14.3 per cent in
1961, 20 per cent in 1962, 8 per cent in 1963, 17
per cent in 1964, and 14 per cent in 1965.[52] Contrary to the pattern established in recent years,
North Korea failed to make public production figures
for 1966 in early 1967. Furthermore, its decision
to extend the Seven-Year Plan for three more years,
announced in the October, 1966, meeting of the KWP,
made it abundantly clear that its economy is lagging
behind the schedule. At the meeting, it was disclosed that the average growth rate of North Korea's
total industrial output during the first six years
of its Seven-Year Plan was 14.3 per cent--3.7 per
cent below the target. In an effort to explain
away the lagging economy, the KWP leadership took
pains to emphasize that the growing military build-
up in South Korea necessitated a corresponding
increase in P'yŏngyang's own military preparedness.
Hence North Korea should not neglect its defense
sector by any means; on the contrary, economic

construction must go hand in hand with "military build-up" (kukpang kŏnsŏl). If a sizable portion of North Korea's resources had to be diverted to "military build-up," it was inevitable that economic construction would be slowed down somewhat, it was argued.[53]

At this point, it may be appropriate to pose a major question regarding the state of the North Korean economy. The question is, just how valid and reliable are North Korean statistics? Although the reliability of economic and social statistics has been generally overrated even in the Western context, Communist statistics suffer from a notoriously low degree of credibility. North Korean statistics are no exception. Their shortcomings, from the point of view of non-Communist analysts, include measurement and observational errors; absence of definitions; the use of percentage, rather than absolute figures; misclassification; double-counting; omissions; and deliberate falsification.[54] On the other hand, the North Korean practice of publishing clearly unfavorable statistics, such as those showing not only failure to attain previously declared targets, but also serious setbacks in different sectors of the economy, leads one to believe that its official statistics have a fair measure of empirical basis. Moreover, Joseph S. Chung has found that they are "at least internally consistent, that is, the relationship between rates of growth in the total output, rate of growth in each of the industrial sectors and change in the relative composition are algebraically consistent."[55]

Even if one makes allowances for the deceptive nature of North Korean statistics, one still gets the impression that giant strides have indeed been taken by North Korea during the post-Korean War period. Yoon T. Kuark estimates that North Korea's national income, measured in constant prices, has grown at the rate of 22.1 per cent a year during that period, whereas South Korea's has increased at the modest rate of 3.6 per cent a year. As already noted, however, the North Korean economy has shown signs of increasing strain in recent years. It may be that, after a decade of sustained growth, the North Korean economy has reached "the point of diminishing returns."[56]

The view that North Korea's exorbitant claims
may yet contain a grain of truth is supported by a
legion of foreign observers who have visited that
country in recent years. Among them is Professor
Joan Robinson of Cambridge University, a world-
renowned economist, who paid a short visit to North
Korea in 1954 and again in 1964. Although her
undisguised sympathy for socialist regimes apparently disqualifies her as the most objective observer
of the North Korean scene, Professor Robinson's
views nevertheless are of considerable interest.
Reporting on her latest visit (October, 1964), she
describes P'yŏngyang as "a city without slums" and
North Korea as "a nation without poverty." According to her, "All the economic miracles of the postwar world are put in the shade" by the spectacular
achievements of North Korea.[57] She writes that the
chief ingredients of North Korea's success formula
are "well conceived economic strategy" and "patriotic rage and devotion expressing itself in enthusiasm for hard work." She hastens to add that
"North Korea did not start absolutely from scratch,"
thanks to the Japanese who "had built up mines and
production of pig iron, wood pulp, and fertilizer."[58]

Professor Robinson takes note of a conspicuous
deviation from the Soviet model in North Korea's
Seven-Year Plan: For the first three years, it
lays primary emphasis on agriculture and light
industry, postponing an all-out expansion of basic
industries to the latter part of the Plan--a strategy later copied by Communist China. Even though
North Korea has been in a great hurry in its pursuit
of economic expansion, as seen by the building up
of a pool of 200,000 technicians and experts from
nearly nothing, it has not subordinated quality to
quantity, the British scholar insists. In her
words, "the proof of the pudding is in the eating:
the trucks are running, the electric pumps are
irrigating the fields, the machine tools are being
exported."[59]

The North Korean experience, Professor Robinson
argues, has implications for the economics of development. For one thing, it demonstrates the role
of national character in economic modernization.
The "intense concentration of the Koreans on national
pride and national wrongs," as epitomized by the
widely advertised phrase, "chuch'e" (national self-
identity or autonomy),[60] has left a deep impression

on Robinson. For another, the "Korean miracle"
shows the "pernicious effect of foreign aid prolonged beyond the first boost." Because North
Korea could not count on foreign aid as a continuous
major source of developmental capital and because
it doggedly followed the policy of self-reliance,
Robinson feels, it was able to accomplish so much.
Moreover, the Korean experience suggests that
economies of scale may not be so important as is
generally assumed, she writes. North Korea explicitly rejected the policy of concentrating on a few
lines and importing the rest, which economies of
scale dictated. Instead, it pursued the policy of
self-reliance. The latter, argues Professor Robinson, had a psychologically beneficial side effect:
It helped to throw off the colonial mentality.[61]

If there is any truth in Professor Robinson's
eye-witness account of North Korea's economic progress, then North Korean claims cannot be totally
brushed aside. In all likelihood, North Korea may
indeed be on the verge of becoming, if it has not
already become, an economically independent nation.[62]
No less important, however, is the disturbingly high
price North Korea has had to pay for what must be
considered as the rare feat of transforming a war-
torn economy into an industrial complex, however
crude some of its components may be. The price has
been human sacrifice and suffering of unimaginable
magnitude. According to Dong Jun Lee, a former
writer for Pravda in P'yŏngyang, who escaped to
South Korea in 1959:

> ...ever since the "Ch'ŏllima Movement"
> got under way the exploitation of
> peasants has reached a new height.
> Shackled to a stifling life of servi-
> tude which defies imagination, North
> Korean peasants, along with the rest
> of our brethren in the north, are
> sick and tired of living under the
> Communist regime of Kim Il-sŏng.
> They are desperately hoping to escape
> from the Communist dictatorship at
> the earliest possible date.[63]

In different words, North Korea's national
power, of which economic power is the core, may be
said to have grown at the expense of individual
freedom and comfort. The Japanese journalists who

visited North Korea in 1960-61, although impressed
by its rapid industrial growth, were nevertheless
constrained to report that the living standards of
the North Korean masses were pitifully low.[64] Not
only have the living standards of the North Koreans
been deliberately depressed in order to divert
more and more funds and resources to the task of
industrialization, but the North Korean people
have been compelled to work with an intensity and
dedication that would appear to surpass the limits
of human endurance in the Western context.

     More recently, however, the KWP leadership has
become increasingly sensitive to the needs of the
masses. What is commonly known as the mass line
in Communist parlance has been receiving a renewed
and repeated emphasis in North Korea in the past
several years. Along with the "technical and cultural revolutions," the twin goals of the Seven-
Year Plan, a "human-relations revolution" appears
to be taking place in that Communist regime. The
widely acclaimed "Ch'ŏngsan-li method" and "Theses
on the Socialist Agrarian Question in Our Country,"
both attributed to Premier Kim Il-sŏng, are symptomatic of North Korea's growing awareness of the
importance of the human factor in the building of
socialism. The Ch'ŏngsan-li method, allegedly
initiated by Kim Il-sŏng during his inspection tour
of Ch'ŏngsan-li agricultural cooperatives in February, 1960, underscores the need to motivate,
rather than manipulate, farmers and to get their
active participation in the cooperative decision-
making process. It urges the leaders of a group
to make on-the-spot inspections, to invite suggestions from rank-and-file farmers, and to enhance
their sense of participation in a common and
mutually beneficial enterprise. Such an approach
will pay rich dividends in the form of increased
productivity, it is argued. Further, it is said
to be transferable to other sectors of the economy
and should therefore be applied to the management
of North Korea's entire economy.[65]

     Kim Il-sŏng's "Theses on the Socialist Agrar-
ian Question in Our Country," adopted as an official
KWP policy in February, 1964, are also notable for
their emphasis on closer ties with the peasant masses. In order to hasten the "inevitable" transition
of North Korean socialism to the stage of Communism,
it is urged that the living standards of the peasant

be upgraded. To abolish the backwardness in the
countryside requires a concerted effort on the part
of the entire Korean people. Industrial workers
should work hand in hand with their peasant brethren
in improving farming methods and in carrying out
the "technical, cultural, and ideological revolutions" in the rural areas. Further, "guidance and
management of the rural economy should steadily be
brought closer to the advanced level of industrial
enterprise management." Significantly, however,
stress is given to "working-class leadership of the
peasantry." There is abundant evidence that these
strictures are being assiduously observed in North
Korea today.[66]

Still another fashionable phrase in North
Korea's current official lexicon is the "Taean
Work System" ("Taean ŭi saŏp ch'egye"). In a speech
delivered at an enlarged meeting of the Party Com-
mittee of the Taean Electrical Machine Factory on
November 9, 1962, Kim Il-sŏng said:

> The Taean Work System is radically
> different from the old; it is an
> advanced system with many factors
> of communist industrial management.
> This new system of work is an excel-
> lent embodiment of the principle of
> collective, communist life: "One
> for all and all for one." In this
> system, superiors help their sub-
> ordinates, the well-informed are
> teaching the less-informed, all the
> people are helping each other as
> comrades, and all the workshops are
> cooperating closely.
> . . . .
> The great power of the new sys-
> tem of work is the great power of
> unity and cooperation, the great
> power of the enthusiasm and creative
> abilities of the awakened masses; it
> is the great power which is born
> when Party leadership penetrates
> deeply into the lower units.[67]

Under this system, all members of diverse factory
work teams are urged to contribute new ideas so
that at least one technical improvement or innova-
tion a month may be realized. It is designed to

stimulate the maximum possible utilization of the
inventive genius of the masses, making it possible
for them to become the "genuine master as well as
manager" of socialist enterprises. In a word, the
system is nothing less than a "concrete application
/in North Korea7 of the revolutionary mass line."[68]

So far, we have sketched the main contours of
North Korea's political and economic developments
during the past two decades. Having achieved
internal political stability under the watertight
reign of Kim Il-sŏng, it has mobilized its entire
resources in the massive task of economic modernization along socialistic lines. Technical and material assistance from "fraternal countries of the
Socialist camp" played an important role in the
early stage of North Korea's postwar recovery, but
has been practically discontinued since 1961.
Despite indications that its Seven-Year Plan of
1961-67 has been falling short of attainment, North
Korea has apparently entered the threshold of economic self-reliance.

Before turning to its behavior on the world
stage, we shall briefly consider the nature of the
decision-making process in the North Korean regime.
The most obvious conclusion that emerges from a
study of both North Korean sources and secondary
analyses of that regime is that it is a one-party
dictatorship, root, stock, and branch. As in all
Communist nations, there is but one effective political party, the Korean Workers Party, which dominates and rules the nation with an iron hand.
Although it pays lip service to the principles of
"democratic centralism" and "collective leadership,"
the KWP is in actual practice controlled by Kim
Il-sŏng and his closest associates in the all-
powerful Political Committee of its Central Committee. This, it should be noted, is the prevailing
pattern in other Communist parties including both
the CPSU and the CCP.

As of August 1, 1961, the KWP counted 1,311,563
members, of whom 1,166,359 were full-fledged members,
the remainder being candidate members.[69] Since
North Korea has a population of about 11,568,000
(as of October 1, 1963), it follows that the KWP
membership embraces nearly 10 per cent of that
country's population.[70] The unusually high proportion of Party members to population in North

Korea is in part attributable to the relatively
liberal requirements for admission. No doubt, the
KWP leadership must have deemed it politically
advantageous to maintain the façade of a mass
party.[71]

At the national level, the KWP's basic decision-
making organ is the National Party Congress, which,
under Party rules, should be called by the Central
Committee at four-year intervals. The actual practice of the KWP diverges from the dictates of its
rules, and only four such congresses have been
held thus far at somewhat irregular intervals. The
First KWP Congress was held in August, 1946;* the
Second Congress in March, 1948; the Third Congress
in April, 1956; and the Fourth Congress in September,
1961. The last was attended by 1,157 delegates and
73 alternates.[72] From October 5 to 12, 1966, a
"leadership conference" (taep'yoja hoeŭi) of the KWP
was held in P'yŏngyang. In his opening address,
Ch'oe Yong'gŏn, the Party's number two boss, frankly
acknowledged that the conference was being held in
lieu of the Party's Fifth Congress, which had been
planned for 1966. He pointed out that, under Party
rules, such a conference is "an important meeting
which discusses and decides on urgent problems
concerning Party policies and strategy." He revealed that the conference was being attended by
1,275 delegates and 48 alternates.[73]

Aside from the realities of Communist politics, the enormous size of the Congress makes it
operationally unfit to actually debate and formulate substantive policies. An organ relatively
better suited to such tasks, but which in reality
is largely relegated to a rubber-stamp function,
is the Central Committee (CC). Theoretically
elected by the Congress, members of the CC are
believed to be actually handpicked by Kim Il-sŏng
and his loyal lieutenants in the KWP hierarchy.
The Fourth Congress "elected" eighty-five CC members
plus fifty-eight candidate members. At the October,
1966, meeting of the KWP, it was extensively reorganized. As a result, a Presidium (Sangmu Wiwŏnhoe)
was created within the Political Committee of the

---

*Actually, this was the first National Party Con-
 gress of the North Korean Workers Party, which was
 eventually merged with its southern counterpart to
 form the KWP.

Chart 1

ORGANIZATION OF THE KOREAN WORKERS PARTY

NATIONAL PARTY CONGRESS
- - - - - - - - - - - - - - - - -
Consists of more than 1,100
delegates and is supposed to
meet every four years. In theory,
this is the most important
decision-making organ of the
Party, but, in reality, it
functions as a rubber-stamp body.

CENTRAL COMMITTEE
- - - - - - - - - - - - - - - - -
Has a membership of over 140.
This is the elite group in North
Korea and has substantial, albeit
not decisive, powers. Manages
Party affairs during the intervals
of National Party Congresses.

POLITICAL COMMITTEE
- - - - - - - - - - - - - - - - -
Consists of eleven regular and
nine alternate members. Second
only to the Presidium in terms of
decision-making authority.

PRESIDIUM
OF THE POLITICAL COMMITTEE
- - - - - - - - - - - -
This is the top decision-
making organ of the Party.
Its six members are lit-
erally the rulers of North
Korea.

SECRETARIAT
- - - - - - - - - - -
Headed by the general
secretary and includes
ten secretaries. Over-
sees the execution of
Party decisions.

CENTRAL INSPECTION
COMMITTEE
- - - - - - - - - - -
Consists of seven
members. Has juris-
diction over Party
disciplines and peti-
tions.

CENTRAL AUDIT
COMMITTEE
- - - - - - - - - - -
Consists of seventeen
members. Audits the
activities and finan-
ces of the central
organs.

CENTRAL ORGANS
- - - - - - - - - - -
Organization Dept.
International Dept.
Propaganda and Agita-
   tion
Science and Education
Commerce and Finance
Heavy Industry
Light Industry
Construction and
   Transportation
Agriculture
Fisheries

Central Committee, and the posts of chairman and
six vice-chairmen were abolished. Additionally, a
Secretariat, composed of a general secretary and
ten secretaries, was established within the Central Committee. The Presidium would be empowered
to "discuss problems of the Party and the State on
a continuing basis," and the Secretariat would be
entrusted with the responsibility of "organizing
Party activities designed to implement the line,
policies, and decisions of the Party." Named to
the Presidium were Kim Il-sŏng, Ch'oe Yong-gŏn,
Kim Il, Pak Kŭm-ch'ŏl, Yi Hyo-sun, and Kim Kwāng-
hyŏp, in that order. Simultaneously, five new
members were "elected" to the all-powerful Political Committee: Kim Ik-sŏn, Kim Ch'ang-bong, Pak
Sŏng-ch'ŏl, Ch'oe Hyŏn, and Yi Yŏng-ho. Nine others
were admitted to the Political Committee as candidate members.* In short, the Political Committee,
the supreme decision-making organ of the KWP,**
would consist of eleven members and nine candidate
members. Of these, the six members of the Presidium
would undoubtedly form the nucleus. As for the
membership of the Secretariat, Kim Il-sŏng became
General Secretary, and his five colleagues in the
Presidium shared the title of Secretary with five
others. The remaining five were Sŏk San, Hŏ Pong-
hak, Kim Yŏng-ju, Pak Yong-guk, and Kim To-man.[74]

Although the full implications of the reorganization are not yet clear, one thing became
unmistakably obvious: the unassailable supremacy
of the partisan group headed by Kim Il-sŏng in
North Korean politics. Strikingly, all six members of the Presidium and all but two of the eleven
regular members of the Political Committee belonged
to that group. Conspicuously absent from the Party's
top leadership roster were such names as Nam Il,
Chŏng Il-yŏng, Kim Ch'ang-man, and Pak Chŏng-ae,

---

*They are Sŏk San, Hŏ Pong-hak, Ch'oe Kwang, O
Chin-u, Yim Ch'un-ch'u, Kim Tong-gyu, Kim Yŏng'ju,
Pak Yong-guk, and Chŏng Kyŏng-bok.

**The Political Committee is empowered by Party rules
to "direct all affairs of the Party in the name of
its Central Committee" during the intervals between
National Party Congresses. This means, in effect,
that it makes all important decisions regarding
the Party and the State.

all of whom had been members of the Political Committee on the eve of the KWP leadership conference.
What these persons had in common was their lack of
affiliation with Kim Il-sŏng's anti-Japanese
guerrilla activities in Manchuria. Both Nam Il
and Chŏng Il-yŏng traced their origins to the
Soviet Union, Kim Ch'ang-man to the Yenan group,
and Pak Chŏng-ae to the domestic Communist faction.
Kim Ch'ang-man had not been seen in public for
several months prior to the formal, if tacit,
confirmation of his purge.[75]

In October, 1967, the Dong-A Ilbo, South
Korea's largest newspaper, reported that a "massive
purge" had occurred in P'yŏngyang in May, 1967, in
which six leading members of the KWP were dismissed
from their Party posts. The alleged victims were
Pak Kŭm-ch'ŏl and Yi Hyo-sun, both members of the
Presidium and the Secretariat, Yim Ch'un-ch'u, a
candidate member of the Political Committee, Kim
To-man, a Secretary, Ko Hyŏk, a Vice-Premier of the
D.P.R.K., and Hŏ Sŏk-sŏn, a member of the Central
Committee. The report, based on information
obtained at P'anmunjŏm, indicated that the purge
had apparently been triggered by the growing influence of Pak and his followers within the KWP.[76]
Although there is no way of empirically ascertaining
the precise extent to which Kim Il-sŏng personally
dominates the KWP's decision-making organ, all-
pervasive signs of personality cult (i.e., the cult
of Kim Il-sŏng) in North Korea today strongly
suggest that his powers may be formidable. Indeed,
it may be safe to describe the present North Korean
regime as the dictatorship of Kim Il-sŏng.

Thus, North Korea's existing governmental, as
distinguished from Party, apparatus, is largely
superfluous, amounting to no more than an echo or
a shadow of the KWP. Its salient features may be
briefly described. The nominal legislative body
of the D.P.R.K. is the Supreme People's Assembly,
composed of 383 deputies elected by the North
Korean people for a three-year term. It is required
by the North Korean Constitution to meet semi-
annually. The Assembly elects a Presidium comprising a Chairman, four Vice-Chairmen, a Secretary-
General, and sixteen members. The present Chairman
is Ch'oe Yong-gŏn, who may be regarded as the cere-
monial head of state in North Korea. The executive
branch of the D.P.R.K. is its Cabinet. Organized

by the Assembly, it consists of a Premier, a first
Vice-Premier, eight Vice-Premiers, and twenty-nine
members, who head various ministries and agencies.
Kim Il-sŏng concurrently serves as the Premier of
the D.P.R.K.[77] The judicial branch consists of
three layers of courts--the Supreme People's Court
at the top, provincial courts in the middle, and
people's courts in the cities, counties, and dis-
tricts at the bottom. All judges are elected for
fixed terms by legislative assemblies at the
respective levels. Although nominally independent,
the North Korean courts are, in fact, subservient
to the KWP.[78]

It may be added parenthetically that the KWP
is not the only political party in North Korea,
although it is the only effective one. As in Communist China, there are a few pseudopolitical
parties as well as a multitude of organizations,
all of which are totally subservient to the KWP.
They include the North Korean Democratic Party,
Ch'ŏndogyo Ch'ŏngu-dang (Ch'ŏndogyo Young Friends'
Party), the Democratic Independence Party, the
Working People's Party, the Democratic Front for
the Unification of the Fatherland, the Committee
for the Peaceful Unification of the Fatherland,
and a host of trade unions and other organizations.[79]

In short, the sole depository of effective
political power in North Korea is the KWP, which
in turn is but an instrument of Kim Il-sŏng. At
the risk of oversimplification, it may thus be
asserted that North Korea's foreign policy is formulated by Kim Il-sŏng in the name of the KWP and
then formalized in the name of the D.P.R.K. To
say this is not to suggest that Kim Il-sŏng is
immune from either domestic or external constraints.
For, manifestly, the range of foreign-policy alternatives available to the North Korean dictator at
any given moment is sharply delimited by a multi-
plicity of variables--such as his perception of
North Korea's national self-interest, his need for
continued political control at home, North Korea's
prior commitments, and the availability of resources,
information, and time, to mention just a few. In
the remainder of the book, North Korea's specific
responses to the stimuli of international politics
will be examined.

NOTES TO CHAPTER 1

1. For information on the extent of Soviet
influence in the initial stage of North Korea's
political development, see Kim Ch'ang-sun, Pukhan
sibonyŏn-sa (Fifteen-Year History of North Korea)
(Seoul: Chimunkak, 1961), pp. 43-73 et passim;
Dong Jun Lee (Yi Tong-jun), Hwansang kwa hyŏnsil:
na ui kongsan chuŭi kwan (Fantasy and Fact: My
Observations of Communism) (Seoul: Tongban
T'ongsinsa, 1961), Chaps. 6, 7; U.S. Department of
State, North Korea: A Case Study in the Techniques
of Takeover, Department of State Publication No.
7118, Far Eastern Series No. 103 (Washington, D.C.:
Government Printing Office, 1961), pp. 100-114;
Philip Rudolph, North Korea's Political and Eco-
nomic Structure (New York: Institute of Pacific
Relations, 1959).

2. U.S. Department of State, op. cit., pp.
2-5. The reliability of information contained in
this State Department study is questioned by some
students of North Korea. Dae-Sook Suh, for instance,
calls the study a "dubious source"; letter from
Dae-Sook Suh, Department of Government, University
of Texas, Austin, Texas, November 29, 1967.

3. There were an estimated 300,000 such Koreans
in the prewar period. For an account of their activities, see Walter Kolarz, The Peoples of the Soviet
Far East (New York: Frederick A. Praeger, 1954),
pp. 32-42. A brief account of the origins of Korean
immigration to the Russian Far East is also provided by Dae-Sook Suh in his The Korean Communist
Movement, 1918-1948 (Princeton, N.J.: Princeton
University Press, 1967), pp. 4-11.

4. See U.S. Department of State, op. cit.
p. 101. This point is specifically questioned by
Dae-Sook Suh.

5. Ibid., p. 100.

6. Kim Ch'ang-sun, op. cit., pp. 58-59.

7. See Suh, op. cit., pp. 292-93.

8.   See Dae-Sook Suh, "The Elite Group of North Korea," paper read at the annual conference of the Association for Asian Studies, Chicago, Ill., March 20-22, 1967. The "partisan group" had previously been known as the "Kapsan faction," but Suh persuasively argues that the latter is a misnomer. In the early stage of the game, the partisan group was not sharply differentiated from the Soviet-Koreans. Thus they were jointly referred to as the "Soviet faction." But later developments clearly established the existence of an inner core centering around the person of Kim Il-sŏng. Membership into this elite was restricted to those Koreans who either shared Kim's anti-Japanese guerrilla activities in Manchuria or operated under his directions in Kapsan, a Korean town near the Manchurian border. See Kim Ch'ang-sun, op. cit., p. 60.

9.   See U.S. Department of State, op. cit., p. 115; Chong-Sik Lee, "Politics in North Korea: Pre-Korean War Stage," in Robert A. Scalapino (ed.), North Korea Today (New York: Frederick A. Praeger, 1963), pp. 8-9. On the activities of the NCKIL, see Suh, The Korean Communist Movement, pp. 226-30; Chong-Sik Lee, "Korean Communists and Yenan," The China Quarterly, No. 9 (January-March, 1962), 182-92.

10. U.S. Department of State, op. cit., p. 115. On the origins of the Korean Volunteer Corps, see Suh, The Korean Communist Movement, pp. 215-25.

11. Ibid., pp. 301-3; Kim Ch'ang-sun, op. cit., pp. 90-92; Chong-Sik Lee, "Politics in North Korea: Pre-Korean War Stage," pp. 5-6.

12. Ibid., p. 4.

13. Suh, The Korean Communist Movement, p. 301.

14. See Yun Sŭng-ho, Hang-il t'ujaeng ki (The Record of Anti-Japanese Struggle) (P'yŏngyang: Kungnip Ch'ulp'ansa, 1963), pp. 14-26; "Kim Il-sŏng changgun ŭi yakjŏn" ("A Brief Biography of Marshall Kim Il-sŏng"), Nodong Sinmun, April 15, 1952. Nodong Sinmun (Labor News) is the organ of the Central Committee of the Korean Workers' Party.

15. Suh, The Korean Communist Movement, pp. 256-93. The quoted passage is from p. 261.

16. Ibid., pp. 257-61.

17. For another illuminating work on the back-ground of the North Korean dictator, see Chong-Sik Lee, "Kim Il-sŏng of North Korea," Asian Survey, VII, 6 (June, 1967), 374-82. Lee's account is in substantial agreement with Suh's.

18. Kim Ch'ang-sun, op. cit., pp. 65-69.

19. See Dae-Sook Suh, The Korean Communist Movement, pp. 316-19, and his letter to the author dated November 29, 1967. Kim Ch'ang-sun's version, however, says that Kim Il-sŏng, not Kim Yŏng-bŏm, became the head of the North Korean Branch Bureau at the October, 1945, meeting. See Kim Ch'ang-sun, op. cit., pp. 94-96.

20. Ibid., pp. 69-73.

21. Ibid., pp. 97-99. The merger took place on August 28, 1946.

22. Ibid., pp. 99-104.

23. Ibid., pp. 107-11.

24. Ibid., pp. 115-21; Pak Tong-un, Pukhan t'ongch'i kiguron (The Government Structure in North Korea) (Seoul: Korea University Press, 1964), pp. 96-97, 204.

25. Chosŏn Minjujuŭi Inmin Konghwaguk Kwahagwŏn, Yŏksa Yŏn'guso, Chosŏn t'ongsa (A General History of Korea) (P'yŏngyang: Kwahagwŏn Ch'ulp'ansa, 1959), Vol. III, pp. 109-10. Cited hereafter as Chŏson t'ongsa.

26. U.S. Department of State, North Korea: A Case Study in the Techniques of Takeover, p. 114. The other facets of the Soviet direction of the North Korean Army discussed above are also revealed by the same source. See ibid., pp. 113-14.

27. For some clues, see Allen S. Whiting, China Crosses the Yalu: The Decision to Enter the Korean War (New York: The Macmillan Company, 1960).

28. U.S. Department of State, op. cit., p. 120.

29. Kim Ch'ang-sun, <u>op. cit.</u>, pp. 123-31.

30. <u>Ibid.</u>, pp. 132-34.

31. U.S. Department of State, <u>The Record on
Korean Unification, 1943-1960: Narrative Summary
with Principal Documents</u>, Department of State
Publication No. 7084, Far Eastern Series No. 101
(Washington, D.C.: Government Printing Office,
1960), pp. 22-23.

32. <u>Chosŏn t'ongsa</u>, Vol. III, p. 264.

33. Kim Ch'ang-sun, <u>op. cit.</u>, pp. 138-50. For
the details of the charges against Pak and others,
see Kim Il-sŏng's main report to the Third Congress
of the KWP on April 23, 1956, in <u>Chosŏn Nodongdang
chesamch'a taehoe chuyo munhŏnjip</u> (<u>Principal Documents of the Third Congress of the Korean Workers'
Party</u>) (P'yŏngyang: Korean Workers Party Press,
1956), pp. 74-83. It is, of course, entirely
possible that Pak and his followers may actually
have attempted to stage a <u>coup d'état</u>. However,
the charge that they were agents of the United
States is preposterous.

34. Kim Ch'ang-sun, <u>op. cit.</u>, pp. 150-60;
U.S. Department of the Army, <u>U.S. Army Area Hand-
book for Korea</u>, Department of the Army Pamphlet
No. 550-41 (Washington, D.C.: Government Printing
Office, 1964), pp. 271-72.

35. <u>Ibid.</u>

36. See <u>Nodong Sinmun</u>, October 13, 1966, and
Suh, "The Elite Group of North Korea." More on this
later in the chapter.

37. Rudolph, <u>North Korea's Political and Economic Structure</u>, p. 35.

38. <u>Ibid.</u>, pp. 35-40.

39. Joseph S. Chung, "Industrial Development
of North Korea, 1945-1964: Some Strategic Quanti-
tative Indicators," in Joseph S. Chung (ed.),
<u>Patterns of Economic Development: Korea</u> (Kalamazoo,
Mich.: Korea Research and Publication, Inc., 1966),
pp. 104-5.

40. Ibid., pp. 105-8.

41. "Total industrial output" or "gross industrial product" should not be confused with Gross
National Product (GNP). As used in and by North
Korea, the former refers to "the total value, in
monetary terms, of goods produced and technical
services rendered by industrial enterprises during
a given period of time." By "the value of technical services" is meant "the value of operations
involving processing of goods produced by other
enterprises, preparing materials discarded by
industrial plants for sale to the people, packing
goods, assembling parts of machines manufactured
by other enterprises, and repair services for other
enterprises on request." This means that the total
industrial output in the North Korean sense, and
in the sense in which it is used in other Soviet-
type economies, "contains elements of double counting, such as counting purchases for inter-enterprise
production more than once." See Chung, "Industrial
Development of North Korea," p. 115.

42. Tōitsu Chōsen nenkan (One Korea Yearbook),
1964 (Tokyo: Tōitsu Chōsen Shimbunsha, 1964),
p. 393.

43. Yoon T. Kuark, "Economic Development Contrast Between South and North Korea," in Chung
(ed.), Patterns of Economic Development: Korea,
p. 156.

44. Tōitsu Chōsen nenkan, 1964, p. 393.

45. Chosŏn chungang yŏn'gam (Korean Central
Yearbook), 1954-55 (P'yŏngyang: Chosŏn Chungang
T'ongsinsa, 1954), pp. 21-24.

46. Tōitsu Chōsen nenkan, 1964, p. 393.

47. See ibid., and Chong-Sik Lee, "Land Reform,
Collectivisation, and the Peasants in North Korea,"
in Scalapino (ed.), North Korea Today, p. 76.

48. The origin of the Great Leap Forward may
be traced to the declaration by the CCP in May,
1958, that its "general line of socialist construction" was "the achievement of more, quicker, better,
and more economical results in building socialism."
See Chalmers Johnson, "Building a Communist Nation

in China," in Robert A. Scalapino (ed.), <u>The Com-</u>
<u>munist Revolution in Asia: Tactics, Goals, and</u>
<u>Achievements</u> (Englewood Cliffs, N.J.: Prentice-
Hall, Inc., 1965), p. 65. As far as can be determined, the word "Ch'ŏllima" made its first appearance in <u>Nodong Sinmun</u> on June 13, 1958. The KWP
organ also carried a feature article on "Ch'ŏllima"
on August 2, 1958.

49. According to a North Korean source, "The
proportion of industry to agriculture was 69 to 31
already in 1958, and in 1960 it was 71 to 29."
See <u>Democratic People's Republic of Korea</u> (P'yŏngyang:
Foreign Languages Publishing House, 1964), p. 20.

50. <u>Tōitsu Chōsen nenkan, 1964</u>, pp. 393-94.
Joseph S. Chung points to some statistical evidence
which tends to suggest that North Korean claims
for the growth of the machine-building industry
during the Five-Year Plan period are substantially
exaggerated. See Chung, "Industrial Development
of North Korea," p. 114. Whether or not North
Korean statistics are generally reliable will be
discussed shortly.

51. <u>Tōitsu Chōsen nenkan, 1964</u>, p. 394.

52. For 1961 to 1963, see <u>ibid</u>. For 1963 and
1964, see <u>Nodong Sinmun</u>, January 16, 1965, and
January 19, 1966, respectively.

53. <u>Nodong Sinmun</u>, October 11, 1966.

54. See Kuark, "Economic Development Contrast
Between South and North Korea," pp. 192-95.

55. Chung, "Industrial Development of North
Korea," pp. 108-9.

56. Kuark, <u>op. cit</u>., pp. 195-96.

57. Joan Robinson, "Korean Miracle," <u>Monthly</u>
<u>Review</u>, January, 1965, p. 542.

58. <u>Ibid</u>., p. 543.

59. <u>Ibid</u>., pp. 543-44.

60. The origin and significance of "chuch'e" are discussed in Chap. 3. See also B. C. Koh, "North Korea and Its Quest for Autonomy," Pacific Affairs, XXXVIII, 3, 4 (Fall, Winter, 1965-66), 294-306.

61. Robinson, op. cit., pp. 547-48. According to North Korean sources, the proportion of foreign-aid contributions to that country's total state revenue during the postwar period declined sharply until it became zero in 1961. The reported percentage figures are: 33.4 per cent in 1954, 21.7 per cent in 1955, 16.5 per cent in 1956, 12.2 per cent in 1957, 4.5 per cent in 1958, 4.9 per cent in 1959, 2.6 per cent in 1960, and zero per cent in 1961-64. In 1964, 98 per cent of North Korea's state revenue came from the so-called socialist enterprises, and the remaining two per cent was derived from taxes. See Chosŏn chungang yŏn'gam (North Korean Central Yearbook), 1954-55 - 1965.

62. The term "economic independence" is used in a relative sense; it means the ability of an economy to sustain itself without foreign aid, but not necessarily without foreign trade. A generally favorable account of North Korea's postwar economic recovery is also found in Hōchō Kishadan, Kita Chōsen no kiroku (The Record of North Korea) (Tokyo: Shintoku Shosha, 1960). Of particular interests are Akimoto Hadeo, "Keizai ni tsuite" ("On the Economy"), pp. 75-104, and "Jukōgyo o meguru wadai" ("Topics on Heavy Industry"). Akimoto represented Tokyo's Yomiuri Shimbun, one of the three largest newspapers in Japan, on the team of seven Japanese journalists who visited North Korea in December, 1959, and January, 1960. The book is a collection of reports written by members of the team.

63. Dong Jun Lee, Hwansang kwa hyŏnsil, pp. 230-31.

64. Hōchō Kishadan, op. cit., pp. 41-43; pp. 128-33.

65. See "Ch'ŏngsan-li kyosi nŭn sahoe chuŭi nongch'on kyŏngni unyŏng ŭi chich'im ita" ("Ch'ŏngsan-li Instructions Provide Guidelines for Socialist Farm Management"), Kŭlloja (The Worker), February, 1966, pp. 2-7. Kŭlloja is the theoretical journal of the KWP, published monthly in P'yŏngyang.

For an English translation of the article, see
U.S. Department of Commerce, Joint Publications
Research Service (JPRS), Economic Report on North
Korea, No. 181; JPRS No. 35,739 (May 27, 1966),
pp. 1-7.

66.   See Kim Il-sŏng, Theses on the Socialist
Agrarian Question in Our Country (P'yŏngyang:
Foreign Languages Publishing House, 1964). For
evidence that Kim's ideas are being translated into
action in North Korea, see recent issues of Nodong
Sinmun. The frequency with which the "Theses" and
the problems connected with their implementation
are mentioned is rather revealing.

67.   Kim Il-sŏng, "On Further Developing the
Taean Work System," Selected Works, Vol. II
(P'yŏngyang: Foreign Languages Publishing House,
1965), pp. 376-77.

68.   Ibid., pp. 375-92; Tōitsu Chōsen nenkan,
1964, p. 478; Chosŏn chungang yŏn'gam, 1965, pp.
106-7; Kim Kyu-wŏn, "Taean ch'egye ha ŭi chibaein"
("The Manager Under the Taean Work System"),
Kŭlloja, June, 1966, pp. 28-34.

69.   See Chosŏn chungang yŏn'gam, 1965, p. 116.

70.   For North Korea's population figures, see
Chosŏn chungang yŏn'gam, 1964, p. 316.

71.   For a comparison between the KWP and the
CPSU regarding their membership requirements, see
Rudolph, North Korea's Political and Economic
Structure, pp. 30-31.

72.   Chosŏn chungang yŏn'gam, 1962, p. 217.

73.   Nodong Sinmun, October 6, 1966. Whereas
"delegates" have full powers, "alternates" have
only the right to speak but not the right to vote.

74.   Nodong Sinmun, October 13, 1966.

75.   For the background of the various KWP
leaders, see Suh, "The Elite Group of North Korea"
and The Korean Communist Movement, passim, and
Chong-Sik Lee, "Stalinism in the East," pp. 117-18.

76. Dong-A Ilbo, October 2, 1967.

77. Both the Presidium of the Supreme People's
Assembly and the Cabinet of the D.P.R.K. have undergone frequent reorganizations. The most recent
reorganization, reported by the North Korean Central News Agency on December 19, 1967, decreased
the number of Vice-Chairmen of the Presidium from
five to four, while increasing the number of Vice-
Premiers from seven to eight. The most interesting
aspect of the reorganization was that Pak Chŏng-ae
and Nam Il, both of whom had been stripped of their
Party posts in October, 1966, were retained in the
government hierarchy. Pak remained as a Vice-
Chairman of the Presidium of the Assembly, and Nam
kept his Vice-Premiership in the Cabinet. For the
preceding information, see Dong-A Ilbo, December 19,
1967. For the previous organizational setup, see
Chosŏn chungang yŏn'gam, 1965, pp. 113-14.

78. For a detailed description of North Korea's
judicial setup, see Ilpyong J. Kim, "The Judicial
and Administrative Structure in North Korea" in
Scalapino (ed.), North Korea Today, pp. 94-100.

79. For a complete list of the front organizations in North Korea, together with their brief
descriptions, see Tōitsu Chōsen nenkan, 1964,
pp. 335-38.

CHAPTER **2** NORTH KOREA
AND THE
SINO-SOVIET RIFT

The rift between the Soviet Union and Communist China, the two giants of the Communist world, is doubtless one of the most significant phenomena of the post-World War II era. Although the conflict did not come into full public view until 1960, its origins are commonly traced to the Twentieth CPSU Congress of February, 1956.[1] An analysis of North Korea's position in the dispute must, therefore, encompass the last decade in full. The increasingly acrimonious quarrel between the two most powerful members of the Communist camp has posed a major dilemma to the budding Communist nation north of the demilitarized zone on the Korean peninsula. Reluctant and, perhaps, unable to offend either side in the dispute, North Korea has taken pains to maintain the façade, if not the reality, of neutrality. With the deterioration of Sino-Soviet relations, however, North Korea was compelled to modify its aloof posture. Sensing a renewed threat from the militantly anti-Communist regime of General Chung Hee Park in Seoul, North Korea drifted toward the Chinese side during the period 1962-64. By early 1965, the honeymoon between Peking and P'yŏngyang was apparently over. Russo-Korean contacts visibly increased, and a corresponding cooling-off in Sino-Korean relations could be discerned. Yet it appears premature, if not inaccurate, to describe North Korea's present intrabloc behavior as Soviet-oriented. Rather, its wavering attitude is symptomatic of its strong desire and growing capacity for autonomy in the arena of intrabloc politics.

THE NORTH KOREAN DILEMMA

The split between Moscow and Peking has confronted North Korea with three possible, if over-
simplified, courses of action: (1) to side with
Moscow, (2) to side with Peking, and, finally,
(3) to remain neutral. This is not to imply that
these alternatives are clearly demarcated and hence
mutually exclusive. For North Korea can experiment
with all three, not simultaneously, to be sure, but
sequentially. That is to say, P'yŏngyang can now
flirt with the Soviet Union, now support the Chinese
position in the dispute, and now take the posture
of nonalignment. Vastly compounding the complex-
ities of the situation, however, are its unbreakable
ties with both countries.

To begin, the D.P.R.K. was literally "fathered"
by the Soviet Union. Had it not been for the latter
it would not have come into being. More importantly
Kim Il-sŏng and his associates could not possibly
have reached the pinnacle of political power in
North Korea without Russian help. Although it is
true that Kim and some of his present associates
had engaged in partisan warfare with the Japanese
in Manchuria, the total impact of their activities
on Japan's military capacity was comparatively
negligible. In different words, the "Korean revolution" was not of their own making but was handed
to them on a silver plate. What happened in North
Korea was not a spontaneous revolution but was
contrived--a revolution imposed from without. Kim
Il-sŏng did not "earn" his claim to leadership
through long and hard years of revolutionary struggle, though struggle he did. He became the Soviet
choice for North Korean leadership mainly through
his demonstrated loyalty to the Soviet Union,
coupled with his apparent capacity to lead. Perhaps, Kim deserves more credit than has so far
been accorded him for his ability to stay in power
for more than two decades. Regardless of the
utterly merciless manner in which he has pursued
his goal, Kim has plainly shown his remarkable
fitness for survival in totalitarian politics.
The fact nonetheless remains that the initial
backing of the Soviet military authorities was
the decisive factor in his rise to power.

Furthermore, the Soviets were so successful in Sovietizing North Korea that a marked similarity, if not identity, of interests existed between the two. No matter where one looked--be it culture, education, government structure, party apparatus, economic planning and organization, judicial system-- one could not but notice overwhelming Soviet influ- ence. If the Soviets brazenly exploited North Korea's industrial and agricultural resources, they also helped in its postwar reconstruction. Last but not least, was not the Soviet Union "the leader of the Socialist camp" as well as "the first social- ist country in the world?"

No less strong are the bonds that unite North Korea and Communist China. No other country has left such an indelible mark on Korean culture as has China. Chinese influence permeated practically every facet of Korean life. The Soviet occupation policy in North Korea carefully sought to neutralize Korea's traditional cultural affinities with China. This policy took on added significance in view of the presence in North Korea of the powerful Yenan group, a potential roadblock to the Soviet design of installing a Kremlin-oriented regime in P'yŏng- yang. It is worth noting that Russian, not Chinese, became the required foreign language in North Korean schools--a policy which has been consistently pursued despite P'yŏngyang's recent flirtation with Peking.

The Korean War marked a new watershed in Sino- Korean relations. By coming to the rescue of the North Korean regime on the brink of annihilation, the Chinese achieved overnight the lofty status of a true friend, benefactor, and comrade-in-arms. The friendship between the two neighboring coun- tries and peoples was thus firmly "sealed in blood." The "Chinese People's Volunteers" did not simply fight side by side with the "heroic Korean people." They also exhibited exemplary behavior toward the people they had come to help. During and after the war, North Korean newspapers were full of stories about how the Chinese soldiers helped the Korean people behind the front lines, even at the risk of their lives. Thus Kim Il-sŏng wrote in Jen-min Jih-pao (People's Daily), the organ of the CCP, on September 26, 1959:

> Chinese People's Volunteers set a
> shining example of noble moral
> character and deeds. Under the
> difficult conditions of the war
> they helped our farmers till and
> seed land and harvest. Braving
> the savage air raids of the U.S.
> imperialists, they saved the lives
> and properties of countless Koreans.
> They economized on their rations so
> that our refugees might partake in
> them. As a result, there developed
> between them and our people noble
> ties of love, self-sacrifice, and
> mutual cooperation.[2]

If there is any truth in such stories, it can readily
be imagined that the North Koreans must have been
tremendously impressed and gratified. The good
deeds of the Chinese must have appeared doubly
impressive to these Koreans who still had vivid
memories of the constant harassments and numerous
atrocities reportedly committed by the Russian
occupation forces.[3]

North Korea's sense of indebtedness to Communist China was sharply heightened by the latter's
extraordinarily generous assistance in the postwar
reconstruction program. Its own pressing needs at
home notwithstanding, the P.R.C. made a grant to
North Korea which initially exceeded that pledged
by the U.S.S.R. An additional factor strengthening
the sense of comradeship between Peking and P'yŏngyang is the stark realization that they both share
an archenemy--"United States imperialism." They
are both persuaded that the United States presents
the most formidable barrier to the realization of
their dreams. Just as Communist China is prevented
from "liberating" Taiwan and from playing what it
considers to be its rightful role in the world
arena by the "U.S. imperialists," so is North Korea's
cherished goal of national unification continually
frustrated by the menacing presence of U.S. troops
in South Korea, so the reasoning goes.

The two Asian regimes, furthermore, share
many problems. For one thing, they are both developing nations, not yet fully recovered from the
scars left by Western and Japanese colonialism.
Although they have had varying degrees of success

in their campaigns to wipe out poverty and to stand
on their own feet, they still remain in the ranks
of "have-not" nations. The Russians, on the other
hand, are clearly in the category of "have" nations.
Their intense dissatisfaction with the status quo,
burning hatred of colonialism, and uncompromising
militancy toward the comparatively affluent nations
of the West, a fortiori the United States and its
close allies, are in a large measure a function of
this common experience and world outlook shaped
thereby. No less important, perhaps, is the racial
background of the two peoples. It may be that the
North Koreans, having been colonized by the Japanese,
are less race-conscious than the Chinese, who have
suffered humiliation under the scandalous "unequal
treaties" imposed on them largely by the colonial
powers of the white West. Yet they are both intensely
aware that, when all is said and done, they are of
the same race and may never be accepted as equals
by the Caucasians, to which category, the Russians,
no less than the Western imperialists, most emphatically belong. Finally, one should not overlook
Kim Il-sŏng's Chinese background--his predominantly
Chinese education and guerrilla experience under
the Chinese in Manchuria. Such a long exposure to
China may or may not have made Kim more sympathetic
toward China, but it is a fact worth noting.

    Here, then, is the crux of the dilemma: North
Korea can ill afford to alienate the Soviet Union,
its liberator, political and economic sponsor, and,
above all, the leader of the socialist camp. Nor
can it afford to antagonize Communist China, its
cultural mentor, savior, erstwhile comrade-in-arms,
and fellow Asian nation. The way out of this
dilemma, as noted, is to be found in the policy of
neutrality. If North Korea can manage to remain
nonaligned, it may hopefully succeed in offending
neither party. And this was precisely the policy
followed by Kim Il-sŏng in the formative stage of
the Sino-Soviet conflict.

AMBIVALENT NEUTRALITY, 1956-61

    The immediate spark for the Sino-Soviet con-
troversy, as mentioned earlier, was provided by the
historic Twentieth Congress of the CPSU, held in
Moscow from February 14 to 25, 1956.[4] In his main

political report to the Congress, Khrushchev made
several major doctrinal innovations. First, he
declared that peaceful coexistence, and not military confrontation, was Soviet policy vis-à-vis
the Western bloc. Claiming that "the peaceful
coexistence of states with different social systems" was a time-honored Leninist principle,
Khrushchev emphasized in the strongest possible
terms that there was no practicable alternative to
peaceful coexistence. In his words, "there are
only two ways: either peaceful coexistence or the
most destructive war in history. There is no third
way." Significantly, he made it plain that he was
speaking for the entire socialist camp. Peaceful
coexistence, he said, was not simply "a fundamental
principle of Soviet foreign policy" but "one of the
cornerstones of the foreign policy of the Chinese
People's Republic and the other people's democ-
racies."5

     The second major doctrinal innovation unveiled
by the Soviet Premier was the jettisoning of the
"Marxist-Leninist proposition that wars are inevitable as long as imperialism exists." Because of the
drastically changed world situation in which the
socialist camp has become powerful enough to compel
the imperialists to renounce war, war is no longer
"fatalistically inevitable," he declared. The new
world climate, Khrushchev insisted, called for still
another modification in orthodox Communist doctrine:
Violence and civil war should not be looked upon
as the only way to remake society. In other words,
there are different paths to socialism. Although
the specific form of transition to socialism may
vary, there is one unalterable principle, that
"the working class headed by its vanguard" must
provide political leadership.6

     The most significant event of the Congress,
however, took place behind closed doors. In a
secret speech, Khrushchev mounted his famous attack
on Stalin, which led to the adoption of a resolution denouncing "the cult of the individual."7
Of all the doctrinal reforms initiated by Khrushchev, the de-Stalinization and antipersonality cult
campaigns proved the hardest for the Chinese to
accept. The immediate reaction in Peking was one
of both consternation and dismay. Not only had
Stalin been enshrined as a demigod in China, but
Mao Tse-tung was closely following his footsteps.
Further, the assault on the cult of the individual
could very well have been aimed at Mao.

If these developments annoyed the CCP leadership, they were not greeted with enthusiasm by the
KWP leadership. Excerpts from Khrushchev's main
political report were published in Nodong Sinmun
on February 16. The following day, the same newspaper editorially endorsed his major doctrinal
innovations. Full support of the Soviet position
was also voiced by Ch'oe Yong-gŏn, North Korea's
chief delegate to the Congress and vice-chairman of
the KWP Central Committee, in his congratulatory
speech to the Congress on February 18. But the KWP
organ gave no hints of Khrushchev's secret denunciation of Stalin other than by reproducing without
comment the resolution of the CPSU Central Committee
on the cult of the individual. The first indication that Stalin had fallen into disgrace in the
Soviet Union came on April 2, when Nodong Sinmun
reproduced a Pravda editorial of March 28, "Why Is
the Cult of Individual Alien to Marxism-Leninism?"
The editorial contained an express criticism of
Stalin. Only a few days earlier, Jen-min Jih-pao,
the CCP organ, had done the same.

On April 7, two days after Jen-min Jih-pao
published an editorial, "On the Historical Experience of the Dictatorship of the Proletariat,"
cautiously revealing for the first time the CCP's
lukewarm attitude toward de-Stalinization, Nodong
Sinmun commented:

> ...The collective principle in
> party leadership is of enormous
> practical significance. The Cen-
> tral Committee of our Party /KWP/,
> mindful of Comrade Kim Il-sŏng's
> repeated emphasis on the matter,
> has therefore spared no effort to
> strictly observe the Leninist
> principle of collective leader-
> ship, to encourage intra-party
> democracy, criticism, and self-
> criticism, and to further
> strengthen ties with the masses.8

No doubt, the preceding was meant as a repudiation
in advance of the possible charge that Kim Il-sŏng
was propagating the cult of the individual in North
Korea. The Chinese editorial was reproduced in
full the following day.

As already noted, however, the KWP leadership
could not but feel the impact of the Twentieth
CPSU Congress. Discontented elements in the Party
began covertly to organize a rebellion. Charges of
dictatorship and personality cult were leveled
against Kim Il-sŏng by influential members of the
Soviet and Yenan factions. When the Third Congress
of the KWP opened on April 23, in P'yŏngyang, the
picture of Kim Il-sŏng was conspicuously absent
from the convention hall--an obvious sign that the
KWP leadership was anxious to avoid any manifestation of the cult of Kim Il-sŏng.[9]

While Kim Il-sŏng was out of the country on a
tour of the Soviet Union and Eastern Europe, the
anti-Kim forces intensified their campaign, now no
longer entirely covert, to loosen, and if possible
terminate, Kim's political control. Shortly before
the North Korean leader returned to P'yŏngyang,
Nodong Sinmun spoke out on the cult-of-personality
controversy. In its editorial of July 16, "Collective Leadership and Centralized Control," the
official voice of the KWP made a thinly veiled
defense of the cult of Kim Il-sŏng and his openly
dictatorial rule. Declaring that a prerequisite to
collective leadership is the establishment of
democratic centralism, that is to say, the enforce-
ment of discipline and control from above or, more
bluntly, dictatorship by the Party elites, it argued
that North Korea could not possibly have survived
all the trials and tribulations to which it had
been subjected but for the "correct and courageous
leadership" of the KWP elites headed by Kim Il-sŏng.
Although the KWP fully endorsed the decision of the
CPSU to root out the cult of personality, it
attached a rather novel meaning to the term: The
cult of personality, Nodong Sinmun implied, was
synonymous with "sectarianism" and hence with "an
intra-party struggle for hegemony." According to
this interpretation, any move to challenge the
authority of Kim Il-song served to perpetrate the
cult of personality!

The power of the masses becomes indomitable
only when the masses are both politically and morally
united and tightly organized, the newspaper said.
"It is therefore incumbent upon the masses," it
continued, "not only to claim their role as the
creators of history and the decisive performers of
revolutionary tasks but also to correctly realize

the part that must be played by the vanguard, that is, the Marxist-Leninist party and its leadership, in organizing and guiding the revolution." The KWP organ tried to show the consistency of the preceding view with orthodox Communist doctrine by quoting directly from Lenin. An important task confronting the KWP, according to Nodong Sinmun, was "to unite ever more firmly behind its Central Committee led by Comrade Kim Il-sŏng, to tighten revolutionary discipline within the Party, and to steadfastly preserve the ideological and behavioral unity of the Party." Any move aimed at weakening Kim Il-sŏng's leadership and hence Party unity was labeled as "petty-bourgeois" and "anarchistic."

Upon his return, Kim Il-sŏng must have felt constrained to further clarify and defend his precarious position. On August 1, Nodong Sinmun published another editorial on the subject. Entitled "A New Milestone in the International Labor Movement and the Might of Proletarian Internationalism," the editorial faithfully echoed Pravda's line that the cult of the individual is totally alien to Marxism-Leninism. Quoting from Kim Il-sŏng's own denunciation of the discredited practice, made in an interview with a visiting Indian journalist, it went on:

> ...the CPSU is entirely justified
> in waging a struggle against the
> cult of personality which has
> impeded both the progressive devel-
> opment of Marxism-Leninism and the
> transition to a Communist society,
> while, at the same time, duly rec-
> ognizing the great contributions
> made by Stalin, the outstanding
> Marxist-Leninist, to the success
> of socialist revolution and con-
> struction in the Soviet Union as
> well as to the international labor
> movement.[10]

The newspaper took note of a "great uproar" created by de-Stalinization among the capitalist and imperialist countries. If they have any hopes of exploiting the situation, they are bound to be disappointed, it said. For, no matter how it may appear on the surface, the socialist camp "is as solid and united as ever, bound together by the

unbreakable chain of proletarian internationalism."
The KWP organ particularly underlined North Korea's
inseparable ties with the Soviet Union. It recalled
that the Soviet Union not only liberated the Korean
people from Japanese imperialism but continuously
provided "huge and selfless assistance, material
as well as moral, to our struggle to build a new
way of life." What is more, it added, the Korean
people were filled with both inspiration and hope
by the success with which the Soviet Union was
pursuing the goal of Communist construction.

As noted, the Twentieth CPSU Congress-inspired
revolt against Kim Il-sŏng ended in total failure,
and North Korea continued to give verbal support
to the antipersonality cult drive, while clearly
betraying it in actual deeds. If he was to stay
in power, Kim Il-sŏng could not live up to the
letter and spirit of the CPSU resolution any more
than Mao Tse-tung could. North Korea, then, reacted
rather cautiously to the unexpected turn of events
in the international Communist movement. Initially
confused and bewildered, it waited until its fraternal parties, in particular the CCP, made known
their reactions. Apparently following the Chinese
lead, it went through the motion of formally embrac-
ing the doctrinal innovations but showed an extreme
reluctance to translate them into practice.

Meanwhile, the rapprochement between the Soviet
Union and Yugoslavia was hailed as a "positive contribution" to the easing of world tensions and to
the restoration of an atmosphere of confidence
essential to harmonious international relations.[11]
The Central Committee of the League of Communists
of Yugoslavia reciprocated by sending a congratulatory telegram to P'yŏngyang on the opening of
the Third Congress of the KWP. The telegram showed
that the Yugoslav Communist Party had been invited
to attend the Congress, but that it "regretfully"
could not accept the invitation.[12] Later, North
Korea enthusiastically applauded the joint Soviet-
Yugoslav communiqué issued on June 20 in Moscow, at
the conclusion of Tito's visit there. Nodong
Sinmun, reproducing the full text of the communiqué,
declared in an editorial that Tito's Moscow visit
turned out to be "an epoch-making event" in the
annals of international Communism.[13] North Korea's
favorable reaction to the readmission of Yugoslavia
into the Communist camp was but a reflection of the

prevailing sentiment in the entire bloc. For Communist China went even further than the P'yŏngyang
regime by formally establishing diplomatic relations with Belgrade. Peking must have been encouraged by the prospect of greater autonomy and equality
in intrabloc relations which the rapprochement
seemed to herald.

North Korea's identitication with the Soviet
Union thus remained intact; it continued to pay
homage to that "great leader of the socialist camp."
Nor was there any noticeable strain in its relations with the P.R.C. Whenever an appropriate occasion arose, North Korea did not fail to reaffirm its
warm friendship and strong ties with the Mao Tse-
tung regime. Thus the opening of the Eighth Congress of the CCP on September 15, in Peking was
hailed as marking a significant watershed in world
history. Nodong Sinmun took pains to point out
that the Soviet Union and the P.R.C. were one in
their pursuit of "peace-loving" foreign policy and
that the international Communist movement was
"invincibly united." Because the Chinese revolution is manifestly a component part of the world
proletarian revolution, it said, there is a "blood
relationship" between the historic victory achieved
by the CCP and the Chinese people on the one hand
and the interests of the Korean revolution on the
other. Significantly, however, North Korea refused
to elevate Communist China to the status of leader
of the socialist bloc, which it reserved exclusively for the Soviet Union. Even in an editorial
primarily aimed at lauding the CCP, the KWP organ
made it plain that the Soviet Union takes precedence
over the P.R.C. North Korea, it declared, was proud
and reassured to have such great allies as the
Soviet Union and the P.R.C.[14]

P'yŏngyang's support of Communist China's
admission into the United Nations was unqualified.
That "artificial barriers" should have prevented
such a great power as the P.R.C., whose people
comprise one quarter of the entire world population, from occupying its rightful place in the
United Nations is an inestimable loss not only to
the authority of the organization itself, but also
to the peace of mankind, it declared. The exclusion
of Communist China, it went on, is wholly contrary
to the purposes and spirit of the U.N. Charter, and
only serves to aggravate world tensions. As a
Nodong Sinmun editorial put it:

It is utterly preposterous to
think that the United Nations
can satisfactorily cope with
the problem of maintaining
peace and security in the world,
particularly in Asia, without
the participation of the People's
Republic of China.

Nor is there anything more
illusory than to believe that
the human trash Chiang Kai-shek
clique, barely eking out its
existence in the corner of Taiwan
with the guns and swords of the
United States, can represent 600
million Chinese.[15]

As 1956 drew to a close, North Korea's loyalty
to the Kremlin showed no sign of abating. The
dramatic events in Eastern Europe--the abortive
Hungarian revolution and the near-revolt in Poland--
failed to stir P'yŏngyang. After deliberately
playing down the event in Hungary,[16] Nodong Sinmun
gave full support to the Soviet handling of the
rebellion, calling the Western reaction to it "a
reckless attempt to interfere with the internal
affairs of other countries."[17] North Korea joined
Communist China in welcoming the Soviet Declaration
of October 31, on intrabloc relations. The declaration, which spelled out the Soviet Government's
willingness to rectify its past "violations and
mistakes which belittled the principle of equal
rights in the relations between the Socialist
states," was acclaimed as both "a great contribution to the solidarity of the Socialist bloc" and
"a severe blow to the capitalist bloc intent on
destroying the Socialist nations."[18]

Exactly a year later, North Korea took part
in the celebration of the fortieth anniversary of
the October Revolution in Moscow. The leader of
the North Korean delegation, Kim Il-sŏng, also
attended the meeting of the twelve ruling Communist
parties, from which Tito was conspicuously absent.
In a speech to the Russian people broadcast over
Radio Moscow, the North Korean Premier and Party
chief praised the accomplishments of the Soviet
Union in most extravagant terms. Fully endorsing
the "consistently peace-loving" Soviet foreign

policy, he declared that "the Korean people stand
shoulder to shoulder with the Soviet people and
will do the same forever."[19] The declaration
which resulted from the meeting of Communist leaders
also had the full blessing of North Korea. Among
other things, the Moscow Declaration stressed the
need for, as well as the fact of, bloc unity and
solidarity and condemned "modern revisionism,"
which was an obvious reference to the defiant attitude of the Yugoslav Communist Party. Although
there are different roads to socialism necessitated
by the historically specific conditions of each
country, Nodong Sinmun promptly commented, it does
not necessarily follow that the universal principles
of Marxism-Leninism can be deviated from at will.
"The so-called national Communism, revisionism,
dogmatism, sectarianism, and all other tendencies
which the imperialists are spreading," it continued,
"undermine the universal truths and purity of
Marxism-Leninism, and we must never allow them to
subvert the international Communist movement."
It is worth noting that North Korea also saw the
Moscow Declaration as a "telling reaffirmation of
the correctness of the Twentieth CPSU Congress
which opened a new era in the international workers'
and Communist movements."[20]

North Korea's relations with both Moscow and
Peking continued to expand in 1958. If the year
was particularly notable for P'yŏngyang's "emulation" of Chinese policies on the domestic front,[21]
it also witnessed stepped-up cultural, economic,
and political intercourse between North Korea and
the Soviet Union. When the Kim Il-sŏng regime
renewed its perennial offensive for the "peaceful
unification" of Korea in February, it received
prompt and unqualified support from both Communist
China and the Soviet Union. Communist China did
not simply stop at giving verbal support to North
Korea's proposed formula for unification, but agreed
to help the latter achieve its goal by withdrawing
the "Chinese People's Volunteers" from Korean soil.
A P.R.C. Government delegation led by Chou En-lai
visited North Korea from February 14 to 21 in order
to work out the details of Chinese evacuation.
Upon arrival at the P'yŏngyang Airport, Chou En-lai
not only reaffirmed the "ever-lasting" Sino-Korean
friendship, but sought to boost North Korea's
national pride by declaring that China was eager
to "learn" from North Korea's experience in socialist construction.[22]

A joint Sino-North Korean communiqué issued on
February 20 announced that the two governments had
agreed on a plan whereby the Chinese People's
Volunteers (CPV) would be completely withdrawn by
the end of 1958. The communiqué challenged the
United States to withdraw its troops from South
Korea also. In a statement issued on the same day
in P'yŏngyang by the headquarters of the CPV, Communist China pledged its determination to defend
North Korea from American aggression in the future.
Should the U.S. imperialists launch another war of
aggression against the Korean people, it said, the
Chinese people would, without a moment's hesitation,
send their "best sons and daughters" to fight
shoulder to shoulder with their heroic Korean
brethren.[23] The Soviet Union lost no time in
voicing full support for this position.[24]

When Jen-min Jih-pao published an editorial
expressly denouncing the "modern revisionism" of
the League of Communists of Yugoslavia on May 5,
it was quickly reproduced in Nodong Sinmun. Pravda
followed suit a few days later. North Korea's own
position, however, was not made public until May 15.
An unsigned article which appeared in the KWP organ
stated that, although the League of Communists of
Yugoslavia had the right to manage its own internal
affairs without interference from fraternal parties,
it must nevertheless willingly subject itself to
"legitimate, comradely criticism" on matters concerning the deviation from and distortion of the
basic principles of Marxism-Leninism, "an underpin-
ning of Communist world outlook as well as the
ideological weapon of all Communists." Significantly, the article added:

>...all Communists worthy of the
>name have always defended the
>Soviet Union. We search in vain
>for a historical example of a
>person who became a genuine Com-
>munist while, simultaneously,
>opposing the Soviet Union. He
>who opposed the Soviet Union
>invariably either inflicted dam-
>age to the revolution or betrayed
>the interests of his people.
>Such is the lesson of history.[25]

This was a relatively mild criticism, for within
three months North Korea was to denounce Yugoslavia
in unrestrained language. Spurred by the Khrushchev-
Mao statement of August 3, declaring their common
determination to "wage an uncompromising struggle"
against Yugoslav revisionism, Nodong Sinmun editorialized that there was no alternative to crushing
the "dirty Yugoslav revisionists whose abominable
identity as faithful servants of imperialism has
been fully exposed."[26]

In terms of domestic economic policy, the
P'yŏngyang regime manifested a clear weakness for
Chinese innovations, of which the Great Leap Forward and the commune movement were most outstanding.
We have already seen that both of these innovations
were "emulated" by North Korea. Even in the absence
of positive proof, both the timing and pattern of
North Korea's Ch'ŏllima (Flying Horse) Movement and
integration of agricultural cooperatives strongly
suggest that they have been inspired by Chinese
experimentation. Glenn D. Paige shows that North
Korea imitated China in at least three other aspects:
It decided "to combine economic and administrative
units at the lowest rural administrative level, ...
to adopt handicraft methods of local industrial production, and to make Party organs directly respon-
sible for economic and administrative decisions."[27]

In November and December, a top-level North
Korean delegation headed by Kim Il-sŏng paid a ten-
day visit to the P.R.C. Kim met with Mao Tse-tung
and other Chinese leaders, discussing ways to
strengthen both Sino-Korean friendship and the
"unity of the Socialist camp." Having reached a
"complete agreement" on their views, Mao and Kim
issued a joint communiqué on December 8 in Peking.
The communiqué expressed full support for the "peaceful initiatives" of the Soviet Union aimed at over-
all arms reduction, cessation of nuclear testing,
and the termination of the allied Berlin occupation;
reiterated their demand for complete withdrawal of
American troops from Korean and Chinese soil alike;
and pledged their unstinting efforts toward the
dual goal of "waging an uncompromising struggle
against modern revisionism" and "strengthening the
unity of the Socialist camp headed by the Soviet
Union."[28]

Additional signs of deepening Sino-North
Korean friendship were provided by a visit of a
North Korean military delegation to Communist China
in November and December, conclusion of numerous
commercial and economic agreements between the two
countries, exchange of scores of educational,
cultural, artistic, and athletic teams, and, finally,
the establishment of both the Sino-Korean Friendship
Association (Peking) and the Korean-Chinese Friendship Association (P'yŏngyang), and the subsequent
observance of a "Korean-Chinese Friendship Month"
in October.[29]

It must be stressed that P'yŏngyang's pro-
Chinese gestures were wholly independent of its
posture toward the Soviet Union. The Sino-Soviet
conflict was still in its embryonic stage, and
North Korea had yet to face the problem of taking
sides in any clear-cut fashion. An increase in
Sino-Korean contacts could thus be coupled with a
corresponding increase in Soviet-Korean interaction.
That was precisely what happened. The Soviet Union
actively championed North Korean causes both in
the United Nations and out, and P'yŏngyang reciprocated by echoing the Kremlin line whenever the
occasion arose. Exchanges of cultural, scientific,
economic, and even military missions were vigorously carried on. The Soviet Union reportedly
even agreed to provide North Korea with technical
assistance in the peaceful uses of atomic energy.
It is worth noting that the founding of the Sino-
Korean Friendship Association in Peking was preceded
by the formation of the Soviet-Korean Friendship
Association in Moscow on July 16.[30]

The Kremlin, of course, could not have remained
completely indifferent to North Korea's emulation
of Chinese practices. By carefully refraining from
making any presumptuous claims offensive to Soviet
sensibilities, however, the Kim Il-sŏng regime
managed to maintain an excellent rapport with Moscow.
Unlike the Chinese, the North Koreans neither adopted
the name "commune" nor boasted of having found a
shortcut to Communism; instead, they retained the
relatively innocuous name of "agricultural cooperative" for their newly integrated collective
farms, which came very close to being carbon copies
of Chinese communes.

At the Twenty-first Congress of the CPSU,
held in Moscow from January 27 to February 5, 1959,
North Korea was represented by Kim Il-sŏng, who in
his congratulatory speech on January 30 reiterated
North Korea's platitudinous support of the Kremlin
line: Khrushchev's denunciation of Yugoslav
revisionism, his insistence that "complete equality
and independence" should govern intrabloc relations, and his denial of an incipient rift between
the CPSU and the CCP were all heartily applauded
by the North Korean ruler.[31]

The Sino-Indian border clash of August and
September, in which the Soviet Union took a neutral
stand, must have posed a dilemma to P'yŏngyang.
Summing up North Korea's record in foreign affairs
for the preceding year, the 1960 Korean Central
Yearbook not only mentioned gains in relations
with such neutral nations as India, Indonesia, the
United Arab Republic, and Burma, but also stated
that North Korea had "expressed complete solidarity
with the justifiable position of the PRC" in the
"Sino-Indian territorial question" which was "part
of an Asia-wide anti-Communist and anti-Chinese
campaign conducted by the U.S. imperialists."[32]
In short, North Korea supported Communist China,
but refrained from directly attacking India. The
latter was only inferentially criticized for having
fallen prey to the anti-Chinese plot of the U.S.
imperialists. This pro-Chinese stand was significant in view of the fact that the Soviet refusal
to back China in the dispute, by the latter's own
admission, infuriated Peking, contributing to the
deterioration of the already-strained Sino-Soviet
relations.[33]

Yet North Korea was at pains to demonstrate
its allegiance to Moscow by hailing both Khrushchev's
visit to the United States in September and Eisenhower's proposed visit to the Soviet Union as
"enormously stimulating events in the improvement
of the international situation." It "fervently
welcomed" the visits which, hopefully, "would promote mutual understanding between the Soviet Union
and the United States, bring the 'cold war' to an
end, ease international tensions, and contribute
to world peace." Assessing the over-all impact of
Khrushchev's American journey, North Korea claimed
a "victory for the peace-loving foreign policy of
the Soviet Union."[34]

As noted, the year 1960 marked the beginning
of open polemics between Moscow and Peking, thus
exposing to the entire world the existence of a
conflict between the two largest Communist nations.
The conflict, to be sure, had been long in the
making, but had thus far eluded the attention of
all but the most perceptive observers of the Communist scene. It became public knowledge, however,
with the publication of the article, "Long Live
Leninism!" in Hung Chi (Red Flag), the CCP theoretical journal, on April 16, 1960. The article,
commemorating the ninetieth anniversary of Lenin's
birth, repudiated the doctrinal innovations of the
Twentieth CPSU Congress, clearly indicating that
they were alien to the teachings of Lenin. It
declared:

> We believe in the absolute correct-
> ness of Lenin's thinking: War is
> an inevitable outcome of systems of
> exploitation and the source of
> modern wars is the imperialist sys-
> tem. Until the imperialist system
> and the exploiting classes come to
> an end, wars of one kind or another
> will always occur.[35]

While recognizing the desirability of peaceful
coexistence with nations having different social
systems, the article directly challenged the notion
that peaceful transition to socialism was actually
feasible under the prevailing circumstances.[36]

To judge from its later reaction, North Korea
must have been in full agreement with the preceding
views; but Nodong Sinmun merely reproduced the
article, withholding any editorial comment.[37] Apart
from its understandable reluctance to offend the
Kremlin, the KWP must have been too preoccupied
with the dramatic events then unfolding in South
Korea to pay much attention to the new developments
in Sino-Soviet relations. The dictatorial regime
of Dr. Syngman Rhee had just been overthrown by
student-led uprisings in South Korea, and North
Korea justifiably saw a golden opportunity to renew
its campaign for North-South negotiations that would
lead to unification of the peninsula under North
Korean influence, if not domination.

Meanwhile, Soviet-Korean relations continued to be warm and close. On August 13, Nodong Sinmun reported that Khrushchev had accepted an invitation to visit North Korea in October, but the visit never materialized. The D.P.R.K. Government, however, was all enthusiasm and gratitude in September, when the Soviet Premier supported its position and proposals on Korean unification at the United Nations.[38]

North Korean sympathy for Chinese views in the no-longer secret ideological quarrel between Moscow and Peking was made plain on the heels of the Conference of Eighty-One Communist and Workers' Parties, which was held in Moscow in November. The "first formal meeting of representatives of all the world's Communist parties to take place since before the Second World War," the conference had the apparent goal of working out a common program for the whole Communist movement and of ironing out the differences between the CPSU and the CCP.[39] The significance which world Communist leaders attached to the conference was indicated by the presence of practically all leading Communists. Two important absentees were Mao Tse-tung and Palmiro Togliatti.[40] Kim Il-sŏng was also absent.[41]

The "Statement" of the Moscow conference was a patchwork of compromises which not only concealed the extent of disagreements between Moscow and Peking, but managed to present the façade of unity. Nodong Sinmun, although jubilant at the "demonstration of the invincible unity of the international Communist movement," made it clear that the KWP shared Chinese views regarding the world situation. Moscow could hardly have been pleased by the North Korean assertion that "the peoples of all countries know that the danger of a new world war has not yet been removed." Nor could it have endorsed the following statements:

> As is indicated by the /Moscow/ Statement, to struggle for peace in the contemporary setting is to be ever on the alert, to ceaselessly expose imperialist policies, to sharply scrutinize the maneuvers and conspiracies of war arsonists, and to unite all the peace-loving forces of the world.

...Peace is not to be begged
for; it must be conquered. To
crush and paralyze imperialism
is the only way to win peace.[42]

The KWP organ also echoed the Peking line that the
peaceful coexistence of countries with different
social systems "does not mean abandoning the class
struggle." Peaceful coexistence, it said, was but
"one form of the class struggle between socialism
and capitalism." "It does not preclude but pre-
supposes a political and ideological struggle with
capitalism," the paper continued.[43]

If the Kremlin was annoyed by North Korea's
pro-Peking attitude, it did not show its feelings.
On the same day that Nodong Sinmun published the
above-mentioned editorial, the Soviet Government
issued a statement reiterating its long-standing
support of North Korean proposals for national
unification. On December 24, the Soviet Union
signed agreements with North Korea, which, among
other things, committed Soviet technical assistance
in the construction and expansion of industrial
and power plants in North Korea in the period 1961-
67. Earlier in the year, the Soviet Union had
agreed to deliver to North Korea 85 million rubles
worth of goods free of charge by the end of the
year. In October, it had also signed a protocol
with P'yŏngyang that would exempt the latter from
repayment of a debt of 760 million rubles and would
also extend the expiration date of another debt
amounting to 140 million rubles for ten years
beginning in 1967.[44] Despite its own economic
difficulties, Communist China also continued its
assistance to P'yŏngyang. In a series of agreements signed in Peking on October 13, it agreed to
make a long-term loan of 420 million rubles to
North Korea during the period 1961-64 and to assist
in the construction of factories there.[45] All this
was clearly intended to help North Korea carry out
its Seven-Year Plan of 1961-67.

If North Korea was immensely encouraged by
the sudden demise of the Syngman Rhee regime in
April, 1960, it was profoundly disappointed by the
equally unexpected military coup in Seoul in May,
1961. Having tirelessly pursued the policy of
stirring up support in South Korea for its formula
for "peaceful unification," the P'yŏngyang regime

followed with keen interest the new developments
in Seoul. While hailing the downfall of Premier
John M. Chang as "just" and "natural," North Korea
expressed alarm at "the consistently reactionary
behavior" of General Chang To-yong, the ostensible
leader of the coup. General Chang was presently
exposed as a mere front man for a group of young
army and marine officers who had masterminded and
executed the revolt. As the militantly anti-
Communist position of the new military regime in
Seoul became increasingly apparent, North Korea
declared that the coup d'état was the "conspiracy
of U.S. imperialists," who, disillusioned by the
impotence of their "puppet," John M. Chang, had
decided to replace him with a "military-fascist
regime."46 That the Kim Il-sŏng regime must have
sensed a real threat from the new South Korean
regime is suggested by the haste with which it
proceeded to conclude mutual-defense treaties with
both the Soviet Union and Communist China.

On May 30, a month before Kim Il-sŏng left for
Moscow and Peking in order to negotiate the above
treaties, a Soviet good-will delegation led by
Alexei Kosygin, then First Deputy Premier of the
U.S.S.R., arrived in the North Korean capital.
Just what he was after remains unclear, but the
speeches he made in P'yŏngyang provide some clues
as to the nature of his mission. Expressing full
support to North Korea's "peace-loving proposal"
to unify the peninsula, Kosygin assured the North
Koreans that "the Soviet people stand ready to provide whatever assistance may be necessary to preserve the hard-won fruits" of the socialist revolution in their country. He hastened to add, however, that the socialist camp did not want war.
In his words:

> We need peace in order to build
> a new way of life. That is why
> the Soviet Government invariably
> carries out the policy of peace-
> ful co-existence and consistently
> advocates general and complete
> disarmament as well as a ban on
> atomic and hydrogen weapons.
> While steadfastly pursuing the
> policy of maintaining and con-
> solidating peace in the world,
> the Soviet Government is

diligently searching for ways
and means to settle international
disputes and to enhance mutual
understanding among nations.

...The fraternal friendship
among socialist nations is a
great fruit of our revolution
which we must safeguard like
the apple of our eyes.[47]

Shortly thereafter, North Korea signed a
"Treaty of Friendship, Cooperation, and Mutual
Assistance" first with the Soviet Union and then
with the P.R.C. The Soviet-Korean treaty, signed
in Moscow on July 6, stipulated that in the event
either contracting party was militarily attacked
by another nation or a coalition of nations, the
other party should, without delay, provide military
and other assistance "with all means at its dis-
posal." It further provided that both parties
would not only refrain from entering into agreements
or coalitions hostile to the other party but that
they would consult each other on important international issues affecting their mutual interests.
The two countries also pledged "all possible"
mutual assistance in the economic and cultural
fields on the basis of the principles of equality,
respect for national sovereignty, territorial
integrity, and noninterference in the internal
affairs of other nations. The treaty, to take
effect upon the exchange of documents of ratifica-
tion in P'yŏngyang, would be valid for ten years.
In the absence of notification by either party
of its intention to abrogate the treaty at least
a year in advance, it would continue to be valid
for the next five years, subject to renewal thereafter in like manner.[48]

In a speech at a Moscow mass rally marking the
friendship between the Russian and Korean peoples,
Khrushchev made it crystal clear that an attack
on North Korea would be construed as an attack on
the Soviet Union. He quickly added, however, that
the Soviet people "sincerely wish that the military
clause of the /Soviet-Korean/ treaty will not have
to be invoked." He underlined the need for peace,
indicating that the Soviet Union placed top priority
on a peaceful, not military, approach to the unification of Korea.[49]

Kim Il-sŏng flew from Moscow to Peking on
July 10. The next day he and Chou En-lai signed
the Sino-Korean treaty on behalf of their respective governments. It was a carbon copy of the
Soviet-Korean treaty but for two seemingly minor
features. Unlike the Moscow treaty, it made no
reference to the need "to maintain and consolidate
peace and security in the Far East and in the world
on the basis of the purposes and principles of the
United Nations." Furthermore, it lacked any
expiration date. It would "remain in effect continuously unless and until both contracting parties
agree to revise or abrogate it."[50] All this made
it extremely difficult to assess the status of
North Korea's relations with the two Communist
giants. Was P'yŏngyang closer to Peking than it
was to Moscow at that particular juncture in Sino-
Soviet relations? On the one hand, North Korea
made it known that it still considered the Soviet
Union as its number one ally as well as protector
by concluding a treaty with the latter first. On
the other hand, the absence of an expiration date
in the Sino-Korean treaty appeared to symbolize
the confidence with which North Korea and Communist
China viewed their fraternal friendship. A diametrically opposed interpretation, of course, should
not be ruled out: By agreeing to an indefinite
duration of the treaty, both parties also left open
the possibility of terminating it any time.

North Korea's ambivalent posture toward the
ever-growing Sino-Soviet feud was further underlined by Kim Il-sŏng's behavior at the Twenty-second
Congress of the CPSU in October. His speech to the
Congress on October 21 was as adulatory as ever.
The CPSU, he assured his audience, was "the acknowledged vanguard of the international Communist movement." By saying these seemingly innocuous words,
the North Korean leader was momentarily siding with
the Soviet Union in opposition to the P.R.C., for
the latter had insisted that the CPSU be referred
to not as "the vanguard" of world Communism but as
"the leader" of the socialist camp. Kim added that
it was not only the duty of all Communists but also
a fundamental principle of proletarian internationalism to unite behind the CPSU. Soviet-Korean
friendship, he said, would be "ever-lasting and
imperishable." Significantly, Kim neither mentioned
Communist China nor ventured even a veiled defense
of the Albanian Party of Labor, the official whipping

boy of the Congress.[51] The following day, however,
Kim Il-sŏng joined in the symbolic defiance of the
Kremlin by placing wreaths on the tombs of both
Lenin and Stalin. Chou En-lai had done the same
a few days earlier.[52] On the home front, meantime,
a Korean-Soviet Friendship Month (October 15-
November 15) had been launched, commemorating both
the Twenty-second CPSU Congress and the forty-
fourth anniversary of the October Revolution. Thus,
at the end of 1961, North Korea continued to maintain its precariously neutral stance in the conflict
between Moscow and Peking.

P'YŎNGYANG-PEKING AXIS, 1962-64

If there is a thread of consistency in North
Korea's mercurial response to the unruly winds of
Sino-Soviet polemics, it is its unshakable desire
to remain neutral. Yet there is no necessary
correlation between a subjective desire, on the one
hand, and the objective conditions conducive to its
fulfillment, on the other. Slowly but surely North
Korea strayed from the path of nonalignment and,
by late 1962, found itself in the camp of Communist
China. This is not to say that it succeeded in
alienating the Kremlin. But on major issues dividing the Communist bloc, it unmistakably sided with
Peking. What is more, the frequency and intensity
of Sino-Korean contacts visibly increased, while
P'yŏngyang's multifaceted intercourse with Moscow
showed a marked decline.

Although the exchange of good-will delegations
representing the supreme legislative assemblies of
both countries in the first half of 1962 served to
reaffirm the already strong bonds of friendship
between North Korea and Communist China,[53] it
remained for a series of developments in the latter
part of the year to make them staunch allies confronting their common ideological enemy, the Soviet
Union. These were the Sino-Indian border clash,
the Cuban missile crisis, and the unprecedented
public snub of the KWP by European Communist
parties at some of their congresses. When the
Chinese invaded Indian territory in the areas of
Ladakh and the North-East Frontier Agency on
October 20, 1962,[54] North Korea was solidly behind
the Chinese move. This was due not so much to

North Korean hostility toward India as to its
growing disillusionment with the Soviet Union.
Ignoring the Soviet position, which not only refused
to condone, much less support, the Chinese action,
but indirectly criticized Chinese recklessness,
P'yŏngyang echoed Peking's charge that "reactionary
elements in India, aided and abetted by the U.S.
imperialists, were stirring up trouble to aggravate
the Sino-Indian border controversy."[55]

     Nodong Sinmun's day-to-day coverage of the
incident was consistently slanted in favor of the
Chinese position, but the paper withheld editorial
comments at the outset. On October 26, however,
it published an editorial, "The Indian Side Must
Immediately Respond to the Chinese Proposal to
Negotiate." Supporting the Chinese argument that
"there has never existed a formally established
boundary between China and India," the editorial
stated:

          It goes without saying that the
          armed aggression committed by
          Indian reactionaries against the
          Chinese people is a criminal act
          designed to frustrate the ideals
          of peace and negotiation and to
          realize their territorial ambi-
          tions by means of "force" only.

               That the Chinese people
          should have resolutely repelled
          the Indian aggression was not
          only inevitable; it was a legit-
          imate act of self-defense on
          their part. The Indian side
          therefore is solely to blame
          for all the bloodshed caused by
          the clash.

The editorial went on to warn that unless India
responded favorably to the Chinese offer to reach
a negotiated settlement, it would have to face
"grave and irreparable" consequences.[56]

     The Cuban missile crisis, occurring almost
simultaneously with the Sino-Indian border dispute,
immediately attracted North Korea's attention, and
a full-scale propaganda offensive was set in motion.
Measured in terms both of the number and scale of

mass rallies waged in support of the Cuban people
and of the space devoted to it in Nodong Sinmun,
the Soviet-American confrontation in Cuba was an
enormously significant event for North Korea. It
received as much attention as, if not more attention than, the student uprisings of April, 1960,
which led to the overthrow of the Syngman Rhee
regime in Seoul. North Korea was as vigorous in
condemning "the criminal act of aggression by the
U.S. imperialists" as it was in expressing support
for "the heroic struggle of the Cuban people to
defend the fruits of their revolution." Echoing
Mao Tse-tung's dictum that "people are mightier
than weapons," Nodong Sinmun voiced confidence in
the ultimate victory of the Cuban people. "To
crush the aggressive maneuvers of the U.S. imperialists," it declared, was "the sacred duty of the
world proletariat and all peace-loving peoples
alike."[57]

     That North Korea shared with Communist China
a profound feeling of disappointment, and even
indignation, over Khrushchev's decision to back
down in Cuba was amply indicated by its renewed
attack on modern revisionism, as well as its
reiteration of the argument that there is no
alternative to crushing imperialism by force.
Imperialism had become ever more militant, it
asserted, but the modern revisionists not only
refused to recognize that fact, they were working
hand in glove with the imperialists to challenge
and undermine Marxism-Leninism. It also charged
that certain fraternal parties had interfered with
the internal affairs of others in violation of the
Moscow Declaration of 1957.[58]

     At the congresses of European Communist parties
that took place in November and December, the Communist camp split more visibly between the pro-
Moscow and pro-Peking groups. North Korea was
consistently on the side of Peking, thus incurring
the overt hostility of all European Communist
parties, except the Albanian Party of Labor. The
public snubbing of the KWP reached a climax at the
East German Party congress in January, 1963, where
the KWP was not only denied a chance to make the
customary congratulatory speech but was system-
atically prevented from presenting its case to its
fraternal parties even in a written form. North
Korea bitterly complained that it had been

outrageously mistreated by the German Party, which
added insult to injury by allowing the "Yugoslav
revisionists" to be heard.[59]

If there were any lingering doubts about
P'yŏngyang's ideological alliance with Peking,
they were expelled by Nodong Sinmun's editorial
of January 30, 1963, entitled "Let Us Defend the
Unity of the Socialist Camp and Strengthen the
Solidarity of the International Communist Movement." It contained the first explicit defense
of the CCP:

> ...To unilaterally attack and
> isolate the Chinese Communist
> Party which occupies an impor-
> tant position in our Socialist
> camp is to endanger the unity
> of our camp and to inflict seri-
> ous damage to our common cause.
>
> In view of the fitful anti-
> Chinese campaign waged by inter-
> national reactionary forces,
> coupled with their increasingly
> obvious scheme to provoke aggres-
> sion and war in Europe and Asia,
> such an act is tantamount to
> joining the anti-Chinese chorus
> of the enemy.
>
> It must be obvious to every-
> one that the unity of our camp
> and the strengthening of its
> influence are inseparably linked
> with the existence of the power-
> ful People's Republic of China,
> which, together with the great
> Soviet Union, the first Socialist
> state in the world, comprises
> two-thirds of the world popula-
> tion. To isolate the CCP and the
> PRC, therefore, is to disrupt the
> unity of the Socialist camp....
> It goes without saying that no
> genuine Communist can sanction
> the disruption of the unity of
> the Socialist camp in this cru-
> cial stage of our common strug-
> gle against imperialism.[60]

The editorial revealed that, at the European Communist party congresses, the KWP had been repeatedly asked, "Which side are you on?" What concerns North Korea most, it said, is not the taking of sides in the ideological quarrel in the Communist bloc but the preservation of both bloc unity and the "interests of those people who are waging a bloody struggle for peace, national independence, and social progress." The editorial declared that the KWP was on the side of "Marxism-Leninism and the interest of revolution and unity." In its view, the unity of the socialist camp would be restored if all Communist parties adhered to the letter and spirit of the Moscow Declaration. It insisted on the importance of upholding the principles of "complete equality; respect for territorial integrity, national independence, and sovereignty; and non-interference in internal affairs of other nations." "All fraternal parties are independent and equal; they must make their policies independently, applying the principles of Marxism-Leninism to the concrete conditions of their respective countries," it said. It added that although there are large and small countries, there cannot be superior and inferior parties. In short, while siding unmistakably with Peking in the Sino-Soviet dispute, P'yŏngyang emphatically asserted its ideological independence in rhetoric.

Consistent with its established practice, the editorial carefully refrained from criticizing the CPSU by name; if the latter was mentioned, it was only to be praised, and not for the purpose of denunciation. Yet few versed in the delicate art of esoteric Communist communication could have failed to identify the target of the following criticism:

> We can and should never tolerate such acts as exposing our internal differences of opinion in front of our enemy, allowing such differences to affect intergovernmental relations, and severing diplomatic ties or expelling ambassadors on account of petty disputes.[61]

The leadership of the CPSU was guilty of every sin
mentioned above in its relations with Albania in
late 1962. As if to underline the identity of KWP
and CCP views on intrabloc relations, the same
issue of Nodong Sinmun also reproduced the full
text of a Jen-min Jih-pao editorial, "Let Us Unite
on the Basis of the Moscow Declaration and Statement."

North Korea's growing disenchantment with the
Soviet Union was also reflected in the decreasing
frequency with which that nation was mentioned,
let alone praised, in Nodong Sinmun. By April,
1963, articles on the U.S.S.R. had practically
disappeared from the pages of the KWP organ. On
the other hand, Sino-Korean interaction picked up
momentum, and in June a top-level North Korean
delegation headed by Ch'oe Yong-gŏn, Chairman of
the Presidium of the Supreme People's Assembly,
paid a three-week good-will visit to the P.R.C.
Among those accompanying Ch'oe were Yi Hyo-sun,
member of the Political Committee and Vice-Chairman
of the KWP Central Committee, and Pak Sŏng-ch'ŏl,
member of the KWP Central Committee and Foreign
Minister of the D.P.R.K. The highlight of the visit
was a conference between the North Korean delegation
and the leadership of Communist China, which produced a joint Sino-Korean communiqué on the relations between the two countries as well as among
socialist countries. Militant in tone, the communiqué particularly stressed that U.S. imperialism
must and can be exterminated. It declared:

> In order to defend world peace
> and promote human progress, the
> Socialist countries and the
> international proletariat must
> enter into the closest possible
> alliance with all oppressed
> peoples and nations, unite all
> the forces that can be united,
> form the broadest possible
> united front against the impe-
> rialists headed by the United
> States and their lackeys and
> wage an unremitting struggle
> against U.S. imperialism--the
> main force of aggression and
> war. Peace cannot be won by
> begging, it can be won only by
> relying on the struggle of the
> masses.[62]

Peaceful coexistence, to which both countries
paid lip service, had a conveniently narrow meaning:
It describes a relationship between socialist and
capitalist states only. It is totally irrelevant
to "the relations between oppressed and oppressor
nations and between oppressed and oppressor classes."
Nor should it be used "as a pretext to liquidate
the anti-imperialist struggle and disclaim the
internationalist duty of supporting the revolutionary struggle of the peoples of various countries."63

After enumerating the various international
issues on which the D.P.R.K. and the P.R.C. have
taken identical stands, the communiqué pointed
out that although the two governments had "consistently stood for general disarmament and the
total prohibition of nuclear weapons," the refusal
of the imperialists to support these objectives
made it imperative that the socialist countries
"strengthen their national defenses, including the
development of nuclear superiority of the socialist
countries." Imperialist power, it suggested, must
be checked by socialist power.64 Then there were
the inevitable attacks on "modern revisionism" and
"dogmatism." In an oblique condemnation of the
Kremlin, which had recently readmitted Yugoslavia
into the Communist orbit, the Sino-Korean statement
accused "the Tito clique of Yugoslavia," a person-
ification of modern revisionism, of having "openly
betrayed the socialist camp," of "serving as a special detachment of U.S. imperialism," and of engag-
ing in "sabotage against the socialist camp, the
national revolutionary movement, and the peoples
of the world." Communists the world over were
urged to "draw a clear-cut demarcation between themselves and the Tito clique and wage an uncompromising struggle against it." Ironically, the
expression "dogmatism," which had been used by
Khrushchev to describe the attitude of Communist
China,65 was chosen to condemn the attitude of
those who "do not use their brains or make a study
of all the relevant facts" and who "on major domestic and international questions, . . . repeat word
for word what someone else says" or "follow closely
in someone else's steps," thus alienating the "Party
from reality and from the masses."66 Finally, the
two governments offered a formula for solving intrabloc differences: They must be adjusted "through
inter-party consultations on an equal footing."

More specifically, they proposed a meeting of representatives of the Communist and Workers' parties
of the world.[67]

When the eighteenth anniversary of the Korean
Liberation arrived on August 15, North Korea was
singularly reserved in its praise of the Soviet
Union. The only favorable mention of the U.S.S.R.
appeared in a Nodong Sinmun editorial, which
expressed "warm thanks to the fraternal Soviet
people who have not only liberated our country but
also rendered material and moral assistance in our
struggle to build a new way of life." Congratulatory messages, however, were exchanged with both
Moscow and Peking, and the composition of the foreign delegations to North Korea's commemorative
activities gave little clue of the extent to which
Soviet-Korean relations had deteriorated. Most
bloc countries, including the Soviet Union and
Communist China, sent nongovernmental teams which
lacked any national figures.

In September, the P.R.C. returned the June
visit of Ch'oe Yong-gŏn and other North Korean
leaders to China by dispatching to P'yŏngyang a
good-will delegation led by Liu Shao-chi. A Sino-
Korean statement following a conference between
the visiting Chinese dignitaries and the North
Korean leadership reaffirmed the views already
embodied in the June communiqué. While the Chinese
delegation was still on North Korean soil, Nodong
Sinmun published an unprecedented indictment of
the Soviet Academy of Sciences for what it called
a "grave distortion of Korean history."[68] To
judge from the fact that it was later reproduced
in Peking Review,[69] the editorial must have been
deliberately timed to please the Chinese visitors.
Among other things, the Soviet Academy was charged
with having ignored ancient Korean history, dis-
torted its medieval history, and erroneously treated
its modern history in compiling World History. The
editorial implied that the Soviet historians had
in effect committed sins typical of "bourgeois
historiology." The significance of the accusations
lay not so much in North Korea's concern for correct
factual description of Korean history, as in the
fact that it represented an indirect assault on
the Soviet Union and particularly the CPSU.

The Sino-Korean ideological alliance in opposition to the Kremlin reached its peak in 1964,
when North Korea's defense of Communist China became
more outspoken, and its indirect but obvious criticism of the Soviet Union less restrained. On
January 27, Nodong Sinmun published a lengthy
editorial, "Let Us Hold High the Revolutionary
Banner of National Liberation." A massive repudiation of the "revisionist" policy of the Soviet
Union, it was a telling evidence of the identity
of views on both intra- and interbloc affairs on
the part of the D.P.R.K. and the P.R.C. Liberally
sprinkled with quotations from Stalin and Kim Il-
sŏng,* the editorial reiterated the familiar argument that the only way to fight imperialism and
neocolonialism is to fight them, and not to compromise with them. What is more, it bluntly suggested that the modern revisionists, a euphemism
for the Soviet Union, had not only prevented
oppressed peoples from winning victories in the
struggle against imperialism--victories which were
well within their grasp--but had made them suffer
unspeakable sacrifices. It was plain that the
editorial was referring specifically to the Soviet
backdown in Cuba in late 1962. The Soviet Union
was also indirectly accused of having provided
assistance to "the reactionary elements of the
countries working hand in glove with imperialism."
What made this doubly intolerable was that such
assistance was used to oppose fraternal social
countries. Again, there was no doubt that the
above was in reference to the Soviet military aid
to India prior to the Sino-Indian border clash in
1962.

If the Soviet Union was walking the path of
modern revisionism, Communist China was "resolutely
defending the principles of Marxism-Leninism and
proletarian internationalism in the international
field," North Korea declared.[70] Further, Peking's
"unshakable peace-loving foreign policy" was

_____
*It is to be noted that even at the height of Sino-
Korean amity and friendship, Mao Tse-tung's thought
was virtually ignored by North Korean leaders and
propagandists. As noted, furthermore, the Chinese
language never enjoyed the same status accorded
the Russian language in North Korean schools, where
the latter was taught as a required foreign language.

contributing a great deal to the easing of world
tensions and to the maintenance of peace in the
Far East and in the world, it added. Significantly,
North Korea argued that no international problem
could be effectively solved without the participation of the P.R.C., which occupied a vast proportion of earth and claimed a quarter of the world's
population. It may be recalled that on previous
occasions the Soviet Union had always been mentioned along with Communist China. That is, North
Korea until recently had argued that no significant
world problem could be solved without the participation of both the U.S.S.R. and the P.R.C. The
omission of the Soviet Union appears to have been
deliberate.

A further clue as to the steadily cooling
Soviet-Korean relations was provided by a Nodong
Sinmun editorial of March 17, marking the fifteenth
anniversary of the conclusion of Soviet-Korean
Agreements on Economic and Cultural Cooperation.
What was striking was that the editorial devoted
only a single paragraph to an appreciation of
Soviet aid to North Korea. The paragraph read:

> The Soviet people have extended
> to us economic and technical
> assistance, particularly in the
> postwar reconstruction period.
> That was a big help in the reha-
> bilitation and construction of
> our people's economy. The Korean
> people will never forget the
> assistance rendered them by their
> fraternal Soviet people.[71]

The bulk of the editorial underlined that North
Korea's rapid economic recovery and rise to a position of self-sufficiency was due mainly to "the
correct policies and wise leadership of the KWP."[72]

A month later, Nodong Sinmun published a long
editorial sharply criticizing what it called "an
extensive campaign" waged by "certain people" to
condemn and ostracize "the fraternal parties which
uphold the principles of Marxism-Leninism." It
identified the CCP as one of the targets but did
not disclose the names of the attackers. Yet there
was no doubt that the editorial, "Thwart the
Maneuvers to Split the International Communist

Movement," was aimed mainly at the CPSU. It was
reproduced in full in Jen-min Jih-pao on April 26,
exactly a week after its appearance in the KWP
organ. The editorial asserted that it was the CPSU,
and not the CCP, that launched open polemics between Moscow and Peking, thus disrupting the unity
and solidarity of the socialist camp. For the
Soviets to accuse the Chinese Communists of undermining bloc unity, it said, is the equivalent of
"a thief crying, 'stop thief!'" "This is an action
designed to conceal their own splitting activities
and shift responsibility on to others," it added.[73]

Charging that "certain people," that is, the
Soviets, had degenerated to the extent of making
"no distinction between revolutionary comrades and
class enemies," the editorial strongly argued that
the socialist camp should repudiate monolithic
control by a single country. The dictates of the
Kremlin, it suggested, should no longer be treated
as sacrosanct. Hence it is perfectly justifiable
for a fraternal party not to join in the CPSU-
initiated campaign against the cult of personality.
Not only is this permissible, but it is mandatory.
For the campaign to combat personality cult is but
a pretext for "persecuting and attacking those who
remain faithful to Marxist-Leninist principles,"
for "interfering in the internal affairs of fraternal parties and countries," and for "inciting
anti-party sectarian elements in these countries
to split fraternal parties and subvert the leadership of fraternal countries." What is more,

> Imperialism and the renegades
> incited by it treasure this
> cloak as a magic cover by
> means of which they have
> launched counterrevolutionary
> riots and stirred up anti-
> Communist waves on an inter-
> national scale. Today they
> are still using it as a weapon
> to assail socialism and Com-
> munism.[74]

The editorial was a brief for two mutually
competitive, if not incompatible, causes. While
championing the cause of bloc unity, it also
asserted the right of each socialist country to go
it alone. Its reasoning ran as follows: A

prerequisite to enhancing the unity and solidarity
of the socialist bloc is the strengthening of its
powers. That calls for the building of an independent
national economy by each socialist country. The
goal of economic integration, as envisaged by the
Council of Mutual Economic Assistance (Comecon),
is plainly "an attempt to control and dominate
economic construction in other countries." The
KWP's long-held, and perhaps justified, bias against
the Soviet policy of intrabloc economic specializa-
tion was expressed in these terms:

> This /the clamor for "economic
> integration"7 is to ignore the
> sovereignty of others as well
> as an attempt to arrogate to
> oneself in every possible way
> all the advantages of the
> socialist camp and reduce the
> economy of other countries to
> the status of an appendage.
> It is a manifestation of typ-
> ical national egoism.75

        The inconsistency of its views notwithstanding,
North Korea appeared genuinely committed to the goal
of economic and political independence. It was
particularly annoyed by the suggestion that Asian
Communist parties are not capable of acting independently because of their lack of experience.
Such an arrogant attitude, in its view, reflected
"great-power chauvinism." Furthermore, the
principle of centralism, which postulates superior-
subordinate relationships as well as the issuing
and taking of orders, was strictly a norm governing
intraparty, but not interparty, relations. In
short, all Communist parties stand on the footing
of absolute equality vis-à-vis one another. Nothing
would be more alien to Marxism-Leninism than blind
subservience to one party, no matter how powerful
it may be. In the words of the Nodong Sinmun
editorial:

> To speak and act as others do
> without a sense of independence
> on one's own part will not help
> strengthen the unity of the
> Communist movement; nor is it
> loyal to internationalism. On
> the contrary, it would cause

> losses to the revolutionary
> work of one's own people and
> the international working
> class and weaken the genuine
> internationalist unity of the
> socialist camp and the inter-
> national Communist movement.[76]

If the unity of the socialist camp is to be
restored and preserved, it is imperative that whatever differences may exist within the bloc be
adjusted internally through comradely discussion
and negotiation and in accordance with the principles of Marxism-Leninism and proletarian internationalism, the editorial declared. It therefore
favored the convening of an international meeting
of Communist parties, but stressed that such a
meeting would bear fruit only if "it is held on
the basis of the principles of independence, equality and comradely consultation and after full
preparations have been made."[77]

If North Korea's public pronouncements were
inadequate to establish P'yŏngyang's ideological
affinities with Peking, there were additional
signs that clearly indicated the KWP's pro-Chinese
orientation. One may thus cite the extraordinary
warmth and vigor with which North Korea interacted
with Albania--a country that had resolutely rejected
Moscow in favor of Peking in the Sino-Soviet rift.[78]
Not only was there a visible increase in the economic and cultural links between P'yŏngyang and
Tirana, but North Korea went out of its way to
express its friendship and solidarity with Albania.[79]
Equally significant was North Korea's wholehearted
support of the Japanese Communist Party (JCP) in
the latter's dispute with the CPSU in July. When
the JCP made known its ideological sympathies for
the CCP through an exchange of a series of letters
with the CPSU, the KWP was solidly behind the
Japanese. In an uncommonly long front-page editorial, Nodong Sinmun, on July 27, pointedly
assailed what it called "the destructive maneuvers
against the Japanese Communist Party." "The attack
on the JCP being carried out by certain people
today," it declared, "is a part and parcel of the
sinister machinations they have been engaged in
continuously ever since the Twentieth CPSU Congress."

North Korea also joined the CCP in opposing
the Soviet-proposed meeting of world Communist
parties. Pointing out that "certain people,"
that is, the CPSU, had openly and unscrupulously
engaged in activities designed to disrupt the unity
of the socialist camp and to frustrate the Marxist-
Leninist policies of fraternal parties, North Korea
asserted that the time was not ripe for "comradely
discussion" capable of yielding any tangible
results. P'yŏngyang foresaw only an exacerbation
of controversy and a further disruption of the
international Communist movement should the projected meeting be convened. In a singularly bold
move, Nodong Sinmun even went so far as to identify
the target of its attack. "The leadership of the
CPSU," it said, was defying the wishes of fraternal
parties in proceeding with the preparation of the
meeting. It added that the CPSU "manifestly has an
ulterior motive," for it knew full well that the
meeting would serve only to disrupt the Communist
camp.[80]

The boldest attack on the Soviet Union ever
to appear in Nodong Sinmun, perhaps, was its editorial of September 7, "Why Downgrade the Results
of the P'yŏngyang Economic Conference?" It was a
rebuttal of a Pravda editorial criticizing the
Asian Economic Conference held in P'yŏngyang from
June 16 to June 23. The conference, in which thirty-
four nations from Asia and Africa participated,
resulted in the so-called P'yŏngyang Declaration,
underlining the need for a self-reliant national
economy in the newly developing countries of Asia,
Africa, and Latin America. The Pravda editorial
entitled "In Whose Interest?" had made dispar-
aging remarks about the conference, suggesting that
it had bordered on a farce. The editorial said
that the conference had added absolutely nothing
to the solution of the economic problems of the
Asian countries, serving only to disrupt the
socialist camp. It further implied that the participants in the conference were economically
illiterate and unfit to represent anybody. That
all this should have profoundly wounded North
Korea's national pride was only natural.

The charges, Nodong Sinmun categorically
asserted, were totally without foundation. They
were complete fabrications, it said. By accusing
the conference of lacking any formal sanction from

established international organizations, the newspaper said, the Soviet Union was merely displaying
its "big-power chauvinistic mentality." The KWP
organ noted that Pravda's criticisms bore a striking resemblance to those of the Voice of America:

> How does it happen that there is
> such a remarkable harmony between
> the voice of Pravda and the "Voice
> of America"? What is surprising
> is that Pravda is even more vicious
> than the "Voice of America." What
> a condescending and arrogant atti-
> tude on its part! What a con-
> ceited, and brazen-faced double-
> talk! Its tone is that reserved
> exclusively for the American
> xenophobes who are accustomed to
> thinking that they alone may decide
> and direct everything, that they
> alone are intelligent, and that all
> others are ignorant.

Nodong Sinmun was curious to know why Pravda was
irritated by the "justifiable" positions of the
P'yŏngyang conference on the need to further
strengthen the struggle against imperialism and
colonialism. "Could it be that /the Soviet Union7
has given up its anti-imperialist struggle, is
afraid of the struggle being waged by others, is
unwilling to support /it7, and dislikes the banner
of anti-imperialist struggle?" it asked.

The editorial was particularly insistent on
the need of each country to be its own master. It
said:

> Any people, any nation, must make
> its own revolution; it must guide
> its national destiny with its own
> hands. People are the master of
> each country; they alone are the
> decisive element in revolution.
> It is only when the people of
> each country are united, mobilize
> their own strength and resources,
> and fight to the last with deter-
> mination and responsibility that
> a revolution in that country can
> succeed.

...No nation, no people, can
ever make revolution and build a
self-reliant economy with external
assistance only; nor can it save
itself from poverty and backwardness that way. We have yet to
find a historical example of such
nation or people. We never will.

Turning specifically to the assistance rendered
to North Korea by the Soviet Union, the editorial
not only minimized the part it had played in North
Korea's economic recovery and construction, but
strongly hinted that the net effect of Soviet aid
was more harmful than helpful to P'yŏngyang.
Acknowledging that the Soviet people did help in
rebuilding North Korea's war-shattered economy,
the editorial stressed that the major burden was
shouldered by the Korean working class, with its
perseverance, creative genius, and wisdom. Then
came one of the most revealing passages of the
editorial:

In the process of providing
assistance in rebuilding /our7
factories, you have sold us
facilities...and materials at
prices far above those prevailing in the international market,
while taking away from us in
return many tons of gold, huge
quantities of precious metals,
and other raw materials at prices
substantially below those prevailing in the international
market.

When you talk about the aid
you have given us, is it not reasonable that you also mention the
above fact--that you took away
from us the fruits of our pains-
taking labor at a time when our
life was most difficult to bear?

As already noted, Western analysts had long sus-
pected Soviet economic exploitation of North Korea.
Here was P'yŏngyang's explicit confirmation that
exploitation had indeed taken place. It might be
said that with the public revelation of what had

theretofore been a closely guarded Communist secret, Soviet-Korean relations had reached their lowest ebb. But, as events were to show, they did not stay there long.

As if to wipe out all remnants of doubt of the KWP's deviation from the Kremlin line, Nodong Sinmun on December 21 published an extravagant eulogy of Stalin, complete with his photograph. The occasion was the eighty-fifth anniversary of his birth. Calling Stalin "a great Marxist-Leninist, an invincible revolutionary fighter for the working class, and one of the truly outstanding leaders of the international Communist movement," the newspaper proclaimed that his name is inseparably linked with the victory of the Russian socialist revolution, the building of socialism in the Soviet Union, and the revolutionary annals of the world Communist movement. "One of Stalin's great accomplishments," the KWP organ said, "is that he not only resolutely defended the revolutionary truths of Marxism-Leninism against revisionism, opportunism, and other hostile ideological tides, but creatively applied and developed them to the historic conditions of proletarian dictatorship." All Communists were strongly urged to emulate Stalin's "uncompromising and merciless struggle" to uphold the purity of Marxism-Leninism.

Finally, it is to be noted that the 1964 edition of The Democratic People's Republic of Korea, an official handbook of North Korea, conspicuously refrained from mentioning the Soviet Union. The 1958 edition of the handbook had contained the following passage:

> On August 15, 1945 the Korean
> people were liberated by the
> great Soviet Army from the yoke
> of the Japanese colonial rule
> which lasted for 36 years.[81]

The 1964 edition changed the preceding passage to read:

> The liberation of Korea from
> the yoke of the Japanese impe-
> rialist colonial rule on August
> 15, 1945 marked a turning point
> in the construction of a free,
> independent new Korea.[82]

Clearly, the change is not merely stylistic but substantive. The mood of North Korea had changed. In 1964, P'yŏngyang not only refused to acknowledge its indebtedness to the Soviet Union, but doggedly insisted on its independence, both political and economic, from external influences. Significantly, the 1964 handbook was equally notable for its omission of any reference to the P.R.C. Its account of the Korean War gave no hint whatever of the sacrifices and bloodshed of the "Chinese People's Volunteers," although it did note that the socialist camp and "peace-loving people throughout the world" had rendered help.[83]

The most outstanding facet of Sino-Korean relations in the period 1962-64, then, is not so much the existence of an ideological alliance between the two Asian Communist countries. Rather, it is the dominant motive which drew the two together and sustained their partnership in the stormy waters of Communist doctrinal polemics. Both were joined by their burning desire for independence. True, there were other common denominators, such as their cultural and racial bonds, wartime partnership, common hatred of "U.S. imperialism," and the like. However, none appeared to be as powerful as their nationalism--their intense craving for a fully independent position in the world, made all the more acute by bitter and humiliating memories of their colonial or semicolonial past. Moscow's attempts to interfere in their domestic affairs by shrewdly, and sometimes not so shrewdly, manipulating the powerful levers of economic and military assistance were understandably detested. Its apparent flirtations with the West, particularly with the United States, the archenemy of both countries, were unbearable. If North Korea sided with Communist China on major issues dividing the Communist camp, it did so not out of reverence for China but in keeping with its own perceived national self-interest. In this very fact lay the weakness of the Peking-P'yŏngyang axis. For the currents of international politics were turbulent and menacing. North Korea's perception of its national self-interest could be no more steady than the hostile tides with which it had to contend.

RAPPROCHEMENT WITH THE SOVIET UNION, 1965-

Even at the height of its ideological partnership with Peking, North Korea never allowed itself
to be totally and irretrievably aligned with the
regime of Mao Tse-tung. To be sure, its responses
to the stimuli of intrabloc politics tended to be
more emotional than rational. Yet one must bear
in mind that P'yŏngyang's emotional outbursts
against the Kremlin had invariably been provoked
by the latter. North Korea was perpetually on the
defensive in its poorly concealed quarrels with
Moscow. The dominant consideration for Kim Il-sŏng
in shaping his posture in the Sino-Soviet schism
had always been his and his regime's self-interest.
With his political control secure beyond challenge,
Kim's personal power and the national power of
North Korea were one and the same. It is not hard
to imagine that three years of largely fruitless
collaboration with Communist China must have
launched him on the path of agonizing reappraisal.
What did he and North Korea gain by their self-
imposed isolation in the Communist camp? Did Communist China provide sufficient technical and
material assistance to offset that which had been
withheld by the more affluent Soviet Union? Was
North Korea's international prestige enhanced in
any way by its refusal to be influenced by the
Kremlin? Had imperialism become any weaker because
of its militancy? Did the Soviet policy of peaceful coexistence really amount to "selling out to
the U.S. imperialists"?

Quite conceivably, the North Korean leader
might have concluded, at the dawn of the new year,
1965, that perhaps too close an identification
with the Chinese side was inimical to P'yŏngyang's
interest and that the cause of North Korea's national
independence would be better served by a reconciliation with Moscow. Then, too, there were a few
other developments that appeared strongly to suggest
the wisdom of winning back Soviet friendship. First,
North Korea was beset with growing difficulties in
implementing its Seven-Year Plan. As noted, even
its own statistical reports admitted that it was
lagging behind the plan. Communist China, plagued
by its own economic problems, which were far more
staggering than North Korea's, was in no position
to help. There was only one direction in which to

turn for help--Moscow. Second, the war in Vietnam had had the effect of driving the Soviet Union closer to the cause of anti-imperialist and national-liberation struggles. By coming to the aid of the "heroic" Vietnamese people who were waging a "courageous struggle against the U.S. imperialists and their lackeys," the Soviet Union had effectively given the lie to the charge that it had turned its back on the oppressed peoples of the world. When the chips were down, the U.S.S.R., the first socialist nation on earth, the vanguard of the international Communist and workers' movement, and the leader of the socialist camp, could be counted on to support the "just struggle against imperialism and colonialism." What is more, because of its superior technical know-how and abundant resources, it could offer better and more aid than could Communist China. The thought of Mao Tse-tung might make determined soldiers out of the Vietnamese people, but they still needed Soviet ground-to-air missiles to shoot down American jets. Kim Il-sŏng was highly unlikely to forget that it takes Soviet might to combat American might. However earnestly Kim might have wished to agree with Mao Tse-tung that "all imperialists are paper tigers," his memories of the catastrophic showdown with the United States in the Korean War were too vivid and his knowledge of the bloodshed in Vietnam too intimate for him to brush aside Khrushchev's wry reminder that "the paper tigers have nuclear teeth." Although Kim still shared with Mao the unflagging hatred of U.S. imperialism, he began to question whether the Chinese were truly capable of stemming its ever-swelling tide.

An additional factor that may have entered into Kim's calculation of the potential benefits of closer P'yŏngyang-Moscow ties is the utility of the Soviet Union in advancing North Korea's unification policy. While ignoring the authority of the United Nations to deal with the Korean question, P'yŏngyang has always been sensitive to the psychological and propaganda impact of U.N. actions. It has thus steadily escalated its diplomatic campaign to increase pro-North Korean sentiment and votes in the world body. The value of the Soviet Union in this regard is self-evident. By contrast, Communist China is practically useless, because it is not even a member of the international organization. Furthermore, the

modernization of North Korea's defense apparatus,
which is a key element in its unification strategy,
urgently called for Soviet military assistance.
Finally, the sudden shift of power in the leadership of the Soviet Union must have spurred P'yŏngyang to re-examine its relations with Moscow. When
the KWP leadership first learned of the unexpected
ouster of Khrushchev in October, 1964, its official
reaction was typically cautious. It said nothing,*
taking the "wait-and-see" attitude. No doubt, Kim
Il-sŏng did not rule out the possibility of being
offered an olive branch from the new Brezhnev-
Kosygin team. In brief, then, P'yŏngyang was ready
for a rapprochement with Moscow.

When it was announced that Premier Aleksei
N. Kosygin of the Soviet Union would visit P'yŏngyang in February, the official announcement said
that he was coming to the North Korean capital at
the invitation of the D.P.R.K. Government. Who
really took the initiative, however, remains
obscure. North Korea could actually have extended
him the invitation. Or, quite possibly, the Soviet
Union could have let it be known that the Soviet
Premier would be interested in talking things over
with the KWP leadership. In any case, Kosygin's
four-day visit to P'yŏngyang (February 11-14)
proved to be a new watershed in Soviet-North
Korean relations.

Coming from Hanoi where he had assured Ho Chi
Minh of continued Soviet assistance to North Vietnam, the Soviet leader had in his entourage top-
ranking military and economic experts. It is con-
ceivable that the possibilities of renewed Soviet
economic and military assistance to North Korea
were explored in discussions between the Soviet
and Korean leaders. In welcoming the Soviet Premier,

---

*Nodong Sinmun made no reference to the event at the
time; the first indication that Brezhnev and Kosygin
had taken over control in the Kremlin came on November 17, 1964, when the paper reported on a courtesy
call to the new Soviet leaders paid by Kim Il, Vice-
Chairman of the KWP Central Committee and First
Deputy Premier of the D.P.R.K., who was in Moscow
leading a North Korean delegation to the commemorative activities of the forty-seventh anniversary
of the October Revolution.

Kim Il-sŏng recalled the "unbreakable bonds of
friendship between the Korean and Soviet peoples,"
pledging that Soviet-Korean friendship and solidarity
would remain "imperishable." Denouncing the aggressive acts of the U.S. imperialists in Vietnam, Kim
expressed his heartfelt thanks to the Soviet Union
for supporting the Vietnamese people. North Korea,
he assured the visiting Soviet leader, was prepared
to furnish all moral and material assistance within
its means, for it was "the sacred duty" of all
socialist countries and Communists to combat imperialism and to support the struggle for national
liberation. Kim was confident that Kosygin's
visit would make a huge contribution to the causes
of Soviet-Korean friendship and bloc solidarity.[84]

In reply, Kosygin reminded the North Koreans
that he was visiting their country for the second
time, having visited it in 1961. He said that he
was struck by the enormous economic progress North
Korea had made in the interval, seeing in its
phenomenal growth a telling evidence of the superiority of the socialist path to economic modernization over the capitalist or any other path. His
major theme, however, was peace. "Imperialism,"
he said, "is still strong, and the fight against it
is not easy." Should the imperialists be allowed to
exploit the internal differences that threatened
to split the Communist camp, he asked? Of course
not, he stressed. There was no more urgent task
facing the Communists, therefore, than to patch
up their differences of opinion. Kosygin stressed
that "the differences of opinion that now exist in
the international Communist movement stem neither
from the essence of Communism nor from the Marxist-
Leninist world view." All Communists, he declared,
were united in their common struggle for the
victory of socialism and Communism as well as in
their common allegiance to Marxism-Leninism, their
only ideology. And the only path to realizing
their objectives, according to Kosygin, was peaceful coexistence.[85]

The Soviet Premier reiterated the Kremlin
line of peaceful coexistence in his speech at a
mass rally in P'yŏngyang the following day. After
assuring the North Koreans that the Soviet Union
had always given top priority to the interests
and goals of the socialist camp and the international Communist movement, he stated:

The march of the Soviet Union and
all other socialist countries on
the path of socialist and Communist
construction is inseparably linked
to the struggle to maintain a lasting peace in the world. Not only
does the Soviet Union unswervingly
and thoroughly defend the cause of
peace, but it also advocates the
peaceful co-existence of nations
with different social systems.
...This the Soviet Union regards as
its internationalist duty. Experience demonstrates that peaceful
co-existence is wholly compatible
with revolutionary struggle....

Of course, there cannot and
should not be peaceful co-existence
between oppressors and oppressed,
between aggressors and victims of
aggression.

The Soviet Union wishes to
live in peace and to cooperate
with all nations. However, those
who think that they can court the
friendship of the Soviet Union,
while simultaneously pursuing a
policy of aggression against other
socialist countries are gravely
mistaken. Cooperate with other
nations we may, but never will
we compromise with acts of law-
lessness and plunder on the international stage. We do not want
to see the international situation
deteriorate. But we are fully prepared to sternly oppose any
encroachment on the interest of
socialism.[86]

If Kosygin's rhetoric did not convert Kim Il-
sŏng, he must have been quite persuasive in his
private conversations with the North Korean dictator. Whatever "deals" may actually have been made,
it appeared plain that the long-strained P'yŏngyang-
Moscow relations had at last returned to normalcy.
The joint communiqué issued by the Soviet and
Korean leaders prior to Kosygin's departure gave

hints that both sides had agreed on stepped-up
economic and cultural interchange. It said that
the mutual obligation to help each other embodied
in the Soviet-Korean treaty of 1961 had received
particular emphasis during talks between the Soviet
delegation and the D.P.R.K. leadership. The communiqué also said that both sides had agreed to "exert
all the efforts that are necessary to maintain,
develop, and strengthen the fraternal friendship
and solidarity among the nations of the socialist
camp and all Communist and workers' parties on the
basis of both the Moscow Declaration of 1957 and
of the Moscow Statement of 1960."[87]

Subsequent developments made it abundantly
clear that North Korea and the Soviet Union had
become friends again. In May, a North Korean
military delegation led by General Ch'oe Kwang,
Vice-Minister of National Defense and Chief of
Staff of the North Korean People's Army, left for
Moscow to participate in the celebrations of the
twentieth anniversary of the Soviet victory over
Germany.[88] While in Moscow, the North Korean
delegation concluded agreements with the Soviet
Union on Soviet military assistance to P'yŏngyang.
According to one source, there were at least three
reasons why North Korea was so anxious to receive
military assistance from the Soviet Union: (1)
American bombings in North Vietnam had pointed to
the need to strengthen North Korea's air-defense
apparatus; (2) North Korea had become alarmed over
the recent supply of sixty F-105 fighter jets to
South Korea by the United States; and (3) North Korea
had become uneasy over its outdated ground weapons
in view of the recent modernization of the R.O.K.
Army with U.S. assistance. The terms of the new
Soviet-Korean military agreements were not disclosed,
but it is presumed that the Soviet Union agreed to
provide North Korea with anti-aircraft weapons
(SA-2), late-model jet fighters, heavy field
artillery, and other weapons.[89]

People-to-people contacts between North Korea
and the Soviet Union, which had been practically
nonexistent in the period 1962-64, were re-established.
Before the year was out, at least half a dozen nongovernmental groups from the Soviet Union had visited
North Korea. They included a women's basketball
team; representatives of Soviet veterans led by
General T. F. Shtykov, the former commander of the

Soviet occupation forces in North Korea and the
first Soviet Ambassador to P'yŏngyang; a national
acrobatic troupe; a delegation from the Soviet-
Korean Friendship Association; and a national
ballet troupe. North Korea reciprocated by sending
various teams to the Soviet Union.[90]

The most obvious sign of P'yŏngyang's altered
stance in the Sino-Soviet dispute, however, appeared
in August, when North Korea celebrated the twentieth
anniversary of Korea's liberation from the Japanese
colonial rule. The Soviet Union chose to honor
the occasion by dispatching to P'yŏngyang a good-
will delegation headed by Alexandr N. Shelepin,
member of the powerful Presidium (recently renamed
the Politbureau) of the CPSU. In marked contrast,
Communist China's delegation was led by Wu Hsin-yü,
member of the Presidium of the rubber-stamp National
People's Congress of the P.R.C.[91] Wu, who was not
even an alternate member of the CCP Central Committee, was no peer to Shelepin in terms of either
prestige or power. It was clear that Peking was
deliberately snubbing P'yŏngyang for its recent
change of heart. As if to show its displeasure
with the Chinese attitude, North Korea withheld
any credit whatever from Communist China for the
latter's military and economic assistance during
and after the Korean War. The Nodong Sinmun editorial of August 15, while praising the Soviet
Union in glowing terms for its part in "crushing
Japanese militarism and liberating our country,"
was conspicuously silent on either North Korea's
traditional friendship with the P.R.C. or its
indebtedness to China for helping to "win the
fatherland liberation war." The omission was
particularly notable, for the editorial pointed
out that the Korean people "will never forget that
countless sons and daughters of the Soviet people
have shed their blood in our fatherland." Had
North Korea forgotten that tens of thousands of
China's "best sons and daughters" had also given
their lives to save it from annihilation?

The year 1966 began with no visible signs of
improvement in Sino-Korean relations. On the contrary, one could sense a definite cooling off in
P'yŏngyang-Peking communications. Although the
January 1 issue of Nodong Sinmun published the
full texts of congratulatory telegrams exchanged
between P'yŏngyang and Moscow, it merely carried

a two-sentence dispatch from the Korean Central
News Agency (KCNA) to the effect that Kim Il-sŏng
and Ch'oe Yong-gŏn had exchanged congratulatory
telegrams with Mao Tse-tung, Liu Shao-ch'i, and
Chou En-lai. Could it have been a journalistic
oversight? When the CPSU held its Twenty-third
Congress in Moscow from March 29 to April 8, the
KWP demonstrated its independence of Peking by
dispatching a delegation headed by Ch'oe Yong-gŏn,
member of the Political Committee of the KWP Central Committee and Chairman of the Presidium of the
Supreme People's Assembly. He was accompanied by
Pak Sŏng-ch'ŏl, a candidate member of the Political
Committee of the KWP Central Committee and Foreign
Minister of the D.P.R.K., and other prominent Party
and government leaders.[92] In an unusually hostile
move, the CCP had boycotted the CPSU Congress, and
the Japanese, New Zealand, and Albanian parties
had followed suit. Ch'oe Yong-gŏn made his congratulatory speech to the Congress on April 1, but
it was a routine tribute to Soviet accomplishments,
coupled with a reaffirmation of Soviet-Korean
friendship and solidarity.[93] The mere fact, however, that North Korea publicly defied Peking by
refusing to follow the latter's lead, and most
probably advice, was of no small significance.
The North Korean team, furthermore, appears to
have been well received by Soviet officials, as
shown by its numerous tours in and around Moscow
during its unusually long stay there.[94]

The number of Soviet-Korean cultural and
economic exchanges continued to rise in 1966.
Thus the Soviet Union held an exhibition of Soviet
people's consumer goods in P'yŏngyang from March 17
to April 6, after which all the goods shown at the
exhibit were turned over to North Korea free of
charge.[95] Then there was a visit to North Korea
by a Soviet Government trade delegation, led by the
Vice-Minister of Trade of the U.S.S.R.[96] North
Korea returned the visit in June when it sent to
the Soviet Union a government economic delegation
headed by Yi Chu-yŏn, member of the Political Committee of the KWP Central Committee and Vice-
Premier of the D.P.R.K.[97] It was also reported
that General Kim Ch'ang-bong, Defense Minister of
North Korea, and General Ch'oe Hyŏn of the North
Korean Army were vacationing in the Soviet Union
and that they were entertained by Soviet Defense
Minister Malinovsky.[98] In the same month, the

Soviet Union launched a "Month of Solidarity with
the Korean People," marking the sixteenth anniversary
of the outbreak of the Korean War. The Solidarity
Month lasted from June 25 to July 24.[99]

Not to be outdone by the Soviets, Communist
China too commemorated the occasion by publishing
in Jen-min Jih-pao a lengthy editorial on the
lessons of the Korean War and by holding a mass
rally in Peking in support of the anti-imperialist
struggle of the Korean people. Both events received
full publicity in North Korea.* Such pro-North
Korean gestures by Peking, however, did not prevent
P'yŏngyang from publishing remarks clearly irritating
to the Chinese. For instance, on July 27, Nodong
Sinmun printed its first explicit criticism of the
Chinese language. Saying that the use of ideographs, rather than a phonetic alphabet, reflected
backwardness, not civilization, the newspaper
stated that "nothing is more deplorable than to
waste one's prime of life, which comes only once,
in learning the Chinese ideographs." It further
pointed out that most advanced nations had not
relied on the Chinese ideographs and called it a
"national disgrace" that Koreans should have so
exalted the Chinese characters at the expense of
their own phonetic alphabet.

Just as the Sino-Korean ideological solidarity
in the period 1962-64 did not signify P'yŏngyang's
subservience to Peking, so the rapprochement between
North Korea and the Soviet Union did not signal
the resumption by the Kremlin of control or influence over Kim Il-sŏng. The significance of the
revitalized Soviet-Korean relations, then, lay not
in North Korea's ideological reorientation but in
its growing nationalism. All successful national
leaders are nationalists, whatever their doctrinal
sympathies may be. Kim Il-sŏng is no exception.
From the beginning of his political career in
North Korea, Kim has assiduously pursued the goal
of building a truly independent nation--a goal
which is embodied in North Korea's national catch-
word, chuch'e. Officially translated as "national
identity,"[100] chuch'e made its unobstrusive entry

---

*The full text of the editorial, translated into
 Korean, appeared in Nodong Sinmun on June 28; a
 five-column article on the rally, based on a KCNA
 dispatch from Peking, was also in the issue.

into P'yŏngyang's clouded political lexicon in late
1955. In a speech before a group of propaganda and
agitation workers of the KWP on December 28, 1955,
Kim Il-sŏng pounded hard on the theme of Korea-
oriented Communism. Reminding his audience that
the ideological work of the Party must be geared
to the peculiar requirements of the Korean revolution, he declared that the study of the history of
Russian Communism, the Chinese Revolution, and the
general principles of Marxism-Leninism had one
paramount goal: "to enable us more correctly to
execute our own revolution."[101]

Particularly deplorable, in Kim's view, was
the failure of the Korean Communists to study
Korean history and culture in any systematic way.
He said:

> ...While we should spare no
> effort to absorb the progres-
> sive elements of other cultures,
> we should at the same time
> develop the strong points of
> our own culture. Otherwise,
> we will lose confidence in our
> own abilities and will degenerate
> into abject copiers of other
> people.

> Make no mistake about it:
> to insist on establishing our
> self-identity /chuch'e/ is not
> to deny the need to learn from
> other countries. We must learn
> from all the socialist coun-
> tries, particularly from the
> Soviet Union.

> The important thing is to
> know the purpose of our learning--
> i.e., to apply the experiences of
> the Soviet Union and other social-
> ist countries to our own revolu-
> tionary tasks.[102]

Kim went on to explain the futility of quar-
reling over the path that Korea must take in over-
coming its difficult problems--that is, the Russian
or Chinese path. "It makes no difference," he
insisted, "whether we eat our meal with the right

hand or the left, with a spoon or chopsticks."
What matters most is the accomplishment of a given
goal, and not the means employed to attain that
goal, he said. It was imperative, then, that the
basic tenets of Marxism-Leninism should be "creatively adapted" to the concrete conditions of
Korea. Kim emphatically repudiated both "dogmatism,"
in the sense of an insistence on the mechanical
application of other people's experience to Korea
without regard to its unique history, tradition,
and ideological consciousness, and "formalism,"
in the sense of a blind adherence to a particular
form of Marxism-Leninism as the only true path to
socialism.[103]

     The nationalistic overtones of Kim's strictures
were somewhat muted by his paradoxical thesis that
nationalism and internationalism are intertwined
and, perhaps, even identical. To love Korea is to
love the Soviet Union and the entire socialist
camp, and vice versa, he argued. "For," in his
view, "the great task of the proletariat transcends
national boundaries and our revolutionary task is
only a component part of the international revolutionary task of the world proletariat." Proletarians in all countries share the common task of
building a Communist society; if there is a difference among them, it is only that some countries
will lead, while others follow, Kim said.[104]

     Kim's 1955 speech on chuch'e was by no means
the first revelation of his intense nationalistic
sentiments. Hardly had he set foot in Korea when
he began to articulate his desire for an independent
Korea. On October 18, 1945, Kim outlined his blueprint for the establishment of what he called "a
new democratic nation" in a banquet held in his
honor by the People's Committee of the Province
of South P'yŏngan.[105] Underscoring the need to
"build a new government with our own hands," Kim
declared that Korea "must strive to become a completely democratic and independent nation which can
stand on a footing of equality with /its/ allies in
the world." This, he was convinced, required the
building of a self-reliant national economy at the
earliest possible date. Political independence, if
it is to be meaningful and enduring, must be underpinned by economic independence, he insisted. Kim
felt that one of the potent weapons with which all
Koreans should arm themselves in pursuit of their

national goals was patriotism. "The Japanese
imperialists," he said, "trampled on the national
pride of the Korean people and inculcated colonial
mentality among our youth." He added that a
revival of Korean national pride was one of the
foremost prerequisites to the task of nation-
building.[106]

Inasmuch as North Korea's policy-making has
thus far been virtually monopolized by Kim Il-sŏng,
it may be asserted that P'yŏngyang's domestic and
international behavior to date has been closely
patterned on Kim's blueprint of building a politically autonomous and economically self-sufficient
Korea. The remarkable extent to which this con-
suming goal has been approximated is indicated by
North Korea's ability to maneuver politically in
the Communist bloc. Its wavering stance in the Sino-
Soviet dispute is symptomatic less of its indecision
than of its markedly enhanced sense of national
self-identity. The Nodong Sinmun editorial of
August 12, 1966, entitled "Let Us Defend Our Independence," was but a public confirmation by the
KWP of a mood that had long been unmistakably
apparent to North Korea-watchers.

Although the editorial undoubtedly took by
surprise most Western journalists, who promptly
called it "North Korea's declaration of independence,"[107] there was little in it that was totally
new. Indeed, its dominant themes were no more than
an echo of Kim Il-sŏng's rhetorical pronouncements
referred to above. The parallels between the two
are too striking to escape notice. Thus the editorial had these subtitles: "One should do one's
own thinking," "One should have confidence in one's
own strength," "Marxism-Leninism is a guide to
action," "One should not mechanically follow other's
experience," "One should have national pride,"
"Independent national economy is the material basis
of independence," "One should respect each other's
independence," and "Let us uphold independence and
strengthen the joint struggle against imperialism."
Kim Il-sŏng was saying these things as early as
1945. As already noted, furthermore, Nodong Sinmun
itself had repeatedly expounded them in recent years.

If the message of the editorial may be summed
up in one word, it is chuch'e. "Communists," it
said, "cannot live ideologically shackled to anyone.

They should live with their own spirit and possess
the unshakable ideas of chuch'e. They should not
dance to the tune of others. If Communists do not
use their own brains they will forfeit independence."
Recalling that the KWP had had to wage a struggle
to overcome dogmatism and "flunkeyism" in quest of
chuch'e, the editorial stated that the key to the
success of socialist revolution and construction is
independence. Although the revolution of each
country is integrally related to the world revolution and must take the international situation
into account, the fact still remains that it is
first and foremost an internal affair and must be
tailored to the requirements of its party and
people. "Revolution can neither be exported nor
imported," the editorial insisted. More than
that, each country should rely primarily on its
own resources and only secondarily on outside aid.
"The experience of our party shows," it said, "that
one can tide over any difficulty and solve any
knotty problem if one has confidence in the strength
of one's people and correctly organizes and mobi-
lizes it." The editorial hastened to add, however,
that assistance to other parties and peoples should
not be ruled out completely. All Communists have
the internationalist duty to assist the revolutionary peoples, it declared. Thus the people of
Vietnam deserve unstinted support from Communists
the world over in their revolutionary struggle
against U.S. imperialism.

The editorial reiterated North Korea's long-
held view that Marxism-Leninism should not be construed too rigidly, as an ideological straitjacket,
but should be given a flexible and realistic interpretation. "The Communist and workers' parties
should evolve their own theory for guiding revolution and construction in their countries by creatively applying Marxism-Leninism to the concrete
conditions of their countries," it said. This is
not the same as condoning deviations from the
orthodox Communist doctrines. As the editorial
put it:

> ...As historic examples show, if
> one is bogged down in the mire of
> revisionism, one emasculates the
> revolutionary essence of Marxism-
> Leninism and denies its universal
> truth. It is also wrong to ignore

the changed situation and concrete, specific conditions of
the country, laying emphasis on
the general principles of Marxism-
Leninism only. We should fight
against all erroneous deviations
from Marxism-Leninism and defend
its purity.

Also repeated was the argument that Communist
parties should be left free to emulate the expe-
riences of fraternal parties and should not be
forced to "swallow /them/ undigested." After
emphasizing the importance of patriotism and a
sense of national pride in the successful execution of revolution, the editorial turned to the
paramount necessity of building an independent
national economy for the preservation of political
independence. It said:

Only by building an independent
national economy can the socialist countries enjoy complete
equality and sovereignty in
international relations. To
disavow the building of an independent national economy amounts
in fact to refusing to recognize
the equality and independence of
each country. The building of
an independent national economy
does not rule our mutual cooperation among the socialist
countries. It is neither seclu-
sionism nor closed-door-ism that
does not admit other things at
all, locking the door....But
mutual cooperation among the
socialist countries should be
conducted in such a way as to
strengthen the independent development of each country.

The editorial went on to underline mutual
respect for independence. "There can be no priv-
ileged party among the Communist and workers'
parties. There are big parties and small parties,
but there can be no superior party or inferior
party nor a party that gives guidance and a party
that receives guidance." Although there was a time

when it was necessary for the international Communist movement to have a single center, conditions have undergone a radical change, it pointed out. Because "the international Communist movement has grown incomparably in scope and strength and socialism has developed into a world system, overstepping the bounds of one country, a single center can never give unified guidance in the world revolutionary movement," the editorial noted.

This was an explicit acknowledgment by the KWP of a fait accompli--that the Communist camp has become "polycentric." The editorial left not an iota of doubt that North Korea resented and would never tolerate any attempt by either Moscow or Peking to dictate its policies. In its words:

> ...No matter what long history or
> rich experience one party may have,
> it cannot impose on other parties
> its line and policy as the general
> line of the international Communist
> movement. Decisions of one party
> are obligatory only within the party.
> Therefore no one can force other
> parties to accept the policy of his
> party or to follow it. In particu-
> lar, it is impermissible for a big
> party or the party of a socialist
> country to impose--abusing its posi-
> tion--its policy and put pressure
> on a small party and the party of a
> capitalist country.

In the final part of the editorial, which dealt with the conflict in Vietnam, the lack of unity in the Communist camp was scored. In what appeared to be an oblique criticism of China's rigid attitude toward the cooperation of the socialist countries in helping the Vietnamese people, the editorial urged that "for the sake of the anti-imperialist joint action and the united front, common points should be sought first of all on this fundamental question /i.e., whether to fight against U.S. imperialism or not, whether to support the revolutionary struggle of the world people or not/, shelving other questions for the time being."

Although the editorial merely reiterated the familiar themes, it was clear that North Korea attached a special importance to it. For the unusually long editorial took all of the front and second pages and a half of the third page of Nodong Sinmun. Moreover, it was reproduced in full as the leading article in the August issue of Kŭlloja, the theoretical journal of the KWP.[108] P'yŏngyang may have been annoyed at being labeled "Moscow-oriented" after its recent rapprochement with the Kremlin, and may have decided to advertise clearly its independence of both Moscow and Peking. If that was indeed North Korea's aim, it was amply accomplished. The P'yŏngyang pronouncement was given immediate and wide publicity throughout the world.

Three days after the publication of the editorial, North Korea celebrated the twenty-first anniversary of the Korean Liberation, but, in contrast to the previous year, no foreign delegations were invited to honor the occasion. It was reported, however, that Izvestia, the Soviet Government newspaper, published an editorial commemorating the occasion. The editorial reportedly praised the accomplishments of the D.P.R.K. as "a shining example /of socialist construction7 to millions of people in Asia, Africa, and Latin America."[109] Despite the cooling-off in Sino-Korean comraderie, the two still continued to interact with each other. On August 19, it was reported that a North Korean team would participate in the 1966 International Invitational Table Tennis Tournament to be held in Peking.[110]

On September 9, the D.P.R.K. marked the eighteenth anniversary of its birth. The Soviet Union sent a delegation headed by the Vice-Chairman of the Presidium of the Supreme Soviet of the U.S.S.R., but the P.R.C. sent none. The only foreign delegations that delivered congratulatory speeches at a P'yŏngyang rally commemorating the occasion were those from the Soviet Union, North Vietnam, and Cuba. However, Peking did not neglect to send a congratulatory telegram, which was reproduced in Nodong Sinmun, and joined other Communist nations in holding a rally to honor North Korea.[111] P'yŏngyang reciprocated by sending a telegram to the CCP leadership and by holding a rally in China's honor on October 1, the seventeenth anniversary of the founding of the P.R.C.[112]

As already noted, the "leadership conference"
of the KWP, held during October 5-12, in P'yŏngyang,
made it emphatically clear that Kim Il-sŏng and
his close associates in the partisan group completely dominated the North Korean power structure.
The purge of Kim Ch'ang-man, until then the only
member of the Yenan group in the powerful Political
Committee of the KWP, may conceivably have been
related to the decline of Sino-Korean amity. It
is equally probable that he was eliminated because
he had lost the confidence of Kim Il-sŏng, regardless of his former ties with Yenan. At any rate,
North Korea continued to harp on the independence
theme, while maintaining correct relations with
Peking and relatively warm relations with Moscow.
Nodong Sinmun, summing up the results of the KWP
conference, editorialized on October 14 that the
existing differences of opinion among fraternal
parties should not prevent "the clear separation
of friends and enemies." Stressing the equality
of all parties in the international Communist
movement, the newspaper said:

> Communists should refrain from
> attempting to impose their ideas
> on others. Nor is there any
> justification for their exerting
> pressure on others and for inter-
> fering in the affairs of other
> people, simply because the latter
> disagree with them and follow
> lines different from their own.

The paper went on to assert the "necessity as well
as the rightfulness of /the KWP's/ independent line
based on Marxism-Leninism." The secret of North
Korea's success thus far, according to the paper,
lay in the policy of pursuing "chuch'e /self-
identity/ in thought, chaju /independence/ in
politics, charip /self-reliance/ in economics, and
chawi /self-defense/ in national defense."[113]

The reported arrival of two Russian-built
ships in the port of Ch'ŏngjin on November 7
served to confirm the resumption of Soviet aid to
North Korea. The ships were reported to be a gift
from the Soviet Union in accordance with a Soviet-
Korean protocol on fisheries cooperation signed
in June, 1966.[114] Meanwhile, a North Korean trade
delegation headed by Pang T'ae-yul, Deputy Minister

of International Trade, visited both Moscow and
Peking.[115] On December 13, it was announced that
North Korea had signed a protocol with the Soviet
Union for the exchange of commodities in 1967.
It was disclosed that the projected volume of trade
between the two countries in 1967 would exceed the
volume for 1966.[116]

As 1967 dawned, Nodong Sinmun repeated its 1966
procedure of reproducing the texts of all New Year
messages (telegrams) from abroad save that from
Peking. As in the previous year, it merely reported
that New Year greetings had been exchanged between
the Party and government leaders of North Korea and
Communist China.[117] In mid-February a high-level
North Korean delegation led by Kim Il, member of
both the Presidium and the Secretariat of the KWP
and First Deputy Premier of the D.P.R.K., arrived
in Moscow in quest of more Soviet economic and
military assistance. The fact that more than two
weeks of negotiations preceded the signing of a
series of agreements suggests the possibility of
hard bargaining between North Korea and the Soviet
Union. Kim met with both Brezhnev and Kosygin, and
conferred at length with a host of lesser figures.
At the signing of the agreements on March 2, both
sides made it clear that the new pacts were specifically aimed at the twin goal of developing the
North Korean economy and strengthening its military
power.[118]

The deepening of Soviet-Korean friendship was
further underlined in late May, when Vladimir
Novikov, Deputy Premier of the Soviet Union, paid
a good-will visit to North Korea. At a banquet
held in his honor, the Soviet visitor took special
note of the "rapidly expanding economic cooperation"
between North Korea and the Soviet Union and other
socialist countries. He expressed satisfaction at
the growing Soviet-Korean relations "not only in
the economic sphere but also in the realms of party,
social, cultural, and other activities." He assured
his North Korean hosts that "the Central Committee
of the CPSU as well as the Soviet Government" would
do "all in their power" to promote Soviet-Korean
relations on the basis of the principles of Marxism-
Leninism and proletarian internationalism. He also
stressed that "the U.S. aggression in Vietnam"
urgently called for "united action on the part of
all socialist countries against U.S. imperialism."[119]

The nature and extent of Soviet military assistance to P'yŏngyang were reported by The New York Times in February, 1968, as follows:

> In the last 12 months, experts /in Washington/ say, Moscow has provided more than half of North Korea's 500 military jet aircraft. The North Korean air force is estimated to include 21 MIG-21, 350 MIG-17 and 80 MIG-15 fighters plus 80 IL-28 bombers. Moreover, since 1965, North Korea's air-defense missile complexes have grown with Soviet help from two to ten, of which at least five are now operational. North Korea is said to have 500 air-defense missiles.
>
> The North Korean army of 350,000 to 400,000 men is equipped almost exclusively with Soviet equipment, including medium tanks, and the North Korean navy is said to have two Soviet W-class submarines, four Komar-type guided-missile ships, forty motor torpedo boats and two coastal defense complexes with Soviet radar and shore-to-ship missiles.[120]

Meanwhile, a report of armed clashes at the Sino-North Korean border pointed toward the steady deterioration of P'yŏngyang-Peking relations. In September, Rear Admiral Nam Ch'ŏl of the South Korean Navy, who had just retired from active duty after serving for more than two years as South Korea's Chief Delegate to the Military Armistice Commission, disclosed in a newspaper article that, according to members of the Neutral Nations Supervisory Commission (which consists of Switzerland, Sweden, Czechoslovakia, and Poland), North Korean and Chinese troops recently exchanged rifle shots at the border in a dispute over the ownership of the Paektu Mountain. The preceding information, Nam wrote, came from those members of the neutral nations group who had recently visited North Korea.[121] When the P.R.C. celebrated the eighteenth anniversary of its founding on October 1,

North Korea apparently failed to send a delegation
to Peking.[122] P'yŏngyang's intention to continue
to maintain ties, however tenuous, with Peking,
however, was indicated by the pro forma renewal
of their annual pact on scientific and technical
cooperation on November 23.[123]

There were a few more developments in the
latter part of 1967 that clearly demonstrated
P'yŏngyang's amicable relations with Moscow. When
the Soviet Union marked the fiftieth anniversary
of the Bolshevik Revolution in November, Communist
China and Albania refused to send any delegations.
North Korea, however, joined other Communist nations
and parties in honoring the occasion by sending a
delegation headed by Ch'oe Yong-gŏn. That Ch'oe,
the titular head of state and the number two man
in the KWP hierarchy, represented North Korea,
instead of Kim Il-sŏng, appeared to be symptomatic
of North Korea's strong desire to underscore its
genuine independence of both Peking and Moscow.
Other Communist leaders who were conspicuous for
their absence in Moscow included Ho Chi Minh and
Fidel Castro.[124]

Another noteworthy development was the singular
enthusiasm with which the Soviet Union championed
North Korean causes at the United Nations. In his
policy statement before the Twenty-second Session
of the U.N. General Assembly on September 22,
Soviet Foreign Minister Andrei A. Gromyko made a
lengthy appeal for membership for North Korea and
East Germany. This was all the more remarkable
in view of the fact that the need for seating
Communist China in the world body was mentioned
tersely, almost as a postscript.[125] Moreover, the
Soviet Union campaigned strenuously on behalf of
North Korea before and during the annual debate on
the Korean question at the United Nations. Not
only did it try harder than ever before to line up
support for resolutions favorable to P'yŏngyang, but
it took the lead in calling for the withdrawal of
all foreign troops from South Korea, for the dissolution of the United Nations Commission on the
Unification and Rehabilitation of Korea (UNCURK),
and for the convening of an international conference to settle the question of Korean unification. Although the preceding efforts ended in
failure, it is nonetheless significant that the
Soviet Union amply lived up to P'yŏngyang's expec-
tations, thus further cementing its ties with the
Kim Il-sŏng regime.[126]

The grave international crisis, precipitated
by North Korea's seizure of the U.S.S. Pueblo in
the Wŏnsan Bay in January, 1968, underscored not
only P'yŏngyang's amicable relations with Moscow
but also the former's obsessive desire for independence.* On the one hand, Moscow's rejection of
Washington's naively published request for good
offices, coupled with its open advocacy of the
North Korean point of view in the U.N. Security
Council, revealed the nature of Soviet-North Korean
bonds. On the other hand, P'yŏngyang's insistence
on direct negotiations with the United States was
indicative of the former's strong desire to underline its political autonomy in the world arena.
In February, 1968, the KWP served another public
notice of its independent posture by rejecting the
Soviet invitation to attend the conference of world
Communist parties, which opened on February 26 in
Budapest, Hungary. Boris N. Ponomarev, a secretary
of the CPSU concerned with foreign parties, visited
P'yŏngyang in early February on his way home from
Tokyo in an effort to persuade North Korea to attend
the proposed conference. In rejecting the bid,
the KWP warned that the conference would be "revisionist" even after it was clear that the Yugoslav
Communists would not be invited. North Korea was
joined in its boycott of the conference by the
parties of Communist China, Albania, North Vietnam,
Cuba, and Japan.[127]

In brief, North Korea's over-all posture in
the Sino-Soviet rift may be summed up as one of
neutrality--not neutrality pure and simple but
with a slight slant in favor of Moscow. Propelled
by economic, military, and other pragmatic considerations to seek its rapprochement with the
Kremlin, P'yŏngyang is extremely reluctant to fully
embrace the Soviet line of peaceful coexistence
with the West. Ideologically, it appears to be
strongly committed to the more revolutionary doctrines of Communist China. Nevertheless, North
Korea remains adamant in its insistence on complete
independence. Not simply in rhetoric but in reality
as well, P'yŏngyang appears to be its own captain
and navigator in its precarious voyage through the
murky waters of international Communist politics.
Its compass appears to be its perceived national
self-interest, and its motto chuch'e.

---

*More on the Pueblo incident in Chapter 3.

NOTES TO CHAPTER 2

1. On the Sino-Soviet dispute, see Donald S.
Zagoria, The Sino-Soviet Conflict, 1956-1961
(Princeton, N.J.: Princeton University Press,
1962); David Floyd, Mao Against Khrushchev (New
York: Frederick A. Praeger, 1964); G. F. Hudson,
Richard Lowenthal, and Roderick MacFarquhar (eds.),
The Sino-Soviet Dispute (New York: Frederick A.
Praeger, 1961); Kurt London (ed.), Unity and Con-
tradiction (New York: Frederick A. Praeger, 1962),
Zbigniew Brzezinski, The Soviet Bloc (2d ed.;
New York: Frederick A. Praeger, 1961), pp. 409-42;
U.S. Congress, House of Representatives, Committee
on Foreign Affairs, Sino-Soviet Conflict: Report
on Its Implications, 89th Cong., 1st Sess., House
Document No. 237 (Washington, D.C.: Government
Printing Office, 1965); Zbigniew Brzezinski,
"Patterns and Limits of the Sino-Soviet Dispute,"
Problems of Communism, IX, 5 (September-October,
1960), 1-7; Richard Lowenthal, "Schism Among the
Faithful," Problems of Communism, XI, 1 (January-
February, 1962), 1-14; Harry Gelman, "The /Sino-
Soviet/ Conflict: A Survey," Problems of Commu-
nism, XIII, 2 (March-April, 1964).

2. Kim Il-sŏng, Kim Il-sŏng sŏnjip (Selected
Works of Kim Il-sŏng) (P'yŏngyang: KWP Press,
1960), Vol. VI, pp. 444-45.

3. One should not rule out the possibility
that the Chinese may actually have offended and
annoyed the North Koreans by their domineering
attitude and behavior. For the ethnocentrism of
the Chinese is well known, and it is difficult to
imagine that the Chinese have completely sublimated
it in their dealings with the North Koreans. Indeed,
Arthur H. Dean, who was the chief negotiator for
the U.N. Command at P'anmunjŏm negotiations, reported
that North Korean delegates were visibly bossed by
their Chinese counterparts. See his article, "What
It's Like to Negotiate with the Chinese," The New
York Times Magazine, October 30, 1966, pp. 44ff.

4. The Chinese themselves are known to have
admitted this in a secret letter to the CPSU dated
September 10, 1960. In the letter, they allegedly
pointed out that Khrushchev's secret speech denouncing Stalin deeply offended their sensibilities,
because they had not been consulted in advance.
See Zagoria, The Sino-Soviet Conflict, pp. 42-43.

5. For the text of Khrushchev's speech, see Floyd, Mao Against Khrushchev, pp. 228-30. The quoted passages are from p. 228.

6. Ibid., pp. 229-30.

7. Ibid., p. 231.

8. Nodong Sinmun, April 7, 1956. See its editorial, "Let Us Thoroughly Study the Documents of the Twentieth Congress of the CPSU."

9. See Nodong Sinmun, April 24, 1956. The paper printed a photograph of the proceedings, from which Kim's picture was absent.

10. Nodong Sinmun, August 1, 1956.

11. This view was expressed as early as May, 1955. See Nodong Sinmun, May 8, 1955.

12. Ibid., April 27, 1956.

13. Ibid., June 23, 1956.

14. Ibid., September 19, 1956.

15. Ibid., November 11, 1956.

16. Nodong Sinmun buried a Korean Central News Agency (KCNA) dispatch on the event in its foreign-news section on Page 4. The dispatch was based on a Soviet account of the Budapest uprising prepared by Tass. See Nodong Sinmun, October 27, 1956.

17. Ibid., November 16, 1956.

18. Ibid., November 11, 1956 (text of the Declaration); for editorial comments, see ibid., November 6, 1956.

19. Ibid., November 7, 1957.

20. Ibid., November 23, 1957.

21. See Glenn D. Paige, "North Korea and the Emulation of Russian and Chinese Behavior," in A. Doak Barnett (ed.), Communist Strategies in Asia (New York: Frederick A. Praeger, 1963), pp. 242-47.

22. Nodong Sinmun, February 15, 1958.

23. Chosŏn chungang yŏn'gam, 1959 (Korean Central Yearbook) (P'yŏngyang: Chosŏn Chungang T'ongsinsa, 1959), p. 145; Nodong Sinmun, February 20, 1958.

24. Ibid., February 22, 1958.

25. Ibid., May 15, 1958.

26. Ibid., August 5, 1958.

27. Paige, op. cit., p. 244.

28. Chosŏn chungang yŏn'gam, 1959, p. 145.

29. Ibid., p. 146.

30. Ibid., pp. 143-45.

31. For the text of Kim's speech, see Nodong Sinmun, January 31, 1959; for the Korean translation of Khrushchev's speech, see ibid., January 30, 1959.

32. Chosŏn chungang yŏn'gam, 1960, p. 172.

33. See Floyd, Mao Against Khrushchev, pp. 261-62.

34. Nodong Sinmun, August 4, 1959; September 16, 1959; September 29, 1959.

35. Floyd, op. cit., p. 269.

36. Ibid., pp. 270-71.

37. Nodong Sinmun, April 25, 1960.

38. For the text of the D.P.R.K. Government statement on Khrushchev's U.N. speech, see Nodong Sinmun, October 2, 1960.

39. Floyd, op. cit., p. 110.

40. Ibid., p. 111.

41. The North Korean delegation was led by Kim Il, a Vice-Chairman of the KWP Central Committee and a member of its 11-man Political Committee. See Chosŏn chungang yŏn'gam, 1961, p. 61.

42. Nodong Sinmun, December 7, 1960.

43. Ibid.

44. Chosŏn chungang yŏn'gam, 1961, pp. 134-36.

45. Ibid., p. 136.

46. Nodong Sinmun, May 17, 18, and 20, 1961.

47. Ibid., May 31, 1961.

48. For the Korean text of the treaty, see Nodong Sinmun, July 7, 1961.

49. Ibid.

50. Ibid., July 12, 1961.

51. Ibid., October 22, 1961. (Emphasis added.)

52. Ibid., October 23, 1961.

53. A delegation representing the National People's Congress of the P.R.C. visited North Korea from April 28 to May 8. It was led by CCP Polit-bureau member P'eng Chen, one of the top casualties in the so-called great proletarian cultural revolution. In return, the Supreme People's Assembly of the D.P.R.K. sent a delegation to Communist China. The North Korean team, which was in China from June 15 to July 2, was led by Pak Kŭm-ch'ŏl, member of the Political Committee of the KWP Central Committee. See Chosŏn chungang yŏn'gam, 1963, pp. 191-92.

54. See Floyd, op. cit., p. 159.

55. Chosŏn chungang yŏn'gam, 1963, pp. 193-94.

56. Nodong Sinmun, October 26, 1962.

57. Ibid., November 6, 1962.

58. Ibid., November 17, 1962.

59. Ibid., January 30, 1963.

60. Ibid.

61. Ibid.

62. Joint Statement of Chairman Liu Shao-chi and President Choi Yong Kun (Peking: Foreign Language Press, 1963), p. 8.

63. Ibid., p. 9.

64. Ibid., p. 11. (Emphasis added.)

65. By "dogmatists" he meant those "who do not believe in the possibility of the victory of social- ism and Communism under conditions of peaceful coexistence with capitalism." See his speech on foreign policy delivered to the Supreme Soviet on December 12, 1962, in Floyd, op. cit., p. 329.

66. Joint Statement of Chairman Liu Shao-chi and President Choi Yong Kun, pp. 15-16.

67. Ibid., pp. 15-16.

68. Nodong Sinmum, September 20, 1963.

69. See Peking Review, December 6, 1963, pp. 18-20.

70. Nodong Sinmun, January 30, 1964. See its editorial, "We Welcome the Establishment of Diplomatic Relations Between the P.R.C. and France."

71. Nodong Sinmun, March 17, 1964.

72. Ibid.

73. Nodong Sinmun, April 19, 1964.

74. Ibid.

75. Ibid.

76. Ibid.

77. Ibid.

78. See William E. Griffith, Albania and the Sino-Soviet Rift (Cambridge, Mass.: The M.I.T. Press, 1963).

79. See, for example, the Nodong Sinmun editorial of May 17, 1964, entitled "The Friendship and Solidarity Between the Korean and Albanian Peoples Are Imperishable."

80. Nodong Sinmun, August 31, 1964.

81. Democratic People's Republic of Korea (P'yŏngyang: Foreign Languages Publishing House, 1958), p. 77.

82. Democratic People's Republic of Korea (P'yŏngyang: Foreign Languages Publishing House, 1964), p. 5.

83. Ibid., pp. 9-10.

84. Nodong Sinmun, February 12, 1965.

85. Ibid.

86. Ibid., February 13, 1965.

87. Ibid., February 15, 1965.

88. Ibid., May 6, 1965.

89. Tōitsu Chōsen nenkan, 1965-66 (One Korea Yearbook) (Tokyo: Tōitsu Chōsen Shimbuasha, 1966) p. 690.

90. See Nodong Sinmun, June-December, 1965, passim.

91. Ibid., August 13 and 14, 1965.

92. Ibid., March 27, 1966.

93. Ibid., April 2, 1966.

94. Ibid., April 9, 1966.

95. Ibid., April 7, 1966.

96. Ibid.

97. Ibid., June 9, 1966.

98. Ibid., June 22, 1966.

99. Ibid., June 29, 1966.

100. See The Pyŏngyang Times, January 6, 1966. Published every Thursday since May, 1965, The Pyŏng-yang Times is North Korea's only English-language newspaper. It is an organ of the D.P.R.K. Government. Actually, the term"chuch'e"is not easy to translate, as witnessed by such varying English renderings as "autonomy" (Glenn D. Paige and Dong Jun Lee), "independence" (Glenn D. Paige), "theme" (Chong-Sik Lee), and "subjective entity" (JPRS).

101. Kim Il-sŏng, "Sasang saŏp eso kyojo chuŭi wa hyŏngsik chuŭi rŭl t'oech'i hago chuch'e rŭl hwangnip halte taehayŏ" ("On Exterminating Dogmatism and Formalism and Establishing Autonomy in Ideological Work"), in Kim Il-sŏng sŏnjip (Selected Works of Kim Il-sŏng), Vol. VI, p. 326. The full text of the speech is on pp. 325-54.

102. Ibid., p. 335.

103. Ibid., pp. 336-37.

104. Ibid., p. 338.

105. For the text of his speech, see Kim Il-sŏng sŏnjip (Selected Works of Kim Il-sŏng), Vol. I, pp. 11-14.

106. Ibid., pp. 13-14.

107. See The New York Times, August 13 and 21, 1966; The Washington Post, August 13 and 21, 1966; The Washington Evening Star, August 12, 1966.

108. See "Chajusŏng ŭl ongho haja" ("Let Us Defend Our Independence"), Kŭlloja, August, 1966, pp. 2-20.

109. Nodong Sinmun, August 17, 1966.

110. Ibid., August 19, 1966.

111. Ibid., September 7-10, 1966.

112. Ibid., October 1, 1966.

113. Ibid., October 14, 1966. (Emphasis added.)

114. Ibid., November 8, 1966.

115. Ibid., November 14 and 29, 1966.

116. Ibid., December 13, 1966.

117. Ibid., January 2, 1967.

118. Ibid., March 4 and 6, 1967.

119. Minju Choson (Democratic Korea), May 23, 1967. Minju Choson is the organ of the Government of the D.P.R.K.--the North Korean equivalent of Izvestia.

120. The New York Times, February 1, 1968.

121. Nam Ch'ol, "P'anmunjŏm," Dong-A Ilbo, September 12, 1967.

122. See Tillman Durdin, "Peking Will Hold Big Rally Today," The New York Times, October 1, 1967. This article, a dispatch from Hong Kong, reported that delegations from Albania, North Vietnam, Pakistan, the Congo (Brazzaville) and "a number of other countries" were already in Peking but failed to mention North Korea. NBC News, however, reported on October 6, 1967, that North Korean representatives were present at the Peking rally. If the latter report is correct, then it is possible that North Korean diplomats in Peking, rather than a special delegation from P'yŏngyang, may have attended the rally.

123. See Dong-A Ilbo, November 27, 1967. The signing of the new pact, to be operative for the year 1968, took place in P'yŏngyang, according to a Hsinhua (New China) news agency dispatch from Tokyo.

124. The New York Times, October 29, 1967.

125. The Chicago Daily News, September 23, 1967.

126.   For Soviet activities on behalf of North
Korea at the United Nations, see Dong-A Ilbo,
October and November, 1967.   See in particular
ibid., October 3 and November 4, 1967.   More on
the United Nations' handling of the Korean question in Chapter 3.

127.   The New York Times, February 23 and 27,
1968.

CHAPTER **3** NORTH KOREA AND

KOREAN UNIFICATION

If North Korean leaders were pressed to
state their foremost wish today, they would probably exclaim in unison: "Choguk t'ongil!" (the
unification of our fatherland). And they would
be joined in their chorus by the North Korean
masses as well. What is more, they would hear
resounding echoes of their wish from the southern
half of the Korean peninsula. In a word, Koreans
of all ideological hues are united in their fervent
desire for national unification. Yet the tragedy
of the Korean situation is that unity prevails
only in the realm of abstract desires and not in
that of concrete proposals. The blueprints for a
unified Korea mapped out by P'yŏngyang and Seoul
are poles apart. Just as P'yŏngyang is determined
to extend its full political control to the area
south of the demilitarized zone, so is Seoul unshakable in its conviction that the only form of unification acceptable to the Korean people is the
creation of an all-Korean government free from
Communist influence, let alone control. The two
rival regimes have yet to find some common ground
on which to launch a serious search for a mutually
acceptable and politically feasible formula for
ending the crippling partition of their land which
is more than two decades old.

THE ORIGINS OF THE KOREAN PARTITION

Before exploring North Korea's policy toward
Korean unification, we should briefly note the
developments that led to the tragic division of
the Korean peninsula.[1] In the course of World War
II, the principal Allied Powers publicly committed

112

themselves to the goal of creating a free and independent Korea in the postwar period. The commitment, first made at the Cairo Conference in December, 1943, by the United States, the United Kingdom,
and the Republic of China, was reaffirmed in the
Potsdam Proclamation of July 26, 1945, to which
the Soviet Union subscribed. The Allied Powers
declared their determination to see "that in due
course Korea shall become free and independent."[2]
When the Japanese offered to surrender on August 10,
1945, the United States decided to divide the
responsibility of disarming Japanese troops in
Korea between Soviet and American forces. This
decision, which was to take on historic importance
within a few years, was taken by the U.S. War
Department in a hasty and haphazard fashion.
Although the presence of Russian troops in the
northern part of Korea left few alternatives to
the Pentagon, a prior calculation of the probable
consequences of all the available options by American decision-makers would no doubt have been
enormously beneficial to Washington, not to mention
the Korean people.[3]

     In any event, the decision stipulated that
Japanese troops north of the 38th Parallel in
Korea should surrender to Soviet troops, and those
south of that parallel should surrender to U.S.
forces. This hastily drawn line of demarcation
has since become an enduring symbol of untold
sorrows, miseries, and hardships to countless
Koreans. As McCune points out:

> ...Persons making or approving
> the dividing line probably had
> no idea that their hasty deci-
> sion would last more than a few
> weeks. Therein lies the tragedy
> of the 38th parallel. A line
> adequate or even advantageous
> for a limited military objective
> was subsequently used to divide
> strongly divergent political and
> economic forces.[4]

     Pursuant to the decision, incorporated in
General Order No. 1, which was communicated first
to Premier Stalin and the British Government and
then to the Japanese Government by General Douglas
MacArthur, Supreme Commander for the Allied Powers,

U.S. troops entered Korea on September 8, 1945.
As noted, Soviet troops had already occupied the
northern half of the Korean peninsula. The division of the country was intended as an interim
measure designed to serve a limited military purpose, but the commander of the Soviet occupation
forces quickly made it clear that his interpretation of his authority was not so restricted. He
proceeded to convert the surrender line into an
administrative-political frontier. After attempting vainly to negotiate with the Soviet commander,
the commander of the U.S. occupation forces recom-
mended that the matter should be taken up at the
governmental level.[5]

    At the conference of the foreign ministers
of the United States, the United Kingdom, and the
Soviet Union held in Moscow in December, 1945, the
Korean question was discussed on "an informal and
exploratory basis." Agreement reached at the
conference envisaged the formation of "a provisional Korean democratic government which shall
take all the necessary steps for developing the
industry, transport and agriculture of Korea and
the national culture of the Korean people." As
a preliminary step, however, a Joint Commission
would be established "consisting of representatives
of the United States command in southern Korea and
the Soviet command in northern Korea." The commission, in consultation with "the Korean democratic
parties and social organizations" and with the
consent of the governments of the four Allied
Powers, would work out the details for setting up
the provisional Korean government. Eventually,
the commission would make recommendations for the
"working out of an agreement concerning a four-
power trusteeship of Korea for a period of up to
five years." This latter would also be preceded by
consultations with the political and social organizations in Korea, the provisional Korean government, and the governments of the four powers.[6]

    The Joint U.S.-U.S.S.R. Commission held
numerous meetings in the period March, 1946-July,
1947, but produced no tangible results. One of
the key issues dividing the two sides was the
scope of Korean political parties and social
organizations to be consulted by the commission.
The Soviet delegation insisted that only those
Korean groups should be consulted that had fully

supported all provisions of the Moscow agreement.
This position was predicated on the fact that all
but Communist organizations had voiced stern opposition to the trusteeship provisions of the Moscow
agreement. The United States took the position
that the "Korean people were entitled to express
their views on the agreement and that acceptance
of the Soviet position would violate the principles
of free speech and democratic procedure."[7]

Seeing that the bilateral talks were getting
nowhere, the United States proposed on August 26,
1947, "four-power conversations on this problem at
Washington on September 8, 1947." The Soviet
Union, however, rejected the proposal, placing the
blame for the impasse squarely on the United States.
It insisted that the Joint Commission had not yet
exhausted all the possibilities for working out
agreed recommendations.[8]

It was against this background that the Korean
question finally found its way into the United
Nations. At the initiative of the United States,
the issue was taken up at the second regular session of the General Assembly, which convened in
September, 1947. According to Soon Sung Cho's
persuasive analysis, the United States was, in
effect, seeking an honorable way out of the Korean
impasse by transfering the thorny problem to the
world body. It did not, Cho suggests, really expect
any tangible solution from the United Nations.[9] In
a countermove, the Soviet Union proposed, first to
the Joint Commission in Seoul and then to the U.S.
Government in Washington, that the Soviet and
American troops in Korea be withdrawn simultaneously
in early 1948 and that the Koreans be left to set
up their own government without external interference. The United States was not agreeable to
the Soviet proposal, for, in its view, "the question of withdrawal of occupation forces from Korea
must be considered an integral part of the solution of the problem of setting up an independent
government for a unified Korea." On November 14,
1947, the U.N. General Assembly passed a resolution incorporating mainly the views of the United
States regarding the solution of the Korean question. First, it created a United Nations Temporary
Commission on Korea to expedite the unfettered
participation of the Korean people and their freely
elected representatives in the solution of their

problems. Second, it spelled out a procedure for
conducting all-Korean elections that would ulti-
mately lead to the creation of a united, independent
and democratic Korean government.[10]

The U.N. Commission, consisting of representatives of Australia, Canada, China, El Salvador,
France, India, the Philippines, and Syria,[11] began
to function in Seoul in January, 1948. However, it
met with stubborn Soviet resistance. The Soviet
commander in Korea not only refused to receive the
commission but denied it access to the Soviet zone
of Korea. The commission sought advice and directions from the Interim Committee of the General
Assembly. In a resolution passed on February 26,
1948, the Interim Committee instructed the commission to "proceed with the observance of elections
in all Korea, and if that is impossible, in as
much of Korea as is accessible to it." This
meant, in effect, that elections were to be carried
out only in the southern half of Korea. On May 10,
1948, elections were held throughout the American
occupation zone, and the commission promptly
reported that their results were "a valid expression of the free will of the electorate in those
parts of Korea which were accessible to the Commission and in which the inhabitants constituted
approximately two-thirds of the people of all
Korea."[12]

On May 31, 1948, the Korean National Assembly,
an offshoot of the May 10 elections, convened in
Seoul, but approximately one third of its seats
were left vacant for later occupancy by representatives of the people of the Soviet zone. It adopted
a constitution on July 12, and elected Dr. Syngman
Rhee as President of the Republic of Korea on July
20. On August 15, the Government of the Republic
of Korea was formally established and its constitution promulgated. The American occupation officially came to an end the same day. The newly
created government in Seoul received a stamp of
approval from the United Nations, which in effect
had performed the role of midwife in the former's
birth. On December 12, the U.N. General Assembly
adopted a resolution declaring:

> ...that there has been estab-
> lished a lawful government (the
> Government of the Republic of

Korea) having effective control
and jurisdiction over that part
of Korea where the Temporary
Commission was able to observe
and consult and in which the
great majority of the people of
all Korea reside; that this Government is based on elections
which were a valid expression of
the free will of the electorate
of that part of Korea and which
were observed by the Temporary
Commission; and that this is the
only such Government in Korea.[13]

On the basis of this resolution, the R.O.K. Government has consistently declared that it is the only
legitimate government in all of Korea that has been
duly recognized as such by the United Nations. A
more restrictive interpretation which has been
advanced by some governments, however, is that
the U.N. resolution simply implies that the R.O.K.
Government is the only lawfully constituted government in the southern half of the Korean peninsula.
Whatever its implications may be, the resolution
was followed by the extension of de jure recognition to the R.O.K. Government by the United States
and some thirty-seven countries.[14]

Meanwhile, a rival regime was set up in the
Soviet zone under Soviet auspices. Following the
election of representatives to a "Supreme People's
Assembly" on August 25, 1948, the Democratic
People's Republic of Korea was formally inaugurated
on September 9. Like its southern counterpart,
the new North Korean Government insisted that it
alone is the true government of the entire Korea,
having been organized through "free" elections
held throughout Korea in which practically all
eligible voters in the Soviet zone and an overwhelming majority of them in the American zone
participated. The D.P.R.K. Government was promptly
accorded de jure recognition by the Soviet Union
on October 12, 1948. The other members of the
socialist bloc followed suit, and, by the time
the Korean War broke out, P'yŏngyang had exchanged
ambassadors with all the bloc countries except
Yugoslavia. This in brief is the background of
the Korean partition. Originally designed as a
purely military line of demarcation of limited

duration, the 38th Parallel has hardened into a
nearly impenetrable political boundary separating
two regimes with a common race, language, and
culture but with widely divergent ideologies and
world outlooks.

THE GOALS AND TACTICS OF
NORTH KOREA'S UNIFICATION POLICY

Although P'yŏngyang's strategic objective has
always remained the Communization of all of Korea,
its operational directions and tactics have been
markedly flexible over the years. Its initial
operational direction appears to have been to build
a revolutionary base. Thus, in the pre-Korean
War stage, North Korea experimented with all con-
ceivable techniques of political violence, ranging
from demonstrations to armed guerrilla warfare,
in hopes not only of undermining the stability of
the political authorities in South Korea, but also
of consolidating Communist organization and support.[1]
Then came the stage of full-scale military invasion.
Despite the lack of incontrovertible evidence, it
seems fairly obvious that Kim Il-sŏng, and most
probably Stalin, planned and launched it mainly to
forcibly unify the peninsula. Having learned the
hard way that force alone would not work, the KWP
leadership turned to a massive psychological offensive combined with underground infiltration.[16]

Relentlessly pursuing this "peaceful" operational direction, North Korea has continuously
challenged South Korea to the conference table and
to enter into economic and cultural contacts with
it. It has laid particular stress on the theme of
national self-determination, arguing that Korean
problems should be resolved by Koreans themselves,
without any external interference. Until 1960,
however, North Korea did not rule out the possibility
of convening an international conference to discuss
the Korean question. From the latter part of 1960,
the self-determination theme became all-pervasive.
Simultaneously, Kim Il-sŏng put forth the so-called
confederation proposal. North Korea appeared to
retreat somewhat in the summer of 1966, when it
reintroduced the idea of an international conference.
However, by 1967, its position had stiffened even
further. Meanwhile, it stepped up its infiltration

campaign, markedly expanding guerrilla activities
against and in South Korea. P'yŏngyang's behavior
clearly reflected its realistic appraisal of its
changing capabilities and needs.

Building a Revolutionary Base, 1945-50

Manifestly, the ability of a political group
to formulate and execute a plan of action is con-
tingent upon its internal unity and cohesiveness.
Because it was not until the latter part of 1948
that the Korean Communists were able to project a
semblance of unity, it would be absurd to assume
that Communist activities were centrally directed
in the chaotic aftermath of Korea's Liberation.
Thus, the initial stage of the Communist experience
with political violence was marked by widely
scattered and poorly coordinated acts of civil
disobedience, sabotage, and terrorism.[17]

The year 1948 saw a marked increase in Communist violence in South Korea, and, as Glenn D.
Paige indicates, a period of guerrilla war began.[18]
The most ferocious events of the period were no
doubt the Cheju Rebellion of April, 1948, and the
Yŏsu-Sunch'ŏn Mutiny of October, 1948. The callous
disregard for human dignity and life, so savagely
demonstrated by the rebelling Communists in these
tragic events, was unquestionably counterproductive
from the Communist point of view: It shocked and
antagonized a vast majority of South Koreans.
Despite their lack of success, it appears that the
overriding aim of the Communists in the pre-Korean
War stage was to build a revolutionary base in
South Korea. They sought tenaciously not only to
incite violence, but also to secure bases of operation for the eventual revolutionary takeover of the
entire South. Their dismal failure may be attributable as much to their shockingly savage techniques and the consequent alientation of the South
Korean masses, as to the ruthlessly effective
suppression of their activities by the South Korean
authorities. Had they relied more on techniques
of persuasion, they might have been more successful.

It is probable that P'yŏngyang initially preferred negotiation to military conquest in its
quest for national unity. Thus, in April, 1948,

North Korea was a host to an all-Korean conference
on unification. The architects of the conference,
however, were South Korean nationalist leaders,
notably Kim Ku and Kim Kyu-sik. The two leaders
had proposed a meeting of political leaders from
all parts of Korea to discuss ways of establishing
a unified Korean government. When the meeting
finally convened on April 19, 1948, in P'yŏngyang,
545 delegates representing political parties and
social organizations throughout Korea were reportedly on hand. With the arrival of more delegates
from the South, the membership of the conference
eventually swelled to 695. Of this, 395 came from
South Korea. All told, fifteen political parties
and forty social organizations were allegedly
represented. The tone of resolutions finally
adopted by the conference strongly suggests, however, that if the meeting was not inspired by
North Korean leaders, it was thoroughly dominated
by them. It fully endorsed North Korea's opposition to the impending unilateral elections in South
Korea, pointing out that the only bar to unification was the American military government in Seoul.
It called on "all foreign troops" to immediately
withdraw from Korea and proposed that an all-Korean
political conference be held to form a provisional
government. The latter, the conference added,
would supervise national elections for a constituent
assembly, which would, in turn, draft a constitution and set up a unified Korean government on a
permanent basis.[19] What the conference conveniently
overlooked were the circumstances which were under-
lying the decision of the U.N. Temporary Commission
on Korea to go ahead with "unilateral elections."
Just why self-sponsored and self-supervised elections would be superior to and more reliable than
U.N.-supervised ones was not made clear. The vigor
with which both the U.S. military authorities in
Seoul and the U.N. commissions were denounced left
no doubt that the conference shied away from proposing realistic solutions, but merely performed
a propaganda function for both P'yŏngyang and Moscow.

The next moves of any significance taken by
North Korea came on the eve of the Korean War. In
retrospect, these moves were clearly a part of
P'yŏngyang's strategy of military conquest of South
Korea. On June 7, 1950, the Enlarged Central
Committee of the Democratic Front for the Unification of the Fatherland adopted a resolution in the
form of an appeal for peaceful unification. The
resolution spelled out the following steps:

1. Elections shall be held throughout Korea
on August 5-8, 1950, for the purpose of establishing
a unified, supreme legislative assembly.

2. The legislative assembly so elected shall
convene on August 15, 1950, the fifth anniversary
of Korea's Liberation, in Seoul.

3. A conference of representatives from all
political parties and social organizations throughout Korea shall be called June 15-17, 1950, in
either Haeju or Kaesŏng. The conference will map
out conditions and procedures for bringing about
peaceful unification.

4. The conference shall specifically exclude
certain individuals and organizations, such as
Syngman Rhee, Yi Pŏm-sŏk, Kim Sŏng-su, Sin Sŏng-mo,
Cho Pyŏng-ok, Yun Ch'i-yŏng, Sin Hŭng-u, the Korean
National Party, and the Democratic National Party.
The previously mentioned individuals were branded
as "traitors of the Korean people."[20] Another
gesture quickly followed. On June 19, the Presidium
of the D.P.R.K. Supreme People's Assembly transmitted a message to the R.O.K. National Assembly
proposing that the two rival assemblies be merged
to form a single legislative organ for all of Korea.[21]

Unification by Force, 1950-53

Plainly, these moves were carefully designed
by P'yŏngyang to camouflage its aggressive inten-
tions. For, by the time both moves were made,
plans were virtually complete for the impending
invasion. It is interesting to speculate how Kim
Il-sŏng would have reacted had the preceding proposals struck responsive chords on the part of
South Korean leaders. Yet the uncompromising nature
of the proposals, coupled with the extremely nebu-
lous political situation in Seoul, had effectively
precluded any serious consideration of the North
Korean gestures. Six days after the second message
was transmitted to Seoul, North Korean tanks and
troops swarmed across the 38th Parallel. The Korean
War had begun.

The story of the three-year conflict need not
be told here. Suffice it to point out that North
Korea failed miserably to attain its initial goal.

Far from unifying the country, the war devastated it. When the Armistice Agreement was signed on July 27, 1953, North Korea found itself precisely where it was on that fateful Sunday morning in June, 1950: It controlled only half of the Korean peninsula.[22] The gamble had been lost. The idea of "unification by force" had turned out to be a grave miscalculation on the part of P'yŏngyang and, perhaps, Moscow. Publicly, however, North Korea never acknowledged that it had suffered a setback. It steadfastly maintained that the war was of Seoul's making, and not P'yŏngyang's. North Korea had simply responded to an unprovoked attack from South Korea, it was argued. Begun as a defensive war from North Korea's viewpoint, the war had gradually been transformed into a "Fatherland Liberation War."

The armistice, from North Korea's official point of view, signified a great victory. In a radio speech to the North Korean people on July 28, 1953, a day after the signing of the cease-fire agreement, Kim Il-sŏng claimed that a great blow had been dealt to the "United States imperialists, their South Korean lackeys, and the entire imperialist camp." The war had demonstrated and consolidated the invincible might of the peace-loving democratic camp headed by the great Soviet Union, while intensifying and aggravating the internal contradictions of the imperialist camp, Kim declared. The imperialist scheme to conquer the world and to enslave the peoples of other lands had thus been frustrated, he added. In his view, the chief ingredient of North Korea's "victory" was the unbreakable alliance between the proletariat and the peasantry, together with the wholehearted support given to this alliance by Koreans in all walks of life. The North Korean leader set forth two paramount goals for his Party, government, and people in the postwar period: the economic goal of rehabilitation and reconstruction, on the one hand, and the political goal of peaceful unification, on the other.[23]

If the armistice signaled the formal, if not actual, jettisoning of North Korea's plan to unify Korea by force, it also dispelled any illusion South Korea might have harbored about crushing its rival regime in P'yŏngyang by military means. Had the "Chinese People's Volunteers" not rushed to North Korea's aid in November, 1950, Seoul's

cherished dream might very well have come true.
Korea might have become one nation under South
Korean control. Syngman Rhee had remained adamant
in his conviction that a military victory was not
only possible, but that it alone promised solutions
to Korea's political questions. It took a considerable amount of persuasion and pressure on
the part of the United States to compromise the
South Korean President to the idea of a cease-fire.
In a letter of June 6, 1953, President Eisenhower
told Rhee that the moment had come to decide whether
to try to bring about Korean unification by military
action "or whether to pursue this goal by political
and other methods." He made it plain that the United
States preferred nonmilitary solutions.[24]

Although Rhee continued to speak publicly in
terms of "marching to the north" to unify the
Korean nation even after the armistice, he was
undoubtedly aware of the futility of his rhetorical
exercise. The R.O.K. Army, heavily dependent on
U.S. supplies and logistics, was in no shape to
undertake a northern expedition singlehandedly.
Seoul's dependence on Washington was epitomized by
the initialing of a U.S.-Korean Mutual Defense
Treaty in Seoul on August 8, 1953. The treaty,
signed in Washington on October 1, 1953, stipulated
that "an armed attack in the Pacific area on either
of the Parties in territories now under their
respective administrative control, or hereafter
recognized by one of the Parties as lawfully brought
under the administrative control of the other, would
be /recognized by each nation as/ dangerous to its
own peace and safety." Each nation pledged that
"it would act to meet the common danger in accordance
with its constitutional processes." To avoid the
possibility that the R.O.K. Government might exploit
this provision to involve the United States in an
unprovoked invasion of North Korea, the U.S. Senate
attached a statement declaring that it was the understanding of the United States that the obligations
mentioned in the treaty applied only in event of
external armed attack and that the treaty should
not be construed as requiring American assistance
"except in the event of armed attack against territory which has been recognized by the United States
as lawfully brought under the administrative control
of the Republic of Korea."[25]

Psychological Warfare Combined with
Infiltration and Violence, 1953-

The adoption by North Korea of the so-called
peaceful approach to unification was not an entirely
voluntary act. It was forced to abandon the military
approach by a combination of internal and external
factors. The most obvious factor was the inability
of the Communist side to win a quick military victory. From the beginning, North Korea relied
heavily on external assistance for the conduct of
the war. The three-year conflict had not only
exhausted North Korea's limited resources, but it
had proved to be an enormously costly burden on
both Moscow and Peking. Quite conceivably, had the
Soviet Union rendered more technical and military
assistance, North Korea, with Communist Chinese
help, could have withstood Allied military pressures
much longer. However, neither the Soviet Union nor
Communist China were willing to prolong the military
venture, which they probably estimated to be unwin-
nable. Moreover, as Soon Sung Cho points out, the
internal political struggle in the Kremlin triggered
by Stalin's death in March, 1953, necessitated a
momentary diversion of Soviet attention from global
strategy to the domestic scene.[26]

Additionally, President Truman's veiled threat
to use nuclear weapons further clouded the prospect
of a possible Communist victory. Then, too, there
was the factor of North Korea's internal politics.
Kim Il-sŏng's perceived political interests dictated
not only that he yield to Soviet and Chinese pressures for a negotiated settlement, but that he find
scapegoats for the failure of the military venture.
He saw a golden opportunity to wipe out the South
Korean Communist faction led by Pak Hŏn-yŏng, which
was bitterly opposed to a cease-fire. Thus Kim
made a virtue of a necessity by utilizing the switch
to the peaceful approach to eradicate his political
rivals.[27]

The Armistice Agreement was silent about the
solution of political questions, but contained a
paragraph recommending "to the governments of the
countries concerned on both sides, that, within
three (3) months after the Armistice Agreement is
signed and becomes effective, a political conference
of a higher level of both sides be held by

representatives appointed respectively to settle
through negotiation the questions of the withdrawal
of all foreign forces from Korea, the peaceful
settlement of the Korean question...."[28]   On August
28, 1953, the U.N. General Assembly adopted a resolution welcoming a political conference on Korea
and recommending that the U.S. Government make
appropriate arrangements with interested governments for such a conference to be held not later
than October 28, 1953.[29]   Pursuant to the preceding
resolution, the United States made an abortive
attempt to arrange a conference with the Communists
at P'anmunjŏm.[30]

A meeting of the foreign ministers of the United
States, France, the United Kingdom, and the Soviet
Union in Berlin in early 1954, however, produced an
agreement. In a quadripartite communiqué issued
on February 18, 1954, the four powers concurred
that "the establishment, by peaceful means, of a
united and independent Korea would be an important
factor in reducing international tension and in
restoring peace in other parts of Asia." They
proposed that the United States, France, the United
Kingdom, the Soviet Union, the P.R.C., the R.O.K.,
and the D.P.R.K., and "the other countries the
armed forces of which participated in the hostil-
ities in Korea, and which desire to attend," should
meet in Geneva on April 26, "for the purpose of
reaching a peaceful settlement of the Korean question." It was further agreed that the problem of
restoring peace in Indochina would also be discussed
at the conference.[31]

The Korean Political Conference opened in
Geneva at the designated date and lasted until June
15. The Allied side was represented by delegations
from the R.O.K. and from all the countries except
the Union of South Africa that had contributed
military forces to the United Nations Command, and
the Communist side consisted of delegations from
the D.P.R.K., the P.R.C., and the Soviet Union. It
quickly became apparent that the two sides were
diametrically opposed to each other on three key
issues: (1) the authority and role of the United
Nations, (2) the principle of free elections, and
(3) the withdrawal of foreign troops. The Allied
side consistently maintained that a "reasonable
Korean settlement" must be predicated on the
following propositions:

1. That the authority and competence of the
United Nations to deal with Korea must be recognized
and that the United Nations should have a primary
role in bringing about a settlement.

2. That genuinely free Korean elections, with
proportionate representation for North and South
Korea, should be held.

3. That U.N. forces should remain in Korea
until the mission of the United Nations had been
accomplished by the creation of a unified, independent, and democratic Korea.[32]

The Communist side totally rejected the first
and third propositions and clearly indicated its
uneasiness over, if not disapproval of, the second.
Soviet Foreign Minister V. M. Molotov, denouncing
the U.N. intervention in Korea as a series of
"illegitimate actions" designed only "to cover up
American aggression," asserted that the United
Nations had degenerated into a "belligerent" in
Korea. Therefore, he added, it was without "capacity to act as an impartial international body" and
could "no longer carry out objective functions in
the settlement of the Korean problem."[33] The preceding view was faithfully echoed by North Korean
and Communist Chinese representatives. The only
formula agreeable to the Communist side was one in
which Koreans would be left to solve their own
problems free from foreign interference. More
specifically, Foreign Minister Nam Il of North
Korea made the following proposal on April 27:

1. General elections shall be held for the
purpose of electing a national assembly and of
forming a united Korean government based on the
free expression of the wishes of the inhabitants
of the whole of Korea.

2. An all-Korean Commission shall be established, with representatives from North and South
Korea, to make the necessary preparations for free
general elections for a Korean assembly, and to
take urgent measures for the economic and cultural
rapprochement of North and South Korea. The members of the commission shall be selected by the
Supreme People's Assembly of the D.P.R.K. and the
National Assembly of the R.O.K., respectively, and
shall include representatives of the largest democratic social organizations in South and North Korea.

3. All foreign military forces shall be withdrawn from the Korean territory within six months.

4. All those countries most interested in the
maintenance of peace in the Far East shall guarantee
the peaceful development of Korea, thus creating
the conditions likely to contribute to a swift conclusion of the task of unifying Korea by peaceful
means as a united, independent, democratic State.[34]

If this proposal appeared relatively innocuous
at first glance, it quickly revealed its true nature.
The nucleus of the proposal was the formation of
an all-Korean Commission, and it proved to be an
insurmountable barrier to agreement. Nam Il insisted
that decisions in the proposed commission would be
made only on the basis of "mutual agreement." That
is, North Korea would be able to exercise a veto
over the unification process, thus ensuring that
unification, if it was ever to be attained, would
come on North Korean terms only. In the view of
the Allied side, to agree to such a formula would
be tantamount to surrendering to the Communists at
the conference table what the U.N. forces so
tenaciously fought to preserve on the battlefield.
None of the Allied nations was inclined to put to
naught the blood and sweat of tens of thousands of
U.N. soldiers. What is more, the refusal of the
Communist side to recognize the authority and competence of the United Nations in the settlement of
the Korean question was intolerable to the Allied
side. U.S. Secretary of State John Foster Dulles
summed up the feeling of the Allied nations toward
the United Nations when he told the conference on
April 28: "It is right that the United Nations
should be sustained as an authority to which all
peoples, for all time, may turn to save them from
the scourge of war and to assure the dignity and
worth and equal rights of nations large and small."[35]

On May 22, Communist Chinese Foreign Minister
Chou En-lai added an item to the North Korean proposal: the establishment of a "neutral nations
supervisory commission" to supervise the proposed
all-Korean elections. The commission would consist of an equal number of Communist and non-
Communist governments and could function only on
the basis of unanimity. The Allied side lost no
time in pointing out that such a commission would
be worse than useless because of the Communist veto,

citing the impotence of a similar body created to
oversee the armistice only a short time ago. The
Allied side was more or less united behind a South
Korean proposal providing for U.N.-supervised
elections throughout Korea within six months on
the basis of a secret ballot and universal adult
suffrage.[36] The number of representatives in a
new National Assembly would be apportioned in
exact proportion to the population as determined by
a U.N.-supervised census. The Constitution of the
R.O.K. would remain in force, subject to amendment
by the all-Korean legislature to be convened in
Seoul immediately after the elections. Furthermore,
Communist Chinese troops would be required to withdraw completely from Korea one month before the
election date, whereas U.N. forces would remain in
Korea until a new, united Korean government had
taken complete control and had been certified by
the United Nations.[37]

Yet, as noted, on the crucial issues of the
role of the United Nations, of genuinely free elections, and of withdrawal of foreign troops, the
Communist side would not compromise. Not only did
it continue downgrading the world organization, but
it flatly insisted that all foreign troops must
withdraw from the Korean soil simultaneously, prior
to elections. The North Korean representative paid
lip service to the principle of proportional representation, but he also made it clear that all
decisions regarding the proposed all-Korean elections and the eventual formation of a united government must be subject to North Korean veto.

This last-mentioned item generated considerable
concern among Allied delegations. Their dominant
mood was aptly summed up by Lester B. Pearson, the
Canadian representative to the conference:

> If the Government of the Republic
> of Korea is really guilty, as
> charged yesterday by the Foreign
> Minister of the Democratic People's
> Republic of Korea, of tyrannical
> and savage repression of freedom
> in elections, how can he expect us
> to take seriously his proposal for
> elections which he says will be
> free because they will be conducted
> under arrangements which must be

agreed to by the representatives
of this government which he so
viciously attacks? Does Mr. Nam
Il really wish us to believe that
representatives of North Korea
feel that they can work amicably
and constructively on the All-
Korean Commission with the representatives of what he contemptuously
calls the "Syngman Rhee clique"?

It is clear, Mr. Chairman, that
the most superficial examination of
the North Korean proposals, with
its veto provisions for the All-
Korean Commission, with its rejection of free elections, guaranteed
by impartial and effective outside
international supervision, with
the voters in North Korea, for
instance, left to the tender mer-
cies of the communist governmental
machinery in expressing their views,
it is clear that such an examination of these proposals shows that
they provide no hope for bringing
about a free, united and democratic
Korea.[38]

On June 5, Soviet Foreign Minister Molotov
proposed a draft resolution, which, while restating
all the essential elements of the North Korean and
Communist Chinese proposals, left controversial
matters unsettled. These were to be "the subject
of further examination." In short, the draft
resolution would merely have created an illusion
of unity. It failed to impress the Allied side.
Finally, on June 15, the Allied side issued a
"Sixteen-Nation Declaration on Korea" formally
acknowledging that the Geneva Conference had been
in vain. The blame for the failure was placed
squarely on the Communist side:

...The principal issues between us,
therefore, are clear. Firstly, we
accept and assert the authority of
the United Nations. The Communists
repudiate and reject the authority
and competence of the United Nations
in Korea and have labelled the United

Nations itself as the tool of
aggression. Were we to accept
this position of the Communists,
it would mean the death of the
principle of collective security
and of the UN itself. Secondly,
we desire genuinely free elections. The Communists insist
upon procedures which would make
genuinely free elections impossible.
It is clear that the Communists
will not accept impartial and
effective supervision of free
elections. Plainly, they have
shown their intention to maintain
Communist control over North Korea.
They have persisted in the same
attitudes which have frustrated
United Nations efforts to unify
Korea since 1947.[39]

The Allied side went on to declare that "it is
better to face the fact of our disagreement than
to raise false hopes and mislead the peoples of
the world into believing that there is agreement
where there is none."[40] Thus ended the Korean
phase of the Geneva Conference--and with it the
faint glimmer of hope for an early, peaceful
settlement of the Korean question.

To the surprise of no one, North Korea promptly
shifted the blame for the Geneva failure to the
"imperialist bloc." In the words of Ki Sŏk-bok,
a member of the North Korean delegation to the
Geneva Conference and Chief of the KWP Foreign
Affairs Department:

The Geneva Conference has clearly
revealed the conflicting foreign
policy lines of the two blocs.
One seeks the national unification
of Korea and the peaceful solution
of the Korean question on the basis
of world peace and international
cooperation. This is the position
taken by the representatives of the
DPRK, the PRC, and the Soviet Union.
The other is fanatically dedicated
to the goals of disrupting Korea's
national unity and of prolonging

> international tensions on the
> basis of war and anachronistic
> colonialism. This is the posi-
> tion taken by the United States
> and its followers.[41]

Ki, however, voiced his conviction that peaceful
unification, obstacles notwithstanding, was still
possible. In his view, the solution of the Indo-
chinese question at Geneva "clearly demonstrated"
that the Korean question, too, can and must be
settled by peaceful negotiation. He prophesied
the victory of North Korea's policy. For it alone
was consistent with the interests and aspirations
not only of the Korean people but also of the
millions of peace-loving people the world over,
he said.[42]

On October 30, 1954, North Korea's Supreme
People's Assembly passed a resolution reiterating
P'yŏngyang's prewar proposal for a conference of
representatives from all political parties and
social organizations in North and South Korea to
discuss the peaceful settlement of the Korean
question as well as the opening of cultural and
commercial contacts between the two parts of Korea.[43]
Like its predecessor, this proposal was brushed
aside by Seoul as a propaganda move unworthy of
serious consideration. The Third Congress of the
KWP, on April 28, 1956, adopted a declaration on
peaceful unification, which recognized the need to
convene an international conference for the solution of the Korean question. On June 2, North
Korean Foreign Minister Nam Il called for a conference of the interested nations to discuss
Korean unification. The chance of such a conference
ever being held, however, was seriously reduced by
Nam's demand for withdrawal of all foreign troops
from Korea.[44] In sum, there was no sign of any
change in North Korea's position on unification.

The proposal to convene an international conference on Korea was again put forth by Kim Il-sŏng
in a speech to North Korea's Supreme People's
Assembly on September 20, 1957. In the speech, Kim
also proposed that after complete withdrawal of
all foreign troops from North and South Korea each
side should reduce its armed forces to 100,000.
He further pressed for an agreement pertaining to
cultural and economic intercourse, as well as the

exchange of mail between North and South Korea.[45]
Two weeks later the North Korean Minister of
Domestic and Foreign Commerce sent a letter to his
counterpart in South Korea--the Minister of Commerce and Industry--suggesting a few concrete steps
to implement the preceding proposal. He suggested
that two localities, Kaesŏng for North Korea and
Ch'ŏlwŏn for South Korea, be designated for the
purpose of exchanging goods. Additionally, he
proposed that a preparatory conference of representatives from either government or business be
held before the end of the year to discuss various
practical problems of commerce, such as the setting
up of a common market, the organization of trade
fairs, the establishment of a standing committee,
and the like. He asked the South Korean Minister
of Commerce and Industry to suggest a time and
place for this conference.[46]

     Meanwhile, the United Nations continued to
honor its commitment to strive for a peaceful
settlement of the Korean question. It relied on
the U.N. Commission for the Unification and Rehabilitation of Korea (UNCURK) and the U.N. Korean
Reconstruction Agency (UNKRA), established by the
U.N. General Assembly resolutions of October 7 and
December 1, 1950, respectively. UNCURK furnished
annual reports to the General Assembly concerning
developments bearing on the question of unification, the operation of the Armistice Agreement, and
the progress of economic rehabilitation and reconstruction in South Korea, whereas UNKRA was charged
with the task of administering the U.N. programs
of emergency relief and economic assistance. UNCURK
consists of representatives from Australia, Chile,
the Netherlands, Pakistan, the Philippines, Thailand,
and Turkey, but since January, 1956, its functions
and responsibilities have been exercised by a
committee consisting of representatives from Australia, the Philippines, Thailand, and Turkey, with
headquarters in Seoul.[47] The U.N. General Assembly
annually debated the Korean question, invariably
passing a resolution reaffirming the U.N. objective
of establishing a unified, democratic, and independent Korea by peaceful means.

     On the armistice front, hardly had the ink
dried on the Armistice Agreement when both sides
began to exchange charges of its violations by the
other side. In view of what the U.N. Command called

"the continued illegal introduction" into North Korea of military supplies and equipment, the Allied side formally informed the Communist side in June, 1957, that it was taking the measures it deemed necessary to restore the military balance the armistice was intended to preserve. Earlier in May, 1956, the U.N. Command had "provisionally" suspended the performance on its part of those provisions of the Armistice Agreement governing the operations of the Neutral Nations Supervisory Commission and its inspection teams. The action had been prompted by the complete impotence of the four-nation body to perform its intended functions. Two members of the commission, Czechoslovakia and Poland, by unabashedly taking side with the Communists, had stripped it of its "neutral" character altogether.[48]

In February, 1958, North Korea renewed its peace offensive, which, unlike its predecessors, evoked some response from the Allied nations. In a statement of February 5, issued in the name of the Government of the D.P.R.K., the P'yŏngyang regime first denounced both the United States and South Korea for obstructing its continued efforts toward peaceful unification. It accused the two governments of repeated and flagrant violations of the Armistice Agreement and of attempting to convert South Korea into an atomic base. It then declared that the following measures "should be taken without delay":

1. The simultaneous withdrawal of all foreign troops from North and South Korea.

2. The holding of "all-Korean free elections" under the supervision of neutral nations. All political parties, social organizations, and citizens should be given complete freedom of movement in such elections.

3. The opening of negotiations for economic and cultural contacts between North and South Korea. Such negotiations must be conducted on the basis of complete equality.

4. The reciprocal reduction of armed forces to "a bare minimum." North Korea has already reduced its army by 80,000 men.[49]

On February 8, <u>Nodong Sinmun</u> reported that the
Government of the P.R.C. had given its full blessing
to the preceding proposals. A week later Chou En-lai
arrived in P'yŏngyang for a week-long good-will
visit, which culminated in the announcement that
the "Chinese People's Volunteers" would be withdrawn from North Korea by the end of 1958. The
Sino-North Korean statement challenged the United
States to reciprocate by withdrawing U.S. troops
from South Korea as well.[50] The Soviet Union
promptly endorsed the preceding action.[51]

These moves apparently intrigued the Allied
side, for in April it initiated an exchange of
memoranda with the Communist side through British
diplomatic channels in Peking. Specifically, the
Allied side wanted to know whether North Korea would
be willing to let neutral nations supervise the
elections under United Nations auspices and whether
representation in the new National Assembly would
be in proportion to the population. However, Peking,
which acted as P'yŏngyang's spokesman, would not
elaborate, insisting only on the withdrawal of all
foreign troops from South Korea. The nearly year-
long diplomatic dialogue proved to be an exercise
in futility.[52]

As already noted, the student uprising of
April 19, 1960, in South Korea appears to have
raised new hopes for "unification by negotiation"
in P'yŏngyang. North Korea frantically intensified
its propaganda offensive against Seoul, renewing
its well-advertised offers for the opening of
North-South contacts and for the holding of an
all-Korean conference on unification.[53] Then on
August 14, Kim Il-sŏng unveiled a new North Korean
formula--the "confederation approach." In a speech
commemorating the fifteenth anniversary of the
Korean Liberation, the North Korean Premier proposed the creation of a confederation of North
and South Korea as a transitional measure. Although
North Korea was unalterably committed to the goal
of setting up a unified Korean government through
free elections, it was willing to settle for a
loose confederation of the fully autonomous North
and South Korean governments on a strictly provisional basis, Kim said. More specifically, Kim
envisaged the formation of a Supreme National
Council consisting of the representatives of the
two governments. The council would be primarily

concerned with coordinating the economic and cultural programs of both sides. By ensuring cultural
and commercial intercourse as well as mutual assistance between the two sides, the council would make
significant contributions not only toward rescuing
the South Korean economy from its bankruptcy, but
also toward improving the living standards of the
Korean people, Kim insisted. It was pointed out
that such an arrangement would promote mutual understanding, eliminate mutual distrust, and create
conditions conducive to the holding of free all-
Korean elections. In short, it was the "most
rational approach to hastening the realization of
the fatherland's complete unification."[54]

As usual, Seoul did not respond directly to
the North Korean overtures. However, it made it
abundantly clear that it saw no merit whatsoever
in Kim Il-sŏng's new formula. Both Premier John
M. Chang and Foreign Minister Chŏng Il-hyŏng
declared, in separate statements, that their government was solidly behind the United Nations' position on the question: that democratic and peaceful
unification is possible only through U.N.-supervised
elections.[55] If the "confederation" proposal failed
to impress the South Korean Government, it did not
wholly escape the attention of the South Korean
people. Some vocal elements in South Korea, particularly the traditionally politically minded
university students, began to wonder aloud if
there was no alternative to what they regarded as
the inflexible and unimaginative approach of the
Chang regime to unification. In November, 1960,
for instance, students at Seoul National University
formed what they called the Alliance for National
Unification (Minjok T'ongil Yŏnmaeng). In a resolution adopted by the newly formed organization,
the students made a strong plea to their elders to
assume moral responsibility for the tragedy of the
Korean partition and to recognize their incompe-
tence to suppress the legitimate ideas and actions
of the new generation pertaining to national unification. They further called on the Chang regime
to resort to "positive diplomacy based on the
realities" of the Korean situation. Specifically,
they asked Premier Chang to visit the United States
and the Soviet Union to meet with the leaders of
these superpowers in an attempt to explore the
possibility of bringing about Korean unification.
Finally, they called for an early implementation

of one of the fundamental human rights embodied in
the Universal Declaration of Human Rights, that
is, the right of free correspondence. In different
words, the students expressed their desire for a
postal service between North and South Korea.[56]
Six months later, the Alliance proposed a few concrete steps toward improving North-South relations:
the convening of a conference of student leaders
from both parts of Korea at P'anmunjŏm on May 20,
1961; an exchange of student reporters; the organization of debates on scholarly subjects as well
as an exchange of artistic, scholarly, and literary
information and personnel; and, finally, the holding
of a good-will sports event between North and South
Korean students.[57]

     North Korea was obviously encouraged by these
moves. On December 29, 1960, Nodong Sinmun ran a
front-page editorial enthusiastically welcoming
what it viewed as South Korea's new mood for
negotiated unification. It expressed particular
satisfaction over the formation of the Central
Negotiating Committee for National Independence
and Unification (Minjok Chaju T'ongil Chungang
Hyŏbihoe) in Seoul on December 27. Noting that
the committee was dedicated to the goal of economic
and cultural intercourse between North and South
Korea, the KWP organ declared that such intercourse was not only desirable but also unavoidable,
because, in its view, the underdeveloped South
Korea must depend upon the industrial and economic
resources of the more affluent North Korea. On
January 20, 1961, the paper carried another editorial calling for North-South negotiations and
contacts. The editorial said:

          The spirit of peaceful unifica-
          tion is visibly overflowing in
          this land of ours. Every Korean
          who has a shred of national
          conscience and who deplores the
          tragedy of our partition, par-
          ticularly the hardships to which
          our South Korean brethren are
          subjected, must carry on the
          struggle to bring about North-
          South negotiations and inter-
          course.

> ...We will negotiate with
> anyone and will work hand in
> hand with anyone regardless of
> his political beliefs, religion,
> and occupation provided he sup-
> port the peaceful unification
> of our fatherland and North-South
> contacts.[58]

If North Korea found cause for optimism in the brief but turbulent interlude between the fall of Syngman Rhee and the rise of a new military leadership in Seoul, it was profoundly disturbed by the developments after the <u>coup d'état</u> of May 16, 1961. While hailing the downfall of the Chang regime as "just and natural," P'yŏngyang immediately registered its disapproval of the new leadership. It saw in the words and deeds of the coup leaders the danger signals of reaction and fascism. Taking note of their anti-Communist stand, North Korea charged that the coup was an American conspiracy aimed at suppressing the patriotic activities of the South Korean people.[59] As North Korea correctly estimated, the total impact of the power shift in Seoul on North Korea's peace offensive was devastating. Individuals and groups advocating negotiation with P'yŏngyang were quickly suppressed. Indeed, one of the avowed aims of the coup was to put an end to the chaos resulting from the clamor for negotiated unification and the unceasing demonstrations and political activities by university students. The new military leaders were ruthlessly efficient in restoring order in South Korea.

After a moderate interval, North Korea resumed its peace offensive. On June 20, 1962, Ch'oe Yong-gŏn, Chairman of the Presidium of the Supreme People's Assembly, renewed North Korea's proposal for reciprocal reduction of armed forces and for a meeting of North and South Korean leaders to discuss unification. Insisting on the withdrawal of U.S. troops from South Korea, Ch'oe suggested that the two sides should conclude a mutual nonagression pact. On October 23, Kim Il-sŏng reaffirmed his commitment to the "confederation" formula which he had put forth two years earlier.[60]

In the meantime, the U.N. General Assembly continued its ritualistic reaffirmation of the U.N. objective in Korea--the creation of a unified,

democratic, and independent Korea--by passing
annual resolutions on Korea. North Korea was no
less persistent in denouncing the preceding routine
and in rejecting the competence and authority of
the world body to pass judgment on the Korean question. The D.P.R.K. Foreign Ministry's statement
issued on September 25, 1963, was typical of the
North Korean attitude toward the role of the United
Nations in settling the Korean question. Condemning
the decision of the General Assembly to include the
Korean question on its agenda for its eighteenth
session, the P'yŏngyang regime argued that Korean
unification was an internal problem which must be
solved by the Korean people themselves and with
which no external authority had any right whatever
to interfere. It pointed out that the U.N. Charter
explicitly prohibits any interference in the internal affairs of other nations, adding that the United
Nations should not violate its own charter. In
order to be faithful to the letter and spirit of
the charter, it continued, the United Nations should
take immediate steps to withdraw all foreign troops,
led by the U.S. forces, from South Korea and to
abolish the U.N. Commission on Unification and
Rehabilitation of Korea. If, however, the world
organization should insist on debating the Korean
question, it must invite all parties concerned to
the General Assembly, including the representatives
of the D.P.R.K., the North Korean Foreign Ministry
maintained.[61]

On December 9, North Korea transmitted its
unification formula to the United Nations as a
countermove against South Korea's earlier sub-
mission of its formula. The Seoul regime had
reaffirmed its previous contention that genuinely
free elections in which seats are apportioned
according to population and which are supervised by
the United Nations were the key to unification.
P'yŏngyang, in contrast, repeated its demands for
the withdrawal of American troops from South Korea,
for the conclusion of a mutual nonaggression pact
between the two parts of Korea, for the reduction
of armed forces to 100,000 or less by each side,
and for the creation of an all-Korean economic
committee. As expected, the U.N. General Assembly
renewed its commitment to the elusive goal of
creating a unified, independent, and democratic
Korea in accordance with the principles and purposes of the U.N. Charter.[62]

Undaunted by its repeated setbacks, North
Korea continued to harp on the theme of negotiation
and North-South contacts throughout 1964. On March
27, the Supreme People's Assembly sent an urgent
appeal to the South Korean National Assembly, its
members, and leaders of major social organizations
in South Korea, calling for an immediate overthrow
of the "traitorous Park Chung Hee regime," which
was on the verge of capitulating to the "Japanese
militarists" in the Korean-Japan normalization
talks. An all-Korean conference to discuss ways
of "saving our fatherland" from the impending
disaster was advocated. The Assembly also restated
North Korea's willingness to render a helping hand
to "the impoverished South Korean masses." "So
as to deliver South Korea from its economic bankruptcy, to assist in its economic development, and
to stabilize the livelihood of its people," P'yŏngyang offered to send, free of charge, large quantities of rice, steel, textiles, cement, lumber,
machinery, and other goods. Additionally, North
Korea would welcome and furnish jobs to South
Korea's "jobless, shivering masses." Seoul's
total indifference to the preceding gesture was
promptly denounced as "sinister" and "unpatriotic."[63]

On December 4, North Korea's Committee for the
Peaceful Unification of the Fatherland issued a
statement. Arguing that to agree to the holding
of U.N.-supervised elections would be tantamount to
giving a stamp of approval to "the act of aggression committed by the American imperialists," the
committee restated P'yŏngyang's "self-determination"
theme--that the problem of Korean unification must
be solved by the Koreans themselves. The elimina-
tion of all foreign influence, including American
troops, from Korea, together with the opening of
North-South contacts, would constitute the first
step toward unification, it insisted.[64]

On January 9, 1965, Nodong Sinmun reproduced
a letter sent by Kim Il-sŏng to a Korean resident
in the United States in which the North Korean
ruler reiterated P'yŏngyang's conditions for the
"peaceful unification" of Korea. The letter was
a reply to an inquiry made by Kim Yong-jung,
Director of the Korea Affairs Institute in Washington, D.C., concerning Kim Il-sŏng's views on
Korean unification. Kim Il-sŏng underlined the
importance of self-reliance in solving Korea's

problems. Repudiating the idea of U.N.-supervised
elections, he pointed out that "the so-called U.N.-
supervised elections" had sanctioned "the repeated,
fraudulent electoral victories of the national
traitor, Syngman Rhee"; presided over the fabrication of the regime of John M. Chang; and, finally,
legitimized the military take-over of Chung Hee
Park. Kim referred to his "confederation proposal,"
stressing that the proposed Supreme National Council
would perform purely nonpolitical functions. He
expressed his willingness to consider any alternative proposal embodying the idea of economic and
cultural cooperation between North and South Korea.
Arguing that the reduction of the existing tensions
between the two sides was prerequisite to political
unity, Kim repeated his proposals for reciprocal
arms reduction and for a mutual nonaggression
treaty. Particular emphasis was laid on the independent nature of the North Korean regime. In his
words:

> Our government has been estab-
> lished by the freely expressed
> will of an independent people.
> We have never relied on foreign
> powers, and we are completely
> independent in all fields,
> political, economic, military,
> and cultural.
>
> Our foreign policy is a
> completely independent policy,
> totally free from intervention
> by any foreign power. Our
> government is fully capable of
> taking whatever measures may
> be consistent with the interests
> of our nation and people.

Kim demanded an immediate withdrawal of American
troops from South Korea, exhorting all Koreans to
rise up in a massive national struggle to save
their nation from the twin threats of American
imperialism and Japanese militarism and to unify
their divided land.

Later in the year, Kim Il-sŏng reportedly
told a group of Cuban journalists visiting North
Korea that "the American imperialist aggressors"
would be compelled to withdraw from South Korea

"as our capacity for autonomy is strengthened, as our anti-American crusade to save our nation picks up momentum, and as the international support for our people's struggle multiplies." As soon as the Americans leave the Korean peninsula, the Korean people will achieve their national unification with their own hands, Kim was quoted as saying.[65]

Although P'yŏngyang continued to stress the self-determination theme in 1966, a slight change in its posture was noticeable. In a memorandum issued on July 21, North Korea stated, for the first time since 1960, that it would agree to the holding of an international conference to discuss the Korean question. After reiterating its familiar themes--the withdrawal of American troops, the dismantling of UNCURK, the condemnation of the United Nations, and the assertion that the Korean people alone must determine how their country would be politically united--North Korea declared:

> The Government of the D.P.R.K.
> also recognizes that it is
> possible to convene a conference
> of nations interested in the
> Korean question for the purpose
> of its peaceful adjustment. Such
> a conference shall consist of the
> representatives of North and
> South Korea plus those of an
> equal number of nations to be
> designated by each side. It
> will discuss and explore meas-
> ures which will bring about not
> only a lasting peace but also
> a peaceful unification of Korea.[66]

It is to be noted that North Korea was careful to insist on equal representation in the proposed international conference and to define the latter's functions in the broadest possible terms. This gesture, then, did not symbolize any meaningful departure from North Korea's previous unification formula. When the twenty-first General Assembly of the United Nations took up the Korean question, North Korea vigorously demanded that its representatives be invited to present its case along with those of South Korea. P'yŏngyang had one of its staunch allies, namely, the African state of Guinea, introduce a resolution in the United

Nations requesting the world body to invite North
Korea. The allies of South Korea, led by the
United States, countered the move by proposing
that the P'yŏngyang regime be invited on a conditional basis--that is, it must recognize the authority and competence of the United Nations to deal
with the Korean question. This proposal, known
as the modified Stevenson formula (named after the
late Adlai Stevenson, U.S. Ambassador to the United
Nations, who in 1960 had put forth a similar, but
not identical, proposal), was eventually adopted in
lieu of the Guinean proposal.[67] However, P'yŏngyang
refused to reverse its position, and continued to
condemn the United Nations as a "despicable tool
of American imperialism."[68]

     In retrospect, the most significant develop-
ment in 1966 appears to have been the decision of
the KWP leadership to harden its over-all posture
toward the unification problem. In his lengthy
report to the leadership conference of the KWP on
October 5, Kim Il-sŏng laid a major emphasis on
the need to strengthen not only North Korea's
military capacity, but also South Korea's "revolutionary capacity." In his words:

>   The greatest national tasks
> confronting the Korean Workers'
> Party and the Korean people
> today are the unification of our
> fatherland and the victory of
> our revolution throughout Korea.
> In order to carry out these
> tasks, we must first of all,
> build an indomitable revolu-
> tionary base in North Korea....
>
>   The most important step in
> our revolutionary struggle and
> industrialization efforts at
> this stage is to restructure our
> entire program of socialist con-
> struction so as to meet the
> needs of the changed situation--
> in particular to parallel eco-
> nomic construction with build-up
> in national defense in response
> to the aggressive maneuvers of
> our enemy.[69]

Kim Il-sŏng went on to caution that "as long as imperialism exists, there will never be an absolute guarantee of peace" and that "war may erupt at any moment." "As our experience shows," he added, "should we suffer severe destruction as a result of a new war, we are capable of rebuilding a new life as long as we have our Party, people, and territory." He argued that a strengthened military capacity would be essential to preserve "the fruits of our revolution" even in the absence of a new aggression from the South. "Only when we are thoroughly prepared militarily," he insisted, "will we be able to prevent our enemy from attacking us and to crush him at one blow should he dare to challenge us." Turning to the goal of strengthening revolutionary capacity in South Korea, Kim made it emphatically clear that the only way to unify the Korean peninsula is "to wage a massive revolutionary struggle for national liberation and against the U.S. imperialist aggressors and the Park Chung Hee clique." He said that such a struggle must be a joint endeavor between North Korea and the South Korean people, voicing P'yŏngyang's determination to render every possible aid to the revolutionary elements of South Korea so that the latter may form a united "popular front" against the Seoul regime and U.S. military authorities.[70]

As 1967 dawned, North Korea's increased intransigence became more apparent. On January 5, Nodong Sinmun published the text of another letter written by Kim Il-sŏng to Kim Yong-jung of Washington, D.C., in response to the latter's earlier letter. In the letter, Kim Il-sŏng, in marked contrast to his earlier position, all but ruled out the possibility of negotiation with "South Korean authorities," arguing that the latter "have never represented the South Korean people, nor do they have authority to do so. It is unthinkable that those who have betrayed their own people and are relying on foreign power to maintain their political control can possibly represent the people." Should South Korean authorities abandon their policy of relying on foreign power in favor of an independent position, however, Kim added, North Korea would consider negotiating with them in a neutral country or any other mutually acceptable place. As if to preclude such a possibility, Kim hastened to enumerate "preconditions" for negotiations: (1) that Seoul must request the withdrawal of U.S. troops from

South Korea, (2) that it must stop sending troops
to Vietnam and withdraw those who are now in that
country, (3) that it must renounce the R.O.K.-Japan
Normalization Treaty of 1965, (4) that it must
release all political prisoners in South Korea,
and (5) that it must stop its "fascist suppression"
and guarantee such "democratic freedoms" as the
freedom of speech, press, assembly, association,
and demonstration.[71]

On April 7, the North Korean Foreign Ministry
issued a strongly worded statement warning that
"should the American imperialist aggressors launch
a new war in Korea, they would be completely wiped
out by the Korean People's Army and the entire
Korean people who are armed." The same warning
was repeated on April 14 and again on May 25.[72]
At the same time, the KWP leadership proceeded to
place the entire country on a war footing under such
slogans as "Arm the entire people!" and "Turn the
entire country into a fortress!" Not only did it
step up production of military hardware, but it
also organized a militia of 1.2 million men and
women. Although called "Red Guards," the militia
units bore no resemblance to the youth movement of
that name in Communist China.[73] Additionally, the
KWP leaders began to glorify the Korean People's
Army. Article after article appeared in North
Korean newspapers extolling the virtues and heroism
of the Army, particularly underlining its close
and unbreakable bond with the people. In June,
ten-day-long exhibition maneuvers were staged by
the Army in an apparent attempt to impress the
people with North Korea's military might. The
maneuvers were given the widest possible publicity,
and the participants were reported to have demonstrated their "revolutionary resolve and combat
capability which were strong enough to crush the
enemy at one blow."[74]

Once again, P'yŏngyang did not stand idly by
when the United Nations went through the annual
ritual of debating and passing resolutions on Korea
in October and November. On the contrary, its
diplomatic offensive at the twenty-second session
of the General Assembly was more massive than ever
before. As already noted, the Soviet Union made
an all-out effort to arouse support for North
Korea, actively assisted by North Korean allies in
Afro-Asia. Although P'yŏngyang unmistakably

reaffirmed its well-advertised position on Korean
unification--that is, its refusal to accept the
authority of the United Nations to deal with the
matter, its demand for both the abolition of UNCURK
and the withdrawal of American troops from South
Korea, and its insistence on the right of the Korean
people to solve the problem--[75]its friends succeeded
in placing on the U.N. agenda draft resolutions
calling for (1) the dissolution of UNCURK within
two months (proposed by Cambodia, the Congo
/Brazzaville/, Guinea, Mali, Mauritania, Mongolia,
and Romania), (2) the withdrawal of all foreign
troops from South Korea (proposed by the Soviet
Union), and (3) an unconditional invitation of
North Korean representatives to the U.N. debate on
Korea (proposed by Cambodia, the Congo /Brazza-
ville/, Guinea, Mali, and Mongolia). In its numerous speeches on behalf of North Korea, the Soviet
Union also advocated the convening of an international conference on Korea--a proposal which
P'yŏngyang had carefully avoided in the period
1960-66. Although all pro-North Korean proposals
were defeated, the vigor with which they had been
pushed by P'yŏngyang's allies both impressed and
alarmed South Korea. As expected, North Korea
spurned the conditional invitation to the United
Nations which one of the pro-South Korean resolutions contained.[76]

    North Korea's vigorous pursuit of the "peace-
ful" approach in the postwar period has been
accompanied by its growing efforts to infiltrate
South Korea. Analysis reveals the marked sensitivity of North Korean tactics to the shifting
mood and politico-economic situation of South
Korea. At least three distinct phases are iden-
tifiable in this period. In the first phase, which
lasted from the armistice in July, 1953, to the
student uprising of April 19, 1960, North Korea
concentrated its efforts on establishing contacts
and bases of operation in South Korea. North
Korean agents dispatched to the South during this
phase consisted mostly of former South Korean residents who had gone to the North during the Korean
War. Armed with huge operating funds, these agents
tried to spread North Korean propaganda, to stir
up anti-American and anti-South Korean Government
sentiment, and to advertise both the "accomplishments" of the P'yŏngyang regime and its "peaceful-
unification" formula. This phase was relatively
free from acts of terrorism.[77]

The second phase of Communist infiltration in the postwar era was the brief interval between the April 19 Revolution and the coup d'état of May 16, 1961. We have already seen how the demise of the staunchly anti-Communist Syngman Rhee regime had encouraged North Korea, which saw in the chaotic but liberal atmosphere of Premier John M. Chang's rule an opportunity to bring South Korea under its political control. Kim Il-sŏng's "confederation" plan was the magic formula with which P'yŏngyang hoped to lure the weary South Koreans into its camp. North Korea vastly increased the number of its agents dispatched to the South, instructing them to peddle the peaceful unification formula among the South Korean masses and, if possible, to build up pressure for North-South negotiations. Reflecting on the failure of the North Korean efforts, Kim Il-sŏng told the Fourth Congress of the KWP in September, 1961, that the absence of a revolutionary vanguard, that is, lack of Communist organization, had prevented the transformation of the April 19 Revolution into a Communist revolution.[78]

The latest phase of Communist infiltration thus began with the coup of May, 1961. In the previously mentioned speech, Kim Il-sŏng spelled out the main ingredients of the new Communist operational direction. He pointed out the absolute necessity of organizing and nurturing a revolutionary party in South Korea. Such a party, in his view, must be deeply rooted among the masses and consist mainly, but not exclusively, of industrial proletariat and peasantry. Guided by such a party, the entire South Korean people "must rise up in a massive struggle to crush the aggressive and bellicose policies of the American imperialists," Kim said. He called on the youth of South Korea to "resist forcible conscription," on its laborers to organize strikes and sabotages, and on the entire South Korean people to "struggle against the construction of military bases and facilities." He further urged the South Koreans to help oust the American imperialists by making the latter's life miserable and unbearable in every possible way.[79] The number of North Korean infiltrators operating in South Korea grew steadily. In the latter half of 1965, North Korea began to resort to guerrilla tactics on an increasing scale. There were only six cases of armed clashes between North

Korean agents and the South Korean police in 1963 and again in 1964, but the year 1965 saw twenty-seven incidents--a four-and-a-half-fold increase.[80]

The most dramatic increase in Communist violence came in 1967. According to statistics released by the United Nations Command in Seoul, the number of North Korean provocations in the demilitarized zone alone in that year was ten times that reported in the previous year. As of October 18, 1967, there were 423 major incidents and 117 minor incidents involving North Korean intruders in the DMZ. In South Korea proper, a total of 215 armed clashes occurred between North Korean agents and South Korean authorities. In the nine-and-a-half month period, 224 North Korean infiltrators were killed, and 50 others captured. As for Allied casualties, there were 122 dead and 279 wounded. In addition, 22 South Korean civilians and policemen were killed, and 53 others wounded.[81]

Then came the boldest move North Korea ever made in the postwar period. On January 21, 1968, a thirty-one-man North Korean commando unit came within a mile of the "Blue House" (the Presidential mansion) in Seoul with the mission of assassinating President Chung Hee Park and his top aides. After a violent clash with the South Korean police, five infiltrators were killed, one was captured, and the remainder fled. By February 16, all but two of the fugitive North Koreans had been killed. They had exacted a heavy toll from the South Korean side: thirty-six dead, including eight civilians and two American G.I.'s, and sixty-eight wounded, including four civilians and twelve G.I.'s. The captured commando, a twenty-six-year-old second lieutenant, disclosed that the thirty-one-man team, made up entirely of officers, had trained for two years for its mission. He further disclosed that a total of 2,400 commandos, all belonging to a special unit of the Korean People's Army formed in July, 1967, were undergoing special training in North Korea for guerrilla missions in the South.[82]

Two days after the abortive commando raid on the "Blue House," North Korean patrol boats seized the U.S. Naval intelligence vessel Pueblo with eighty-three men aboard in the Wŏnsan Bay, touching off a major international crisis. In a P'yŏngyang radio broadcast on the same day, North Korea

asserted that the Pueblo had "intruded into the
territorial waters of the Republic and was carrying
out hostile activities"--an assertion categorically
denied by Washington. The United States insisted
that the ship was over 16 nautical miles from land--
at least 4 miles outside the 12-mile limit that
North Korea claims for its territorial waters. The
following day, P'yŏngyang radio broadcast what it
claimed was the voice of Commander Lloyd M. Bucher,
the captain of the Pueblo, reciting an alleged
confession of espionage in North Korean waters.
Amid clamor for stern retaliatory measures, Washington responded to P'yŏngyang's challenge to American power with singular restraint. President
Johnson called up 14,787 Air Force and Navy
reservists, ordered the nuclear-powered aircraft
carrier Enterprise to take up a position off the
South Korean coast, and went on television to
emphasize the gravity of the situation and to declare
that the United States would "continue to use every
means available to find a prompt and a peaceful
solution to the problem." After failing to enlist
the good offices of Moscow, Washington took the
issue to the U.N. Security Council, where it faced
stiff opposition from the Soviet Union, which
vigorously defended the North Korean position.
North Korea promptly declared that it "resolutely
opposes the discussion of the illegal complaint
of U.S. imperialism at the United Nations Security
Council, will not recognize any resolution to be
concocted to cover up U.S. imperialist aggression,
and will declare /such a resolution/ null and void."
It defiantly added that the whole North Korean
nation was prepared for combat and would meet any
American attack with an "exterminating blow."[83]

     Then, on January 31, North Korea hinted that
it might be ready to talk directly with the United
States. The hint came in a statement following
discussions between North Korean leaders and two
Romanians visiting P'yŏngyang. In the statement,
broadcast in English by the P'yŏngyang Radio,
Kim Kwang-hyŏp, a member of both the Presidium and
the Secretariat of the KWP Central Committee, said:

          It is a miscalculation if the
          United States imperialists think
          that they can solve the incident
          of the intrusion of the Pueblo
          into the territorial waters of

> our country by military
> threats, or by the method
> of aggressive war, or through
> illegal discussion at the
> United Nations.
>
> It will be a different
> story if they want to solve
> this question by methods of
> previous practice. But they
> will get nothing if they
> persist in their present
> method.[84]

The phrase "methods of previous practice" was a
reference to the release of two pilots negotiated
by the Armistice Commission in May, 1964. The
United States apologized for the incident, in which
a helicopter had strayed over the DMZ. Encouraged
by the prospect of a possible solution, the United
States immediately approached North Korea at
P'anmunjŏm, thus initiating the process of secret
negotiations between the two. By March 9, the two
sides had held eleven meetings, but were no nearer
the solution of the problem than they were when
they began the secret talks on February 2.[85]

To speculate on North Korean motives in the
Pueblo incident, it is necessary to dwell on the
probable reasons for its increased militancy first.
There appear to be a number of reasons for the
recent acceleration of what South Korea describes
as "Viet Cong-type guerrilla activities" of North
Korean agents. First and foremost, they reflect
the growing uneasiness on the part of P'yŏngyang
over the recent upsurge of the South Korean economy.
As a result of the successful completion of its
First Five-Year Economic Plan of 1962-66, South
Korea has made impressive headway in its developmental efforts. One of the key contributing
factors, no doubt, has been its participation in
the Vietnam War, which has been pouring millions of
dollars into the Korean economy in the forms of
salaries and wages earned by Korean military and
civilian personnel in Vietnam and of export earnings
from Vietnam.[86] In his policy speech to the National
Assembly on October 16, 1967, South Korean President
Chung Hee Park reported that in the first nine
months of 1967, the first year of the Second Five-
Year Economic Plan, South Korean exports had reached

$245 million, which is equal to the total value
of exports for the previous year. He added that
industrial production in the first eight months of
the year had increased 25 per cent over the com-
parable period in 1966. He predicted that the
over-all economic growth rate for 1967 would surpass
10 per cent and that, if present trends continued,
the targets of the Second Five-Year Plan might be
reached ahead of schedule.[87]

South Korea's economic growth has grave implications for North Korea's strategy for the Communization of South Korea. For it undermines the
efficacy of North Korean propaganda, which has
unceasingly pounded on the theme of stark economic
contrast--that while North Korea has proudly
entered the threshold of economic self-reliance,
South Korea continues to lead a parasitic existence
on the handouts of American capitalism. Unification
on North Korean terms thus promises the only honorable and sensible way out of Korea's national
disgrace, P'yŏngyang has insisted. To the extent
that economic privation breeds discontent, North
Korea's message has potential appeal to some of
South Korea's impoverished masses. By the same
token, the attractiveness of North Korea as an
alternative to South Korea decreases as economic
conditions improve in the latter. To hamper South
Korea's economic growth in every possible way,
then, is to promote the perceived self-interest of
the present North Korean regime. By stepping up
guerrilla activities in the South, P'yongyang can
not only inflict direct damages on the South Korean
economy but also warn foreign investors in South
Korea, both present and prospective, of the hazards
of their investment.

Apart from their disruptive impact on the
economy, terrorist activities can also create
psychological tension among South Koreans and
undermine the stability of the Seoul regime, all
of which P'yŏngyang regards as advantageous. North
Korea's growing indignation over the Vietnam War,
and particularly over the participation of 47,000
South Korean troops in it, also seems to have contributed to its belligerency. Clashes in the DMZ
and Communist-triggered violence in South Korea
proper serve as a grim reminder, to South Korea and
the United States alike, of the continuously explo-
sive nature of the Korean situation. By underlining

the undiminished danger of Communist aggression, North Korea can not only keep South Korean and U.S. forces ever on the alert but also prevent South Korea from diverting more military manpower to the "service of American imperialism in a reactionary war against national liberation" in Vietnam.

The guerrilla actions also perform a useful latent function in North Korea's internal politics: They serve to divert attention from the lagging economy and to explain away the failure of North Korea's grandiose Seven-Year Economic Plan. The North Korean people are being told that the recent incidents in the DMZ and beyond, all provoked by the other side, are symptomatic of South Korea's massive preparation for a renewed aggression, that North Korea must build up its military capabilities, too, and that, consequently, it must divide its efforts between economic construction and military preparedness.

We may now turn to P'yŏngyang's motives for precipitating the Pueblo crisis. Given North Korea's commitment to operational autonomy in the world arena, it is extremely unlikely that the decision to seize the ship was made outside P'yŏng-yang. In view of its own vulnerability to retal-iation by the United States, the Soviet Union, had it been consulted in advance, would probably have counseled against the seizure. Nor is it plausible that the seizure was part of a well-coordinated international Communist strategy to disperse the power and attention of the United States. To accept such a view is to assume the unity and cohesion of the Communist bloc, which do not exist. On the other hand, given the vociferous anti-Americanism and intransigence of North Korea, it takes little imagination to assume that P'yŏngyang was the sole architect of the plan to harass and humiliate the United States.

Kim Il-sŏng's elated reaction to the seizure is readily understandable. Not only did it give him the ineffable joy of humiliating the United States, his archenemy, before the whole world, but it immediately elevated him to the focal point of world attention--an immensely thrilling experience for the supremely egocentric North Korean Premier. Moreover, in his view, his stature in the Communist camp and the Third World alike received a major boost. He had been preaching relentlessly that imperialism should be dealt a severe blow whenever and wherever possible. Now he could proudly point to his latest triumph.

On the home front, the North Korean ruler could hold up the Pueblo, a genuine American spy ship, and its crew before his suffering but submissive compatriots as proof of the aggressive nature of "American imperialism," exhorting them to make further sacrifices in North Korea's war-preparation program. Thus he told the North Korean people that the alleged intrusion of the U.S. vessel into North Korean territorial waters was a "piratical act" and a "link in the chain of premeditated maneuverings of United States imperialism for unleashing a new war in Korea." He warned that "the aggressors can be crushed at one stroke if they pounce upon us."[88]

The seizure was also consistent with North Korea's loudly proclaimed thesis that all Communist nations are duty-bound to help the Vietnamese people by intensifying the anti-imperialist struggle all over the world. Although P'yŏngyang was fully aware of the hazard of its adventure, it probably gambled that the United States would not overreact to its provocation because of the Vietnam War--an assumption whose validity was to be borne out by subsequent developments. Another factor which may conceivably have entered into North Korean calculations is the possibility of alienating Seoul from Washington. By inducing the latter to negotiate with it directly and by extracting some concessions, P'yŏngyang could strain R.O.K.-U.S. relations.

If this was indeed one of North Korea's aims, it was at least partly realized. South Korea was enraged by the conciliatory approach of the United States and in particular by the latter's secret talks with North Korea over Seoul's head at P'anmunjŏm. It was annoyed by what it regarded as Washington's overconcern with the crew of the Pueblo and cavalier attitude toward the more basic problem of coping with increased Communist bellicosity. In an unprecedented move, the R.O.K. National Assembly, dominated by President Park's Democratic-Republican Party, passed a unanimous resolution expressly criticizing the United States. What is more, there were anti-American demonstrations

in Seoul and along the DMZ for the first time since
the Korean War, and <u>Dong-A Ilbo</u>, Seoul's most
influential newspaper, editorially lamented what
it called "the diplomacy of humiliation" being
pursued by the United States, saying that the
Korean people were saddened by its myopic and "un-
great-power-like" behavior. Should the United
States yield to Communist pressure, admit the
Pueblo's alleged violation of North Korean territorial waters, and apologize to the P'yŏngyang
regime in order to obtain the release of the crew,
its prestige and authority as the leader of the
free world would plummet to the ground, the newspaper added. Such a "sell-out" would be not only
an abject admission that "the United States is a
paper tiger" but an open invitation to still bolder
Communist challenges in the days ahead, it said.[89]

Finally, the intrinsic value of the Pueblo
and its crew should not be overlooked. According
to columnists Drew Pearson and Jack Anderson,
President Johnson revealed to Congressional leaders
that "the loss of the Pueblo had dealt U.S. security
a 'severely damaging blow,' since the ship had the
most sophisticated and modern intelligence mechanism
on board. The equipment was fifteen years ahead
of anything Soviet Russia possesses." Moreover,
"twenty-seven men in the Pueblo's crew...were the
most highly trained and skilled experts in the
cryptographic and intelligence fields."[90]

In short, there is no question that North
Korea has scored a major propaganda victory in the
Pueblo incident. The incident has served Kim Il-sŏng
admirably well in his campaign to rally the North
Korean people to the "patriotic cause of struggling
against American imperialism and its lackeys and
for the liberation of South Korea." It may also
have boosted his stature in some Communist and most
Third World nations. In the long run, however, it
may very well turn out to be counterproductive.
For the incident, coupled with the abortive commando
raid on the Presidential mansion in Seoul, has had
the effect of galvanizing both Seoul and Washington
into reassessing and fortifying their preparedness
for a possible North Korean aggression. Not only
has the United States reinforced its military
arsenal in South Korea, but it has also pledged
stepped-up military assistance to Seoul. President
Johnson thus requested from Congress $100 million

in special military aid to South Korea and dispatched Cyrus R. Vance, former Deputy Secretary of
Defense, to Seoul as his special representative
for discussions on the "grave threat" to South
Korea. The Vance Mission also had the objective
of ironing out differences between Washington and
Seoul over the handling of the Pueblo crisis.
Although the mission appears to have had but limited success, it did reaffirm the commitment of
the United States to defend South Korea against
Communist aggression.[91]

Simultaneously, President Chung Hee Park
announced a plan to form an armed militia of 2.5
million men, with units in the smallest villages,
as a shield against North Korean incursions. The
militia would be armed with light weapons produced
in South Korea. By March 14, more than 1.6 million
military reservists had already been organized
into a militia made up of thousands of units in
villages and at places of employment. The organization of the remaining reservists was scheduled
to be completed by the end of March. Furthermore,
the R.O.K. armed forces, 15,000 men short of their
authorized strength of 623,000 men, were brought
to full strength by delaying the discharges of
enlisted men.[92] At the graduation exercises of
Seoul National University on February 26, President
Park underlined South Korea's heightened sense of
alarm when he said, "While we have been concentrating on economic construction, the enemy has
completed its plans and preparations for an armed
aggression and has entered into a stage of action."
"Faced with this cold reality," he said, "we must
stage a struggle to defend ourselves. From now
on, we must carry out an intensified struggle
against the Communist aggressors. Any compromise
with the Communists means defeat, and defeat means
death to us. We cannot sit back and die."[93]

Meanwhile, North Korea has not written off
less violent techniques of infiltration. The skill
with which it had infiltrated the South Korean
intelligentsia was dramatically revealed in the
summer of 1967, when the South Korean Central Intelligence Agency announced the arrests of nearly 200
South Koreans on charges of espionage. Both the
timing of the announcement and the manner in which
some of these alleged spies had been rounded up
immediately touched off an international controversy.

The fact that these arrests were made and disclosed
to the public in the midst of widespread protest
in South Korea over alleged election irregularities
was interpreted in many quarters as a diversionary
tactic--a transparent attempt by the South Korean
Government not only to divert the attention of the
people from internal political troubles to the
external threat of Communist infiltration but also
to use such a threat as a pretext for curbing the
expression of dissent by the people, in general,
and the students, in particular. Even more controversial were the mysterious and presumably
underhanded techniques which South Korean secret
agents employed in arresting core members of the
alleged spy ring. Some twenty of them had been
apprehended in West Germany and France and flown
to Seoul by South Korean agents without the knowledge, let alone permission, of the two governments
concerned. A few had been arrested in the United
States and brought to Korea with the apparent
sanction of the U.S. Government. Bonn and Paris
promptly lodged strong protests with South Korea,
and the latter apologized. A few South Korean
diplomats were expelled from West Germany, and
Seoul's Ambassador to Bonn resigned.[94] In December,
West Germany further expressed its displeasure with
Seoul by indefinitely postponing the signing of two
aid agreements with the latter, for which negotiations had already been completed.[95]

Charges against many of the arrested were
later dropped, but thirty-four persons were indicted,
tried, and convicted by the South Korean Government
in November and December, 1967. The Seoul District
Court sentenced two to death, four to life imprisonment, and the remainder to three to fifteen years
of imprisonment. Of the thirty-four, there were
eight couples, two artists of international stature
who had been living in Germany and France, respectively (one is a composer and the other a painter),
seven college professors, five doctorate holders
in law, political science, and medicine, and five
doctoral students in European universities. Both
the detailed reports of the South Korean CIA and
the transcripts of their sworn testimony in court
indicate that they had been lured into P'yŏngyang's
espionage network by financial rewards; curiosity;
disenchantment with the Seoul regime; and a desire
to reunite, albeit momentarily, with parents,
siblings, and relatives residing in North Korea.

The North Korean Embassy in East Berlin had been both the initial contact point and the channel of communication thereafter. All told, they collectively had received a total of $77,022 in U.S. currency from North Korea, and had made 142 trips to East Berlin and 19 trips to P'yŏngyang. A few had even joined the KWP. However, it does not appear that they actually collected any valuable information for North Korea, which in effect had made a long-term investment in them in the hope of gradually infiltrating South Korea's intellectual community, thus laying the groundwork for more revolutionary action at a later stage.[96]

To what extent has North Korea's vigorous psychological offensive been productive? What of its latest shift of emphasis to more violent techniques? As already noted, P'yŏngyang's strategic objective has remained remarkably constant over the years, that is, the political domination of South Korea by whatever means available. North Korea's proposal to open cultural, economic, and postal intercourse with South Korea, its "confederation" plan, its demand that South Koreans must be guaranteed the fullest possible degree of political freedom, and many other seemingly innocuous suggestions represent measures carefully tailored to North Korean needs and interests. If implemented, P'yŏngyang seems to reason, these measures would pave the way for Communist political take-over. It would be assured of greater access to the South Korean population and, consequently, of greater opportunities for propaganda and organization.

North Korea's own estimate of its capacity to win the hearts and minds of the South Korean people appears to be rather inflated. Most adult citizens of South Korea have vivid memories of the nightmarish three months of the Communist occupation in 1950. Those who have been eye witnesses to, as well as victims of, the terror and atrocities of the North Korean reign are extremely unlikely to turn a sympathetic ear to Communist rhetoric. Although the success with which North Korea has wooed South Korean intellectuals in Europe reveals the vulnerability of South Koreans, the chief ingredient of North Korea's short-lived success in its East Berlin operations appears to have been the lure of money to the financially distressed Koreans.

On the other hand, time may gradually wipe out North Korea's unfavorable image. The new generation of South Koreans is without any first-hand experience with Communist practice. Its antipathy toward the P'yŏngyang regime may be surpassed by its aspirations for unification and a more prosperous future. It is no accident that the most vocal proponents of North-South negotiations have thus far been found among South Korea's traditionally politically minded and increasingly rebellious university students. Significantly, an opinion survey conducted by the South Korean Government in February, 1964, found that 16.3 per cent of the respondents favored negotiation between the two Koreas to bring about unification. In the same poll, 23.4 per cent preferred free elections throughout Korea under U.N. supervision.[97] In another survey conducted by the newspaper Chosŏn Ilbo in January, 1964, an overwhelming majority of the respondents expressed their support for cultural exchange with North Korea. Seventeen per cent supported the idea without reservation, and 50 per cent supported it but doubted its feasibility. Only 33 per cent voiced their disapproval.[98]

The sharp increase in Communist violence in recent months is likely to alienate a growing number of South Koreans. Furthermore, it has resulted in the strengthening and modernization of the R.O.K. armed forces. The Seoul regime has also strengthened its counterintelligence and counter-insurgency apparatus. Not only that, it has begun to reappraise its unification policy in light of P'yŏngyang's energetic diplomatic offensive in Afro-Asia and, through its supporters, in the United Nations.[99] Finally, as noted, the changed economic climate of South Korea progressively undercuts the efficacy of North Korean propaganda.

In all likelihood, the shouting, and sometimes shooting, war between P'yŏngyang and Seoul will go on unabated in the foreseeable future. Barring revolutionary upheavals that may drastically alter the ideological posture of either regime or radical metamorphosis in the international scene, the manifest and latent goals of the two governments are likely to remain permanently irreconcilable. Meanwhile, the Korean people, united as they are in language, culture, race, and, most importantly, their burning desire for unification, will have to learn, if they have not already learned, to live with a semipermanent partition.

NOTES TO CHAPTER 3

1. For a detailed and illuminating treatment of the problem, see Soon Sung Cho, Korea in World Politics, 1940-1950: An Evaluation of American Responsibility (Berkeley: University of California Press, 1967).

2. See "Statement Released After the Cairo Conference by President Roosevelt, Generalissimo Chiang Kai-shek, and Prime Minister Churchill, December 1, 1943" in U.S. Department of State, The Record on Korean Unification, 1943-1960, p. 42.

3. Cho, op. cit., pp. 47-58; Shannon McCune, "The Thirty-Eighth Parallel in Korea," World Politics, I (1948-49), pp. 223-32.

4. Ibid., p. 226.

5. U.S. Department of State, The Record on Korean Unification, pp. 4-5.

6. Ibid., pp. 47-48.

7. Ibid., pp. 48-54.

8. Ibid., pp. 56-59.

9. Cho, op. cit., pp. 161-68.

10. Ibid., pp. 8-9; "Resolutions of the U.N. General Assembly Establishing the U.N. Temporary Commission on Korea and Providing for a Program for Korean Independence, November 14, 1947," in ibid., pp. 69-71.

11. The Ukrainian Soviet Socialist Republic was assigned a seat in the commission but refused to send a delegate. Tōitsu Chōsen nenkan, 1964, p. 143.

12. U.S. Department of State, The Record on Korean Unification, pp. 10, 71.

13. Ibid., pp. 10-11, 76.

14. _Ibid._, p. 11. For the legislative history as well as an analysis of the different interpretations of the controversial resolution, see Cho, op. cit., pp. 215-24.

15. For an excellent analysis of North Korea's experience with political violence, see Glenn D. Paige, "Korea," in Cyril E. Black and Thomas P. Thornton (eds.), _Communism and Revolution_ (Princeton, N.J.: Princeton University Press, 1964), pp. 215-42.

16. _Ibid._, pp. 230-37. For an incisive analysis of North Korea's unification policies, see Soon Sung Cho, "The Politics of North Korea's Unification Policies, 1950-1965," _World Politics_, XIX (January, 1967), pp. 218-41.

17. Paige, "Korea," pp. 220-22.

18. _Ibid._, pp. 223-27.

19. _Tōitsu Chōsen nenkan, 1965-66_, pp. 219-20. See also Cho, _Korea in World Politics_, pp. 195-203.

20. _Tōitsu Chōsen nenkan, 1965-66_, p. 242.

21. _Ibid._

22. It is to be noted that, strictly speaking, there has been a slight change in the physical boundary between the two Korean regimes. The demilitarized zone (DMZ) does not coincide exactly with the 38th Parallel. However, the change has not substantially altered the size of the territory over which each regime has control.

23. _Nodong Sinmun_, July 28, 1953, extra edition.

24. U.S. Department of State, _The Record on Korean Unification_, p. 23.

25. _Ibid._, p. 24.

26. Cho, "The Politics of North Korea's Unification Policies," p. 221.

27. _Ibid._, pp. 220-22.

28. U.S. Department of State, The Record on Korean Unification, p. 22.

29. Ibid., pp. 148-50.

30. How the Communist side torpedoed that attempt is vividly described by Arthur H. Dean, chief negotiator for the U.N. Command, in Dean, "What It's Like to Negotiate with the Chinese," op. cit.

31. U.S. Department of State, The Record on Korean Unification, pp. 152-53.

32. Ibid., pp. 25-26.

33. Ibid., p. 27.

34. Ibid., pp. 158-59.

35. Ibid., p. 167.

36. South Korea, backed by the United States, had initially favored elections in North Korea only to fill the vacancies in the South Korean National Assembly.

37. Ibid., p. 26.

38. Ibid., p. 171. These remarks were made on May 4, 1954.

39. Ibid., pp. 186-87.

40. Ibid., p. 187.

41. Nodong Sinmun, August 17, 1954. Ki, a member of the Soviet-Korean group, was purged in 1956 together with Pak Hŏn-yŏng. Letter from Dae-Sook Suh, Department of Government, University of Texas, Austin, Texas, November 29, 1967.

42. Nodong Sinmun, August 17, 1954.

43. Tōitsu Chōsen nenkan, 1965-66, p. 245.

44. Ibid., p. 246.

45. Ibid., p. 247. For the full text of Kim's speech, see Chosŏn chungang yŏn'gam, 1958, pp. 30-36.

46. Chosŏn chungang yŏn'gam, 1958, p. 55.

47. U.S. Department of State, The Record on Korean Unification, pp. 33-34; Tōitsu Chōsen nenkan, 1965-66, p. 216.

48. U.S. Department of State, The Record on Korean Unification, pp. 34-37. The other two members were Sweden and Switzerland.

49. Nodong Sinmun, February 6, 1958.

50. Ibid., February 20, 1958.

51. Ibid., February 22, 1958.

52. U.S. Department of State, The Record on Korean Unification, pp. 216-29.

53. Nodong Sinmun, April 19-May 7, 1960.

54. Chŏson chungang yŏn'gam, 1961, p. 25. See also Tōitsu Chōsen nenkan, 1965-66, pp. 249-50.

55. Tōitsu Chōsen nenkan, 1965-66, p. 250.

56. Ibid.

57. Ibid., p. 251.

58. Nodong Sinmun, January 20, 1961.

59. Ibid., May 18 and 20, 1961.

60. Tōitsu Chōsen nenkan, 1965-66, p. 252.

61. Nodong Sinmun, September 26, 1963.

62. Tōitsu Chōsen nenkan, 1965-66, pp. 253, 268.

63. Ibid., p. 253; Chŏson chungang yŏn'gam, 1965, p. 111. North Korea had made similar offers in the past. Thus, in May, 1957, it offered to send rice to South Korea to help the latter's "famine-stricken peasants." Tōitsu Chōsen nenkan, 1965-66, pp. 75-76. In August of the same year,

the North Korean Red Cross Society proposed to send $2 million worth of relief material to South Korea. Ibid., p. 76. In September, 1959, North Korea offered to furnish flood victims in South Korea with rice, textiles, shoes, cement, and lumber. Nodong Sinmun, September 24, 1959. In October of the same year, P'yŏngyang renewed its offer to send food, clothing, and machinery to South Korea and to help build factories there. Ibid., October 26, 1960. Another North Korean offer to help flood victims in South Korea came in June, 1963. Ibid., June 29, 1963.

64. Tōitsu Chōsen nenkan, 1965-66, p. 254.

65. Nodong Sinmun, July 6, 1965.

66. Ibid., July 22, 1966.

67. See Dong-A Ilbo, October 3, 1967. An article by Chin Ch'ŏl-su, its special correspondent at the United Nations, analyzes North Korean tactics at the United Nations in recent years.

68. Nodong Sinmun, December 5, 1966.

69. Kim Il-sŏng, "Hyŏn chŏngse wa uri tang ŭi kwaŏp" ("The Present Situation and the Tasks of Our Party"), Kŭlloja, October, 1966, p. 24.

70. Ibid., pp. 25-54.

71. Nodong Sinmun, January 5, 1967.

72. Ibid., April 8 and 15, 1967; Minju Chosŏn, May 26, 1967.

73. The New York Times, February 9, 1968.

74. Minju Chosŏn, June 11, 1967.

75. Minju Chosŏn, October 25, 1967.

76. Dong-A Ilbo, October and November, 1967.

77. For an official analysis of North Korean infiltration techniques by the South Korean intelligence authorities, see Dong-A Ilbo, June 24, 1967.

78. Chosŏn chungang yŏn'gam, 1962, p. 41.

79. Ibid., pp. 41-42.

80. Dong-A Ilbo, June 24, 1967. Note that
these figures are based on the records of the South
Korean police only. If we included the incidents
involving both R.O.K. and U.S. forces, we would
have much larger figures.

81. Ibid., November 3, 1967. See also The
New York Times, November 3, 1967.

82. For details regarding the raid and its
aftermath, see Dong-A Ilbo, January 22-February 16,
1968.

83. The New York Times, January 24-28, 1968.

84. Ibid., February 1, 1968.

85. Ibid., February 3, 1968; Dong-A Ilbo,
March 11, 1968.

86. For an informative analysis of South Korea's
recent economic growth, see Joe Won Lee, "Planning
Efforts for Economic Development" in Joseph S.
Chung (ed.), Korea: Patterns of Economic Develop-
ment, pp. 1-24; and "A Perspective for Economic
Development in South Korea," Paper read at the
Conference on Korean Studies, Western Michigan
University, Kalamazoo, Michigan, April 6-7, 1967.

87. Dong-A Ilbo, October 16 and 17, 1967.

88. The New York Times, February 9, 1968.

89. Dong-A Ilbo, February 6 and 7, 1968.

90. See their syndicated column in The Chicago
Daily News, February 8, 1968, p. 10.

91. The New York Times, February 10-18, 1968.
Although Seoul demanded Washington's commitment to
immediate action against North Korean aggression,
it only got a promise of "immediate consultations."
As a result, South Koreans became further disen-
chanted and began to discuss the need for more
"self-reliance" in defense of their country. There
was even talk of repudiating the arrangement held

over from the Korean War whereby South Korea's armed forces are under "operational control" of the commander of the United Nations Forces, an American Army General. The R.O.K.'s complete dependence upon U.S. forces for petroleum supplies, arms, and ammunition, however, made it unrealistic for Seoul to defy Washington.

92. Ibid., February 9 and March 17, 1968; Dong-A Ilbo, February 7 and March 16, 1968.

93. Ibid., February 26, 1968; The New York Times, February 29, 1968.

94. The New York Times, July 5 and 6, 1967. See also editorials on the episode in ibid., July 6, 1967, and The Washington Post, July 6, 1967.

95. Dong-A Ilbo, December 14, 1967.

96. For the CIA reports, see Dong-A Ilbo, July 8, 11-17, 1967. For the transcripts of the trials (in summary), see ibid., November and December, 1967.

97. See Thus Neutralized Unification is Impossible for Korea (Seoul: Ministry of Public Information, Republic of Korea, 1965), p. 52.

98. Ibid., p. 56.

99. For evidence of mounting pressure for such a reappraisal in South Korea, see the Dong-A Ilbo editorials of October 23, November 2, and November 18, 1967. The R.O.K. Foreign Ministry publicly acknowledged that such a reappraisal is under way. See ibid., November 21, 1967.

4

NORTH KOREA'S RELATIONS WITH THE THIRD WORLD AND BEYOND

Thus far we have examined the manner in which North Korea has tackled two of its most pressing and crucial problems--the Sino-Soviet conflict and Korean unification. No picture of P'yŏngyang's international position would be complete, however, without a delineation of its posture toward the rest of the world. Of particular importance are its relations with the Third World, Vietnam, and Japan. Its approach to the West, already examined in an implicit and fragmentary fashion, also needs to be made more explicit.

NORTH KOREA AND THE THIRD WORLD

The term "the Third World," supposedly derived from the French tiers monde, is used in a broad sense: It refers to the totality of those nations that are neither patently Western nor patently Communist. The overwhelming majority of such nations are newly independent, underdeveloped, and non-European. Sharing many problems, attitudes, and interests, they frequently act as a bloc in the international arena. To treat them as an ideologically cohesive grouping, however, would be erroneous. The term is used here not as a rigorous analytical category but simply as a loose descriptive designation.[1] The inclusion of Cuba in the present section is a matter of sheer convenience.

Factors in P'yŏngyang--Third World Interaction

For the first five years after its inception,
North Korea's contact with the outside world was
strictly confined to the then cohesive and monolithic Communist camp. The only Communist country
from which P'yŏngyang remained aloof was the rene-
gade Yugoslavia. In the postwar period, however,
North Korea has made a determined effort to expand
its international relations, wooing the newly
emerging and noncommitted nations of Asia, Africa,
and Latin America with relentless vigor. In late
1967, North Korea maintained diplomatic relations
with twenty-seven nations, of which fourteen were
outside the Communist bloc. In addition, it had
consular relations with three and maintained trade
centers in three more.[2]

North Korea's pursuit of cultural, economic,
and diplomatic exchanges with nonbloc countries
has been closely related to the tempo of its economic recovery and modernization at home. In the
few years immediately following the armistice,
North Korea concentrated all its energy and attention on the vitally urgent task of putting its
economy into shape. As it made some notable headway in its industrialization program, North Korea
began to court and acquire new friends and trading
partners outside the Communist orbit. The continent of Africa, with its mushrooming ministates,
provided a fertile ground for the eager, but
inexperienced North Korean diplomats. Of the
thirty-three states with which P'yŏngyang maintains formal ties, eleven are located in Africa.
North Korea follows a set pattern in wooing foreign states: First, it establishes contacts in
the cultural and economic realms only. This
typically calls for a tentative agreement between
both sides. A stream of visitors, both governmental and otherwise, follows. Then negotiations
may get under way for the setting up of consular
relations. In many cases, however, this step is
skipped, and diplomatic relations are established
directly.

The relative success with which North Korea
has cultivated the friendship of many Third World
nations may be attributed to a fortuitous combination

of both psychological and material factors. The
psychological factors conducive to North Korean
diplomacy in the Third World include the latter's
pervasive anticolonial and anti-Western sentiment,
modernizing nationalism, and need for international
recognition. Long victimized by the colonial
powers of the West, most newly emerging nations
of Asia and Africa are instinctively attracted to
North Korea's militant denunciation of colonialism,
both old and new. In P'yŏngyang's strident nationalism, in words and deeds alike, they find immense
encouragement and moral support. Moreover, newly
independent nations have an intense need for international recognition, which can be met in part by
diplomatic, economic, and cultural intercourse with
any and all nations. On the material side, North
Korea's fairly impressive record in economic development and its consequent ability to provide both
aid and trade to the new nations have facilitated
its diplomatic efforts. To the impatient Third
World nations desperately groping for developmental panaceas, North Korea appears to present
a model of planned modernization worthy of emulation.

     What, then, does P'yŏngyang hope to gain from
its diplomacy and trade in the Third World? Manifestly, it has much to gain and little to lose.
As a newcomer to the world scene itself, its need
for international recognition is equally acute.
The opportunity to boast of its accomplishments
must be a source of profound satisfaction. The
possibility of economic gains, however small, from
foreign trade must also enter into North Korean
calculations. Most important, however, is the
value of the Third World in promoting P'yŏngyang's
paramount objective of Communizing South Korea.
Not only can Third World nations lend moral support
to P'yŏngyang and reinforce its propaganda, they
can also act as the guardians of North Korean
interests in the United Nations. Although P'yŏngyang has consistently refused to recognize the
legal and moral competence of the world body to
deal with the Korean question, it has nevertheless
made quite clear its sensitivity to United Nations
action. To increase support for its position at
the world forum has indeed been one of North
Korea's major international preoccupations in
recent years. In sum, the coincidence of mutual
interests has been instrumental in building

Chart 2

NATIONS THAT HAVE RELATIONS WITH NORTH KOREA

Name of Country	Date of Establishment

A. Diplomatic Relations

1.	U.S.S.R.	Oct. 12, 1948
2.	Mongolia	Oct. 15, 1948
3.	Poland	Oct. 16, 1948
4.	Czechoslovakia	Oct. 21, 1948
5.	Romania	Nov. 3, 1948
6.	Hungary	Nov. 11, 1948
7.	Bulgaria	Nov. 29, 1948
8.	Albania	May 17, 1949
9.	Communist China	Oct. 6, 1949
10.	East Germany	Nov. 7, 1949
11.	North Vietnam	Jan. 31, 1950
12.	Algeria	Sep. 25, 1958
13.	Guinea	Oct. 8, 1958
14.	Cuba	Aug. 29, 1960
15.	Mali	Oct. 31, 1960
16.	Uganda	Mar. 2, 1963
17.	Yemen	Mar. 9, 1963
18.	United Arab Republic	Mar. 24, 1963
19.	Indonesia	Apr. 16, 1964
20.	Mauritania	Nov. 11, 1964
21.	Cambodia	Dec. 20, 1964
22.	Congo (Brazzaville)	Dec. 24, 1964
23.	Ghana	Dec. 28, 1964
24.	Tanzania	Jan. 13, 1965
25.	Syria	Jul. --, 1966
26.	Burundi	Mar. --, 1967
27.	Somalia	Mar. --, 1967

B. Consular Relations

28.	Burma	May 15, 1961
29.	India	Mar. 1, 1962
30.	Ceylon	Jan. 25, 1964

C. Trade Relations[a]

31.	Iraq	Jul. 23, 1959
32.	Austria	Dec. 7, 1960
33.	Uruguay	May 17, 1963

[a]Included in this category are those nations with which North Korea has exchanged permanent trade missions. It should be stressed that P'yŏngyang also maintains trade relations with all the nations with which it has diplomatic and consular relations plus some other nations.

Sources: Chosŏn chungang yŏn'gam, 1965, pp. 123-24; Nodong Sinmun, July 26, 1966, and March 14, 1967; Minju Chosŏn, May 19, 1967.

a bridge between P'yŏngyang and the Third World.
The relative absence of competition from South
Korea has no doubt helped P'yŏngyang's endeavors.

A Chronological Survey

Chronologically speaking, P'yŏngyang's first
ally in the Third World appears to be Indonesia.
In May, 1956, representatives of Indonesia's labor
unions paid a good-will visit to North Korea. A
year later, on May 15, 1957, North Korea signed a
trade agreement with Indonesia in Djakarta. In the
same year North Korea signed trade pacts with India,
Burma, and Egypt. It was also busy cementing its
bonds with the Third World by sending its delegates
to the Afro-Asian Lawyers' Conference, held in
Damascus in October, and the Afro-Asian Solidarity
Conference, held in Cairo in December. Negotiations
for trade and cultural pacts with Arab nations
must have been carried out by the North Korean
delegates to these conferences. For, in addition
to the Cairo agreement, North Korea secured a cultural pact with Syria in January, 1958. This opened
the way for exchange of cultural and artistic teams
as well as other good-will missions between P'yŏngyang and the Arab world.[3]

When Egypt and Syria merged into the United
Arab Republic in February, 1958, P'yŏngyang lost
no time in extending its recognition to the new
state, and contacts between the two were stepped
up. Thus North Korea played the host to U.A.R.
journalist, sports, and military teams, while dispatching its own teams to the Middle East. In
July, North Korea opened a trade center in Cairo.
Meanwhile, P'yŏngyang recognized the new Iraqui
regime which toppled the Government of King Faisal,
establishing political, economic, and cultural
ties with it. A ten-member "people's delegation"
from that country visited the North Korean capital
in December to map out the details of cultural and
economic cooperation. During the Lebanese and
Jordanian crises, North Korea loudly scored the
"armed intervention of Anglo-American imperialism"
in the Middle East, voicing its full support of
"the anti-imperialist struggle as well as the
struggle for national independence and sovereignty
of the Arab people." It called on the United States

and the United Kingdom to put an end to their
"aggressive acts" and to withdraw their troops from
Lebanon and Jordan without delay. Consistent
with its all-out anticolonialist stand, P'yŏngyang
gave full moral support to the Algerian people for
their struggle against French colonialism, and in
September, 1958, it recognized the provisional
government of Algeria. In November of that year,
Kim Il-sŏng met with the representatives of the
Algerian Government in Peking and discussed the
possibility of strengthening ties between the two
countries. North Korea also accorded recognition
to Guinea upon the latter's declaration of independence from French rule in October, 1958.[4]

In Asia, North Korea busily interacted with
Indonesia, India, Burma, and Ceylon. All four
championed the North Korean cause during the annual
United Nations debate on Korea. North Korean trade
centers began operation in New Delhi, Djakarta, and
Rangoon. Scores of delegations were exchanged.
Particularly noteworthy is the fact that North
Korea furnished Ceylon with relief funds when the
latter suffered a flood in January, 1958.[5]

North Korea's friendly relations with the
Third World intensified in 1959. Not only did
P'yŏngyang further develop its economic and cultural partnerships with India, Indonesia, Burma,
and the U.A.R., but it added a new trading partner
to the list, Iraq. The representatives of the
D.P.R.K. Government were invited to attend the
celebration of the first anniversary of the "Iraqui
revolution," and while in Bagdad concluded agreements on trade and cultural exchange. Trade centers
with consular functions and diplomatic immunity
were to be set up in the capitals of both countries
shortly. In May, a good-will delegation from
Algeria visited P'yŏngyang, and, in June, North
Korea recognized the newly independent African
nation of Togo. P'yŏngyang-New Delhi relations,
however, were momentarily strained in mid-1959
because of the Sino-Indian border clash. North
Korea, as noted, sided with Peking but took pains
to blame the "American imperialists" for the incident.[6]

There was no visible letdown in 1960 in the
vigor with which North Korea conducted its diplomacy in quest not only of new allies but of stronger

ties with old friends. India, Indonesia, and Burma
continued to maintain their friendly postures toward
P'yŏngyang, and the latter reciprocated. When the
student uprisings broke out in South Korea in
April, these countries faithfully echoed North
Korea's wholehearted support of the students as
well as its ferocious denunciation of the soon-to-
be-toppled Syngman Rhee regime. They further joined
P'yŏngyang in demanding an immediate withdrawal
of all foreign troops from South Korea as an indispensable preliminary step toward Korean unification.
Trade and cultural relations were stepped up as
well. The Indian-Korean Cultural Association in
New Delhi sponsored a Korean night, a photo exhibit
showing North Korea's progress toward socialist
construction, and a North Korean trade fair. The
Central Committee of the North Korean Red Cross
sent its Indonesian counterpart 10,000 rubles in
the form of relief funds for Indonesian refugees
from insurgency-torn areas. What is more, Indonesia
sent two of its students to Kim Il-sŏng University
for further study, thus initiating an educational
exchange program with P'yŏngyang. North Korea's
sense of national pride must no doubt have been
enhanced by the realization that its universities
could now attract foreign students. A Burmese
governmental trade mission visited North Korea,
making trade arrangements. The terms of trade
clearly indicated North Korea's rate of economic
recovery. For it was to export to Burma machinery,
steel, chemicals, textiles, lumber, food, and other
commodities, while importing from the latter mainly
agricultural and consumer goods. P'yŏngyang also
strengthened its ties with Laos by lending its vocal
support to the latter's struggle against "American
imperialism and its lackeys." A mass rally was
held in the North Korean capital to express Korean-
Laotian solidarity.[7]

Korean-Arab friendship continued to deepen.
North Korean trade and cultural delegations visited
Iraq, the U.A.R., and Yemen. A Korean-Yemeni trade
pact, along with an agreement to establish permanent trade missions in both countries, was signed.
A high-level delegation of the provisional government of the Republic of Algeria visited P'yŏngyang.
A joint Korean-Algerian communiqué expressed the
solidarity between the two peoples in their joint
fight against imperialism, and included North
Korea's high praise for "the heroism displayed by

the Algerian people in their struggle against French
colonialism and for national independence and freedom." In return, the Algerian representatives fully
endorsed P'yŏngyang's prescription for Korean uni-
fication--that peaceful unification must be worked
out by the Koreans themselves after, and only after,
American troops have been completely withdrawn
from South Korea. In a follow-up action, the
North Korean Ministry of Foreign Affairs issued a
statement late in the year strongly condemning and
protesting against "the massacre and other criminal
atrocities committed against the Algerian people
by the French imperialists." The statement repeated
P'yŏngyang's earlier demand that French troops leave
Algeria immediately.[8]

In other parts of Africa, North Korea kept the
ball rolling. In October, it established diplomatic
relations with Mali. P'yŏngyang also extended its
recognition to Togo, Dahomey, and Nigeria. In a
conspicuous display of humanitarianism, the North
Korean Red Cross in April forwarded a sum of 5,000
Swiss francs to Morocco for relief of earthquake
victims. Cameroon sent two teams of visitors to
North Korea, one representing its youth and the
other organized labor. North Korean representatives
took part in the second Executive Committee meeting
of the Afro-Asian Solidarity Conference, held in
Accra, Ghana, in April, reportedly winning additional verbal support for North Korea's unity formula
from Afro-Asian countries. When a crisis developed
in the Congo following its independence from Belgium,
North Korea lost no time in denouncing Belgian and
then American imperialism, claiming that only the
"imperialists" were to blame for the chaos and
bloodshed in that strife-torn country. Condemning
United Nations action in that area as a cover for
"the wanton aggressive acts of American, Belgian,
and other imperialists," North Korea demanded
immediate release of Lumumba and his colleagues,
and called for the liquidation of the "imperialists'
puppet" Mobutu.[9]

North Korea left no doubt whatever that it
considered Cuba as one of its staunchest allies.
Not only did it sign agreements with Havana regarding the establishment of diplomatic relations, the
exchange of diplomatic personnel, and cultural
cooperation on August 29, but it was soon beseiged
by an unending stream of Cuban visitors, both

governmental and otherwise. Nodong Sinmun spared
few words in describing the warmth of Korean-Cuban
friendship as well as the bravery and heroism of
the Cuban people in their anti-imperialist struggle.[10]
Cuba reciprocated by supporting North Korea's position on unification, by joining in the anti-
imperialist chorus, and by lauding the achievements of North Korea in its socialist construction.
P'yŏngyang came into contact with three additional
Latin American countries. In June, a group composed of Argentine and Chilian artists and writers
visited the city. In November, a cultural delegation from Colombia comprising legislators, writers,
and artists made a North Korean journey.[11]

The year 1961 saw further escalation of North
Korea's diplomatic offensive in the Third World.
India, Indonesia, Burma, and Laos were still its
best Asian friends. A North Korean trade mission
led by Yi Chu-yŏn, Vice Premier and Minister of
Trade, visited New Delhi in May and was received
by Prime Minister Nehru. It also reached agreement
with India on the exchange of trade centers, and
other trade matters. In December, P'yŏngyang was
emphatic in supporting the Indian invasion of the
Portuguese colony of Goa. The same trade mission
that visited India went directly to Indonesia.
While in Djakarta, the mission conducted lengthy
negotiations with the Indonesian authorities on
trade, which culminated in the agreement to establish consular relations between the two countries.
Indonesians representing all walks of life visited
P'yŏngyang throughout the year. The visitors
included the Indonesian Ambassador to Peking, representatives of the Indonesian Communist Party, and
leaders of the Indonesian-Korean Friendship Association. An Indonesian art exhibit was held in P'yŏngyang, and a team of Indonesian entertainers performed
in both P'yŏngyang and Hamhŭng. The North Korean
Red Cross donated a sum of relief money for flood
victims in Indonesia. A North Korea trade delegation was also active in Rangoon, where it secured
an agreement to establish consular relations. It
was further agreed that trade as well as cultural
contacts between the two countries would be stepped
up. A Burmese trade and good-will delegation
visited North Korea and was warmly received by Kim
Il-sŏng. Another Burmese governmental delegation
and a Burmese volley ball team made North Korean
trips.[12]

In the Arab world, North Korea deepened its
friendship with the U.A.R., Iraq, Syria, and Algeria
When a North Korean governmental delegation visited
Cairo, President Nasser reportedly conveyed his and
his people's thanks to North Korea for its support
in the Suez crisis. The delegation secured an
agreement to establish consular relations between
P'yŏngyang and Cairo. Continuing its journey to
Iraq, it worked out arrangements for cultural
exchange. The Iraqui Ambassador to Peking paid a
courtesy call on Kim Il-sŏng in P'yŏngyang. Kim
Il-sŏng sent a warm congratulatory telegram to
Algeria on the third anniversary of the establishment of its provisional government, renewing North
Korea's verbal commitment to the cause of "Algeria
for Algerians." Representatives of the Algerian
Communist Party visited P'yŏngyang, and an Algerian-
Korean friendship week was observed by Algerian
students, thus strengthening "the militant solidarity" between them and their North Korean counterparts.[13] A North Korean delegation also visited
Morocco in June, obtaining an agreement for political, economic, and cultural cooperation. Additionally, North Korea and Yemen signed a trade
agreement. In October, P'yŏngyang recognized the
new Syrian Government.[14]

Guinea, Mali, Ghana, the Congo, Togo, Cameroon,
Kenya, Somali, and Tanzania were the other African
nations with which North Korea interacted in 1961.
A North Korean governmental team visited both
Guinea and Mali in the summer, concluding various
agreements relating to trade and cultural exchange.
What is more, the two African nations were later
added to the growing list of North Korea's diplomati
partners; that is, diplomatic relations were finally
established with them. Ghana was also visited by
the North Korean group mentioned above. As was the
case in Guinea and Mali, the North Korean visitors
were received by the chief executive of the host
country, namely, President Nkhruma. A joint
communiqué condemning imperialism and affirming
solidarity between the Korean and Ghanaian peoples
was later issued. North Korea expressed its grief
over the murder of Congolese Premier Lumumba and
reiterated its denunciation of Western imperialism
led by the United States for its "barbaric acts."
Meanwhile, P'yŏngyang played the host to nongovernmental delegations from Togo, Cameroon, and Kenya.
A sum of 2,000 pounds sterling was donated by the

North Korean Red Cross to the flood victims of
Somali.[15] North Korea sent a congratulatory telegram to Tanzania upon the latter's declaration of
independence in December.[16]

Once again Cuba was North Korea's close ally.
In April, P'yŏngyang vigorously denounced what it
called "the piratical armed aggression against the
Cuban people committed by the American imperialists."
It was referring to the abortive invasion of Cuba
by U.S.-trained Cuban revolutionaries--an invasion
in which the United States played a pivotal, if
unsuccessful, role.[17] A North Korean trade delegation led by Vice-Premier Yi Chu-yŏn visited Havana
in the summer. A communiqué issued at the end of
its visit declared that Cuba and North Korea had
discussed matters of mutual concern and had reached
complete agreement. In September, a Cuban delegation led by Labor Minister August Martines Sanches
participated in the Fourth Congress of the KWP
held in P'yŏngyang. The first North Korean Ambassador to Havana presented his credentials to Castro
in April, 1961. Countless Cuban groups, including
a ballet troupe, visited North Korea, which in turn
sent a legion of governmental, Party, and cultural
personnel to Cuba.[18]

The story for 1962 was simply more of the same.
Economic and cultural exchange was carried out with
the same enthusiasm. North Korean good-will and
trade delegations visited Ceylon, Cambodia, Nepal,
Togo, Tunisia, Algeria, Sudan, and Somalia. Agreements were reached to establish diplomatic relations
with Algeria and consular relations with Cambodia
and to exchange trade centers with Togo, Ceylon,
and Somalia. Visitors, both governmental and otherwise, came to North Korea from the Third World in
growing numbers. P'yŏngyang thus entertained guests
from Guinea, Mali, Kenya, Laos, Cambodia, India,
Ceylon, Indonesia, Iraq, Chile, and Cuba, to name
just a few. North Korean delegates were invariably
present at the increasingly frequent Afro-Asian
conferences, be they cultural, economic, or ideological in orientation.[19]

In 1963, a total of fifty-six delegations from
Afro-Asian countries journeyed to North Korea.
P'yŏngyang, in turn, sent its representatives to
Cambodia, Kenya, Mali, Algeria, Yemen, Indonesia,
Burma, Ceylon, Uruguay, Chile, and Colombia. It

established diplomatic relations with the U.A.R.,
Yemen, and Uganda and set up a trade center in
Ceylon. An agreement to set up a trade center in
Uruguay was also reached. As in previous years,
North Korea was most friendly with both Indonesia
and Cuba.[20]

The most eventful year in North Korea's brief
diplomatic history is undoubtedly 1964. In that
year, North Korea sponsored the first international
conference ever held in P'yŏngyang, played host to
two chiefs of state, sent a top-level delegation,
led by its own head of state, on an extended good-
will tour of five Afro-Asian nations, and established diplomatic relations with five nations, all
in the Third World. From June 16 to 23, P'yŏngyang
was the scene of a thirty-four-nation Asian Economic
Conference.* The conference discussed the problems
and methods of building a self-reliant economy in
the newly emerging nations and explored the possibility of mutual assistance and cooperation among
them. Although the P'yŏngyang Declaration, adopted
at the end of the conference, promised little, if
any, positive action but merely underlined the need
for independent national economies, there was little
doubt that North Korea's international prestige as
well as self-esteem had received a major boost.
When Pravda later downgraded the event, P'yŏngyang
reacted indignantly.[21]

In October, President Modibo Keita of Mali
and his wife made a six-day state visit to North
Korea. A joint communiqué signed by Kim Il-sŏng
and Keita expressed their mutual admiration, Korean-
Mali solidarity, and the common determination to
fight against imperialism and colonialism, both old
and new. It also contained a scathing criticism
of the racist policies of both South Africa and
Southern Rhodesia, together with "an unreserved
support for and solidarity with the heroic struggle"
of the African people there for their freedom and
independence.[22] Hardly had the Mali leader left
P'yŏngyang when another distinguished visitor
arrived in the North Korean capital. President

---

*It should be stressed that the number of countries
formally represented at the P'yŏngyang meeting was
considerably less. For quite a few delegations
represented not governments but nonruling Communist or socialist parties.

Sukarno of Indonesia began his four-day state visit
on November 1. His visit, Nodong Sinmun editorialized, made a huge contribution not only to the
friendship and solidarity between the Korean and
Indonesian peoples, but also to the "common great
tasks of the peoples of Asia, Africa, and Latin
America." A Kim-Sukarno communiqué took note of
"the grave threat posed by the imperialists to world
peace, the safety of mankind, and the freedom and
independence of the newly emerging nations," underscoring the urgent necessity of a united common
front of all the oppressed peoples against imperialism and neocolonialism.[23]

North Korea's diplomatic endeavors for the
year were climaxed by Ch'oe Yong-gŏn's good-will
visits to Africa and Asia. From November 19 to
December 22, Ch'oe and his entourage visited the
U.A.R., Algeria, Mali, Guinea, and Cambodia. In
addition, they made brief stopovers in the Soviet
Union, Yemen, Pakistan, Burma, and the P.R.C.,
where, in Ch'oe's own words, they received "warm
welcome and valuable assistance from the respective
governments and peoples alike." The visits were
obviously intended not simply to promote good-
will, but also to produce more tangible results.
Numerous cultural, economic, and diplomatic agreements were thus concluded between the five countries and North Korea. The towering purpose of the
tour, however, appeared to be to enhance P'yŏngyang's
international prestige. In his report to the Presidium of the D.P.R.K. Supreme People's Assembly
on his Afro-Asian journey, Ch'oe voiced his opti-
mistic conviction that the nations of Africa and
Asia, freshly freed from the degrading yoke of
Western colonialism, were marching triumphantly
toward economic and political autonomy. Noting
that factories, business enterprises, and farms
in the five countries were being run far more effi-
ciently than they had been in the colonial days,
the Chairman of the Presidium declared:

>   ...The iron-clad determination
> to be the master of one's own
> destiny, to oppose the subjuga-
> tion policy of the imperialists,
> and to safeguard one's hard-won
> independence at all costs--that
> is the foundation stone of all
> the results the newly independent

peoples of Asia and Africa are
achieving today. Not only have
/they/ become the masters of
their own nations, but they have
provided a convincing proof that
they can build better nations
with their own hands.

Ch'oe stressed that the unity and solidarity of all
emerging nations and peoples, to which his visits
allegedly made a positive contribution, would both
ensure the speedy eradication of imperialism and
bring about lasting peace on earth.[24]

Meanwhile, five nonbloc nations were added to
the steadily growing list of North Korea's diplomatic
partners: Diplomatic missions at the ambassadorial
level were established in Indonesia, Mauritania,
Cambodia, the Congo (Brazzaville), and Ghana, in
that order. In addition, a North Korean consulate
general was set up in Ceylon. Cultural and economic
intercourse with the nations already friendly to
P'yŏngyang also continued unabated. Finally, North
Korea participated in 114 international organizations and meetings of all sorts during the year.[25]
All in all, 1964 was a singularly busy and fruitful
year for the diplomatically adolescent North Korea.

North Korea's relations with the Third World
continued to deepen in 1965. Particularly intense
was its intercourse with the continent of Africa.
P'yŏngyang thus gained another diplomatic partner
in Africa, Tanzania. When Gambia became independent,
North Korea was among the first nations to bless it
with formal recognition. African visitors kept on
pouring into P'yŏngyang, among whom were President
Alphonse Massanba-Debat of the Republic of the
Congo (Brazzaville) and Madame Sekou Touré, wife
of the President of Guinea. A significant milestone
in North Korea's diplomacy was reached, however,
when Premier Kim Il-sŏng made a state visit to Indonesia from April 10 to 15. For it was the first
diplomatic excursion by the North Korean leader
into the Third World. Never before had he visited
a non-Communist country. By journeying to Djakarta,
Kim Il-sŏng was returning Sukarno's visit to North
Korea in late 1964. A Kim-Sukarno communiqué, issued
at the end of the visit, repeated familiar themes:
a denunciation of imperialism, colonialism, and neocolonialism; a call for a united anti-imperialist

front on the part of all oppressed peoples and
nations; an expression of mutual admiration for
each other's "great leadership"; and a reaffirmation of Korean-Indonesian solidarity and friendship. To no one's surprise, Kim commended Indonesia
for the "courage and wisdom" it had shown in withdrawing from the United Nations. For he shared
Sukarno's belief that the world body "is not an
instrument suitable for building a new world but a
tool readily manipulated by the imperialists to
preserve the spiritual and material interests of
their old order." The Indonesian move, Kim stated,
had encouraged the revolutionary struggle of people
the world over who opposed all forms and manifestations of the subjugation of one people by another.[26]
In August, the Asian Soccer Games were held in
P'yŏngyang, in which six nations took part--North
Korea, Indonesia, North Vietnam, Communist China,
Cambodia, and Guinea. North Korea swept the games
by defeating all the visiting teams.[27]

Although there were few exciting events on
North Korea's diplomatic front in 1966, the two-way
commercial and cultural traffic between P'yŏngyang
and the emerging nations remained at the usual pace.
One upsetting event, no doubt, was the unexpected
political upheaval in Indonesia, a country with
which North Korea had built especially warm ties.
Nodong Sinmun, however, chose to bury the event and
its implications for North Korean foreign policy
in an editorial dealing with North Korean-Japanese
relations. It reported that the representatives of
the KWP and the JCP had lodged "a strong protest
against the barbaric persecution and massacre of
Indonesian Communists and other democratic elements
by the right-wing reactionaries of Indonesia at the
instigation of American imperialists."[28]

Eager to please the Arab nations, P'yŏngyang
has gone out of its way to denounce and denigrate
Israel whenever the occasion has arisen. From
April 26 to May 2, North Korea observed what it
called "the Week of Support for the Struggle of
the Palestine People," during which it unleashed
a diatribe against "the Israeli Zionists who are
illegally and forcefully occupying Palestine under
the manipulation of the imperialists led by the
United States."[29] Meanwhile, North Korean delegations scurried about the Middle East, transacting
business and negotiating further agreements. In

July, Syria agreed to elevate its relations with
North Korea to the diplomatic level.[30] In October,
a North Korean embassy opened its doors in Damascus.[31]
A North Korean delegation led by Kang Yang-uk, Vice-
Chairman of the Presidium of the Supreme People's
Assembly, visited Tanzania during its tour of Middle
Eastern states.[32] African visitors to North Korea
included a group of Somalian legislators, headed
by the speaker of its national assembly.[33]

P'yŏngyang busily exchanged good-will delegations with its Asian neighbors as well. A Cambodian
soccer team and a Burmese cultural delegation thus
visited North Korea, and a North Korean delegation
headed by Vice-Premier Yi Chu-yŏn toured Burma,
Cambodia, and Pakistan.[34] Shortly after the North
Korean delegation returned from its Asian tour,
Cambodia announced that it had expelled the South
Korean Consulate General from Phnom Penh and had
broken off relations with Seoul--a move that was
loudly applauded by P'yŏngyang.[35] According to
South Korean explanations, however, it was not
Phnom Penh but Seoul that had initiated the break.
South Korea is said to have closed its mission in
Cambodia in protest against the latter's handling
of a would-be North Korean defector. The North
Korean, a member of an athletic team and a repatriate
from Japan, had sought political asylum in the
Japanese Embassy in Phnom Penh, but the Japanese
Ambassador had surrendered him to Cambodian author-
ities, who subsequently turned him over to North
Korean officials.[36]

North Korea's deepening solidarity with Cuba
was shown by the ever-increasing volume of personnel
exchange between the two countries. Hardly a week
passed without the arrival of a Cuban good-will
delegation. The most distinguished Cuban visitors
to North Korea in 1966 were Osvaldo Dorticos
Torrado, President of the Republic of Cuba and
Member of the Politbureau of the Central Committee
of the Cuban Communist Party, and Raul Castro Rus,
Second Secretary of the Central Committee of the
Cuban Communist Party and Vice-Premier and Minister
of Trade of the Republic of Cuba. In a P'yŏngyang
rally honoring their visit, Raul Castro Rus dramatically emphasized Havana-P'yŏngyang solidarity
in these words:

> If you wish to know what Comrade
> Fidel Castro thinks, ask Comrade
> Kim Il-sŏng. Then you will dis-
> cover that the two think exactly
> the same thoughts. The peoples
> of Cuba and /North/ Korea agree
> with and support each other on
> every issue they are facing today.
> The relations between the parties
> and governments of the two coun-
> tries firmly rest on the founda-
> tions of sincerity and purity.[37]

North Korea's diplomatic activities in 1967
began with the dispatch of a good-will delegation
led by Kang Yang-uk, Vice-Chairman of the Presidium
of the Supreme People's Assembly, to Africa on an
extended tour. From mid-February to mid-April, the
North Korean team made official visits to Burundi,
Zambia, Yemen, and Somalia, and an unofficial visit
to Tanzania. It also stopped briefly in Cairo and
Moscow. The major accomplishment of the tour was
the conclusion of agreements establishing diplomatic
relations with Burundi and Somalia. In his report
to the Supreme People's Assembly on the African
visit, Kang Yang-uk said that North Korea's "spectacular economic and industrial progress, its independent policy, and ideology of chuch'e" were the
objects of inspiration and emulation in the newly
developing countries of Asia and Africa. He stressed
the common determination of North Korea and the rest
of Afro-Asia to struggle against the "aggression
and racist policies of the imperialists headed by
the United States." Because they are united in
their opposition to imperialism and because "united
people are invincible," they are certain to deal
a fatal blow to the imperialists, Kang said.[38]

When the Israeli-Arab war broke out in June,
North Korea quickly expressed its full support of
the Arabs. Kim Il-sŏng sent identical telegrams to
all the heads of the Arab governments strongly
condemning both "the aggressive maneuvers of the
Israeli expansionists" and the alleged intervention
of the United States and the United Kingdom. The
intervention, Kim said in the telegram, "constituted
a brigandish act of aggression imperiling the
national independence and security of the Arab
people as well as a serious threat to the peace in
the Middle East and the World alike." Expressing

the indignation of the North Korean people over the
newest manifestation of "Anglo-American imperialism,"
Kim pledged full North Korean support and assistance
to the Arabs. The D.P.R.K. Government issued a
lengthy statement on the crisis echoing the preceding
sentiment.[39] The news of the Arab defeat was
deliberately played down.[40]

     When the opportunity came to reciprocate North
Korean friendship and support, the Third World
nations generously responded. In the annual United
Nations debate on Korea in October and November,
they aided P'yŏngyang with unparalleled enthusiasm
and persistence. As noted, Cambodia, the Congo
(Brazzaville), Guinea, Mali, and Mauritania joined
the Soviet Union in pro-North Korean oratory and
maneuvers. The failure of their efforts in the end
is less significant than the fact that the majority
of Third World nations in the international organization supported North Korea. As Chart 3 shows,
P'yŏngyang not only had the unanimous support of
all Communist nations, including Yugoslavia, but
it had the solid backing of most Third World nations.
Another development that dramatized North Korea's
firm ties with the Third World was the humiliating
treatment accorded the South Korean delegation by
Algeria at the ministerial conference of eighty-six
developing nations in October, 1967. The host
country, Algeria, apparently under North Korean
pressure, temporarily confined the South Korean
delegation led by Foreign Minister Ch'oe Kyu-ha
to its quarters. The ban on its movement was later
lifted.[41]

     One minor setback for North Korea in 1967 was
the change in Indonesia's posture toward South
Korea. An Indonesian good-will delegation led by
the Speaker of its National Assembly visited South
Korea from October 13 to 16, negotiating the establishment of consular relations between Seoul and
Djakarta. The visiting Indonesians, however, made
it clear that Djakarta would continue to maintain
relations with North Korea.[42] To Seoul's dismay,
furthermore, Indonesia continued to support North
Korea's position at the United Nations. The visit
of Kenya's foreign minister to Seoul in October
and November did not prevent the African nation
from casting a pro-P'yŏngyang vote at the world
body.[43] Meanwhile, North Korean Chief of State
Ch'oe Yong-gŏn led a five-man delegation to Havana

Chart 3

NATIONS SUPPORTING NORTH KOREA
IN THE UNITED NATIONS, 1965-67[a]

Country	1965	1966	1967
U.S.S.R.	x	x	x
Ukrainian S.S.R.	x	x	x
Byelorussian S.S.R.	x	x	x
Albania	x	x	x
Bulgaria	x	x	x
Czechoslovakia	x	x	x
Hungary	x	x	x
Poland	x	x	x
Romania	x	x	x
Yugoslavia	abstain	x	x
Cuba	x	x	x
Mongolia	x	x	x
Burma	abstain	x	x
Cambodia	absent	x	x
Ceylon	abstain	x	x
Nepal	abstain	x	x
Pakistan	abstain	x	x
Afghanistan	abstain	x	x
Indonesia	absent	x	x
U.A.R.	abstain	x	x
Syria	x	x	x
Iraq	x	x	x
Yemen	absent	x	x
Sudan	abstain	x	x
Burundi	abstain	absent	x
Ghana	x	abstain	abstain
Guinea	x	x	x
Mali	x	x	x
Somalia	absent	absent	x
Tanzania	x	x	x
Uganda	x	x	x
Algeria	x	x	x
Congo (Brazzaville)	absent	x	x
Mauritania	x	x	x
Kenya	absent	abstain	x
Ethiopia	abstain	x	x
Nigeria	abstain	x	x
Zambia	absent	absent	x
Jamaica	abstain	x	abstain

[a]Based on Dong-A Ilbo, November 2, 1967. Whether or not a
particular nation supported North Korea in a given year
is determined by its over-all voting record. Since there
has typically been more than one resolution on Korea at
the United Nations each year, many nations have given
qualified, rather than full, support to North Korea. If
a nation has cast at least one vote favorable to North
Korea and has abstained in other cases, its position in
that year is considered to be supportive of North Korea.
It should be pointed out that only the Communist bloc
nations and Algeria have given consistent and unqualified
support to P'yŏngyang in this period.

183

in mid-November, suggesting that the bonds between
the two countries were as firm as ever.[44] No doubt,
their independent positions in the Sino-Soviet
struggle, common hatred of American imperialism,
and common commitment to protracted guerrilla warfare against it were among the factors drawing
them together.

In brief, North Korea's well-calculated campaign to woo the Third World has been both successful and productive. One of its side effects has
been to compel South Korea to reappraise its policy
and posture toward the newly emerging nations.
From August 21 to October 9, 1967, two South Korean
good-will delegations--one led by Yi Tong-wŏn, a
former foreign minister and a member of the National
Assembly, and the other by Yang Yu-ch'an, a former
ambassador to the United States--toured eighteen
African nations. Upon returning to Seoul, they
reported that to counter North Korean influence
in the area would require an imaginative program of
technical and economic assistance. They pointed
out that in the past several years North Korea had
built rice mills, match factories, ceramic factories,
flour mills, and other factories at the cost of
about $100,000 each in Algeria, Mali, Somalia,
Tanzania, the Congo (Brazzaville), Burundi, and
other countries. Moreover, the delegation led by
Yi Tong-wŏn, which was touring East Africa, encoun-
tered enormous obstacles posed by North Korea,
which had sent its own delegation to the area at
the same time.[45] In November, after analyzing
U.N. votes on Korea, the R.O.K. Foreign Ministry
disclosed that a major overhaul of its diplomatic
apparatus and policy was in the offing. Specifically
it would (1) reorient its policy toward the Third
World to one based primarily on economic assistance,
(2) reorganize and expand its African and Middle
East sections, (3) vastly increase South Korea's
permanent missions in Third World nations, (4)
explore nonpolitical contacts with such nations
through international economic cooperation, and
(5) reformulate its strategy in the United Nations.[46]

NORTH KOREA AND THE VIETNAM CONFLICT

Of all the nations in the Communist bloc, no
nation, perhaps, has rendered more verbal support
to the "struggle of the Vietnamese people against

imperialism and for their liberty and independence"
than has North Korea. The intensity of North Korean
sympathy for the plight of the Vietnamese people,
as well as its genuine indignation over America's
role in the war, is matched only by the rapidity
with which the war has escalated. Whether P'yŏngyang has been equally generous with material assistance to both Hanoi and the National Liberation
Front (NLF) of South Vietnam can only be speculated
on. However, there is a reasonable ground for sup-
posing that at least a modest amount of North Korean
economic, technical, and military aid is being
regularly channeled into Hanoi. Although North
Korea has repeatedly expressed its willingness to
send "volunteers" to South Vietnam to help repel
"the American imperialist aggressors," Hanoi has
thus far been cool to the offer.[47]

The sources of North Korean attitude and
behavior are not hard to find. What is happening
in Vietnam, as P'yŏngyang sees it, is proof that
American imperialism is the common enemy of all
the people who either have recently been freed
from the yoke of colonialism or are still enslaved
by it. Ever mindful of the annoying presence of
American troops in South Korea and unable to jettison
the humiliating memories of the Korean War, North
Korea remains convinced that the root cause of its
misery and frustrations is the United States. In
Vietnam, it sees history repeating itself. The
legitimate aspirations of the Vietnamese people
are being mercilessly thwarted by the formidable
might of "American imperialism." P'yŏngyang burns
with indignation; it cannot bear to see it happen
again. The "American aggression" must be stopped,
and the Vietnamese people saved. In its view,
American power is by no means invincible. It can
be checked, even crushed. But that requires the
concerted efforts of all socialist nations, large
and small. Nothing short of a united Communist
front will do the job. North Korea would surely
jump at the opportunity to take revenge on "the
American imperialists" as a member of a multinational
Communist force in Vietnam. To be sure, it would
mean a considerable sacrifice in terms of North
Korea's own domestic programs, but the KWP leadership is more than willing to pay this price for the
liquidation of "American imperialism" from Asia,
if not from the face of earth.

North Korea established diplomatic relations
with Hanoi in January, 1950. The two have remained
close allies ever since. In 1957, Ho Chi Minh paid
a state visit to North Korea, a visit which was
returned by Kim Il-sŏng the following year. Cultural and economic intercourse between the two
countries has been carried on with mounting vigor
in recent years. Significantly, North Korea sent
teams of technicians to North Vietnam in 1960 and,
most probably, in the ensuing years as well.
Politically, the two regimes have consistently
supported each other's positions on significant
issues and, in particular, in times of crisis.
With the escalation and growing Americanization of
the Vietnamese conflict, North Korea has become
one of the staunchest allies of Hanoi and the NLF
alike.[48]

P'yŏngyang was most enraged by South Korea's
decision to dispatch troops to join the Allied
forces in Vietnam. Arguing that the decision was
imposed on the Seoul regime by the "American imperialists," it denounced both the United States
and South Korea in the strongest possible terms.
It accused "the Park Chung Hee clique" of "selling
fellow countrymen as cannon fodder for the brigandish
American imperialists," adding that there was no
more "despicable act of treason" in the annals of
Korea.[49] A few months later, North Korea offered
to match Seoul's troop contributions to Vietnam--
"be it a division or an army corps."[50] In early
1966, Ho Chi Minh and Ch'oe Yong-gŏn exchanged
letters reaffirming the common determination of
both countries and peoples to "fight to the bitter
end to repel the American aggressors." Ho sought
and received a renewed pledge from North Korea
for "more support and assistance." In making that
pledge, Ch'oe emphasized that "the Korean and Vietnamese peoples are both brothers and comrades-in-
arms standing side by side on the common front
against American imperialism."[51]

In his congratulatory speech to the Twenty-
third Congress of the CPSU in Moscow on April 1,
Ch'oe restated P'yŏngyang's position in these words:

> ...The American aggression in
> Vietnam is a grave act of prov-
> ocation aimed at opposing the
> socialist camp, suppressing

national liberation move-
ments, and disturbing world
peace.

/The aggression/,
together with the heroic
struggle the Vietnamese
people are waging against
it, has become the focal
point of the struggle be-
tween the forces of impe-
rialism and anti-imperialism
today.[52]

It is only through united action, he added, that
the socialist camp can emerge victorious in the
crucial struggle.[53]

In the ensuing months, North Korea intensified
its propaganda offensive on Vietnam by constantly
organizing mass rallies, by devoting an inordinately
large amount of space to the war in its newspapers,
and by ceaselessly reiterating its firm verbal support for both Hanoi and the NLF. Thus, on July 18,
Kim Il-sŏng sent a cable to Ho Chi Minh, offering
to send "more positive assistance" to the Vietnamese
people, including "volunteers."[54] In September, a
North Vietnamese governmental delegation visited
P'yŏngyang to sign two agreements, one providing
for North Korean assistance to North Vietnam and
the other stipulating terms of reciprocal trade.
The amount and content of North Korea's proposed
assistance to Hanoi, however, were not disclosed.[55]

At the "leadership conference" of the KWP
held in P'yŏngyang in October, Kim Il-sŏng included
in his main report to the conference North Korea's
formula for resolving the Vietnamese conflict. He
insisted that a joint Communist expedition to Vietnam, and it alone, would defeat the imperialists.
Reminding his audience of North Korea's standing
offer to send volunteers to Vietnam, Kim indicated
that they should be joined by volunteers from other
Communist countries. Offers to send volunteers,
to be sure, had been made by practically all bloc
nations; however, the novelty of Kim's pronouncement lay in the insistence that they should be
sent, regardless of Hanoi's attitude. He saw the
Vietnam War as a potential stepping stone to the
restoration of intrabloc unity. As he put it:

> We deem it necessary for the
> socialist countries, first of
> all, to dispatch international
> volunteers to assist the fighting
> people of Vietnam. This will be
> the first step toward the realiza-
> tion of joint action against impe-
> rialism.

With their volunteers fighting together in Vietnam,
Kim said, individual parties could "gradually
narrow differences and create an atmosphere conducive to mutual contacts." He made plain his dissatisfaction with both Moscow and Peking in regard
to Vietnam, neither of which, in his view, had
done nor was doing enough to help the Vietnamese
people.[56]

In late 1966, the North Korean Foreign Ministry
issued statements on Vietnam almost every week.
Invariably, they condemned the "American aggression"
and pledged North Korean support, repeating its
standing offer to send volunteers anytime.[57] At
the same time, mass rallies in support of the Vietnamese people grew in number. P'yŏngyang also
strongly objected to South Korea's reported plan
to send more troops to Vietnam.[58] Meanwhile, the
U.S. State Department confirmed the presence of an
estimated twenty North Korean pilots in North Vietnam. Initially, they were reported to be flying
MIG's and training North Vietnamese pilots, but,
in September, 1967, it was confirmed that they
actually participated in combat also. By this time,
the number of North Korean pilots in Vietnam was
estimated to be "between twenty-five and fifty."[59]

The year 1967 saw no visible change in North
Korea's militant support of the Vietnamese people.
P'yŏngyang and Hanoi continued to exchange visitors
as well as messages of mutual support and friendship. In February, it was revealed that there were
some North Vietnamese students enrolled at Kim
Il-sŏng University in P'yŏngyang.[60] The North
Korean Foreign Ministry faithfully followed its
ritual of issuing statements on Vietnam at regular
intervals.[61] In August, an economic delegation
representing North Vietnam arrived in P'yŏngyang
for the apparent purpose of negotiating renewal
of aid and trade agreements.[62] In sum, P'yŏngyang's
moral and material support of Hanoi and the NLF

showed no sign of tapering off. All indications
were that it would be as enduring as the war
itself.

NORTH KOREA AND JAPAN

For a capitalist nation, Japan's relations
with North Korea have been singularly close. This,
of course, is not to imply that the two countries
are to be considered as either friends or allies.
Although the two governments have steadfastly
refused to recognize each other either explicitly
or implicitly, they have nevertheless initiated
and maintained extensive "unofficial relations"--
known in international law as "relations officieuses."[63] North Korea has insisted on drawing
a fine line of demarcation between people and
government, between economics and politics, and
between trade and diplomacy. Thus, in P'yŏngyang's
view, if the Japanese Government is reactionary,
capitalist-oriented, and subservient to American
imperialism, the Japanese people are progressive,
courageous, and independent-minded. The lack of
any formal political contacts with the successive
regimes, however, has not prevented the D.P.R.K.
from seeking and establishing economic relations
with Tokyo.

Actually, North Korea's relations with Japan,
like all bilateral interactions, have been strongly
influenced by the attitudes and actions of "the
other side." If it had its choice, P'yŏngyang
would undoubtedly welcome more amicable relations
with Tokyo. The latter's strong ties with the
United States and, more recently, with South
Korea cannot but antagonize the former. What is
more, P'yŏngyang's attempts to normalize relations
with Tokyo have continuously been brushed aside by
the Japanese. Japan's utility to North Korea is
readily apparent. As the world's third industrial
power, Japan can be an extremely valuable trading
partner. Its geographical proximity to North Korea
serves to enhance its attractiveness. With its
huge Korean minority, largely alienated and Communist-
oriented, Japan provides North Korea with both an
ideal propaganda outlet and a useful base for
espionage and infiltration operations directed
against South Korea.

P'yŏngyang's first unofficial contact with
Japan after the establishment of the D.P.R.K. in
1948 appears to have been made in November, 1953,
when a "Japanese people's goodwill delegation"
led by Oyama Ikuo, a member of the Japanese Diet
and Chairman of the Japan Peace Preservation Committee, arrived in the North Korean capital for a
week-long visit.[64] The visit marked the beginning
of an unending stream of unofficial Japanese visitors, who included politicians, businessmen,
labor-union leaders, and student leaders.

In August, 1954, North Korean Foreign Minister
Nam Il issued a statement protesting Japan's alleged
suppression of Korean residents, thus initiating
a formal, albeit indirect, dialogue between P'yŏngyang and Tokyo. In February, 1955, Nam Il declared
that North Korea was prepared to enter into negotiations with Japan for the purpose of establishing
cultural and trade relations between the two countries. The North Korean action apparently had been
prompted by the Hatoyama Government's policy of
normalizing relations with Communist nations.
Informal contacts between the two countries followed quickly, and a campaign to promote trade with
North Korea got underway in Japan. In October of
the same year, two Japanese missions consisting of
socialist members of the Diet and businessmen
arrived in P'yŏngyang for unofficial talks, which
produced nongovernmental agreements on the terms,
conditions, and manner of trade between the two
countries. With the conclusion of another agreement in Peking in February, 1956, the door to
North Korean-Japanese trade was finally opened.[65]

Meanwhile, Japan made plain its desire to
differentiate between economics and politics by
refusing to admit North Korean delegates to a
World Conference Against Atomic and Hydrogen Bombs
held in Hiroshima in August, 1955. P'yŏngyang,
for its part, continued to condemn the Japanese
Government for the latter's alleged maltreatment
of the Korean minority in Japan. The official
animosity between Tokyo and P'yŏngyang, however,
did not pose any barrier to the flow of Japanese
visitors to North Korea, and their number increased
markedly.[66]

In September, 1957, Kim Il-sŏng, in a speech
before the Supreme People's Assembly of the D.P.R.K.,
reiterated North Korea's desire to normalize relations with Japan, saying that harmonious P'yŏngyang-
Tokyo relations "would not only be of mutual benefit
to both peoples concerned but would also be conducive to the preservation of peace in Asia."[67]

In 1958, remarks attributed to two top-ranking
Japanese officials infuriated P'yŏngyang. In June
of that year, Sawada Renzo, Japan's Chief Delegate
to Japan-R.O.K. talks, was quoted as saying that
the purpose of the talks was to "cooperate with
South Korea in an endeavor to push the 38th Parallel
up to the Yalu River." In October, Prime Minister
Kishi told an NBC reporter that Japan's right of
self-defense must extend to South Korea and Taiwan.
These remarks immediately drew condemnation from
North Korea, which construed them as manifestations
of "a brazenly hostile attitude toward the Korean
people on the part of the surviving Japanese militarists."[68] Shortly before the Kishi remarks were
made, Nam Il, Foreign Minister of North Korea, had
declared in an interview with a correspondent for
Akahata (Red Flag), the organ of the Japanese Communist Party, that North Korea stood ready to
negotiate with Japan for normalization of relations, arguing that such a step would be consistent
with the national interests of both countries.
Nam Il pointed out that it was the stubbornness of
the "reactionary government of Kishi" that impeded
friendly relations between the two countries.
Deploring the "inhuman treatment" accorded Korean
residents in Japan by the Kishi Government, he
asserted that their "rightful wish" to return to
North Korea must be honored by Tokyo.[69]

Simultaneously, North Korea launched an inten-
sive campaign in Japan to exert pressure on the
Kishi Government to agree to repatriate Korean
residents to the Communist regime. The main burden
of organizing and carrying out the campaign was
borne by the General Federation of Korean Residents
in Japan (Chōren), which was thoroughly subservient
to P'yŏngyang and to which an estimated 60 per cent
of the Korean population in Japan owed their allegiance.[70] The Chōren conducted a door-to-door
campaign to obtain signatures for a petition calling
on the Kishi Government to allow Korean residents
to repatriate themselves to North Korea. It was

aided by a coalition of Japanese left-wing intellectuals, public figures, and political and social organizations. An impressive number of persons belonging to Japanese political parties, ranging from Liberal-Democratic to Communist, rallied their support behind the proposed repatriation plan. There was virtually no organized opposition. It should be stressed that the overwhelming support generated in Japan for the North Korean cause did not necessarily indicate either the effectiveness of the propaganda offensive of both P'yŏngyang and Chŏren or the general sympathy of the Japanese people toward the plight of Koreans in their land. Although these factors must certainly have played a part, there was a more important factor influencing the Japanese attitude. The Korean minority had long been a troubling problem for the Japanese policy-makers and public alike. Impoverished and suffering from social and economic discrimination, the Koreans had a high crime rate and had become a heavy burden on Japanese society. Many Japanese must undoubtedly have seen in the North Korean proposal an opportunity to rid themselves of a painful nuisance.[71]

In the face of mounting pressure, the Kishi Government decided in early 1959 to consider the North Korean proposal. However, it avoided any direct negotiations with North Korea by entrusting the Japanese Red Cross Society to handle the matter. The delegates of the latter began negotiations with those of the North Korean Red Cross Society in Geneva on April 13, 1959. The move was instantly met with a vehement protest from South Korea, which threatened to use force if necessary to prevent what it called the "deportation" of South Korean citizens to North Korea. The Kishi Government countered by invoking the doctrine of the freedom of domicile recognized by both the Universal Declaration of Human Rights and the Japanese Constitution. Seoul's protests notwithstanding, the Geneva negotiations continued. But it required seventeen meetings for both sides to reach a "basic agreement." A draft agreement was completed on June 18, and the final document was signed in Calcutta, India, on August 13.[72] Under the agreement, which has been renewed every year, more than 88,000 Korean residents in Japan have repatriated to North Korea thus far.[73]

Meanwhile, trade between the two countries continued. Because of Tokyo's ban on direct trade, however, the volume involved was almost negligible. The total value of North Korean-Japanese trade (i.e., the value of both exports and imports from P'yŏngyang's point of view) for 1957, for example, was estimated at about $6 million.[74] In April, 1961, the Japanese Government lifted some of its restrictions on Japanese trade with North Korea but continued to prohibit direct trade. It was not until November, 1962, that Tokyo finally revoked its ban on direct trade. The volume of trade between the two countries has steadily increased since then.[75]

As Soon Sung Cho points out, the change in the Japanese trade policy, which paved the way for more lively economic exchange between Japan and North Korea, coincided with the beginning of the Seven-Year Economic Plan in North Korea. Although Tokyo's decision was probably influenced more by its desire to appease interested Japanese businessmen than by P'yŏngyang's indirect pressure, its total effect was to appreciably enhance North Korea's economic interests. The geographical distance of the latter's potential suppliers of machines and materials in Europe, its strained relationship with the Soviet Union, and the inability of Communist China to export industrial items had combined to make Japan North Korea's ideal trading partner. From Tokyo's point of view, trade with North Korea, no matter how profitable it may be, entailed the grave danger of alienating the United States and South Korea. One was Japan's number one trading partner and ally, and the other was both a valuable market and a strategically important neighbor with which Japan was trying to normalize relations. The marked caution displayed by Tokyo in its approach to trade with North Korea is readily understandable.[76]

The total value of trade between North Korea and Japan rose from about $1 million in 1960 to $8 million in 1961. It increased to $9.5 million in 1962, $14.7 million in 1963, $31 million in 1964, and $31.2 million in 1965. These figures, however, constituted a negligible fraction of Japan's total trade. For example, the figure for 1965 accounted for about one fifth of 1 per cent of Japan's international trade. What is more, it was less than one seventh of the value of trade

between South Korea and Japan. The relatively small
quantity of economic transactions, however, should
not blur the significant fact that in the years 1963,
1964, and 1966, North Korean exports to Japan
exceeded its imports by an impressive margin--
almost by 2 to 1 in 1963 and 1964 and a greater
margin in 1966. South Korea, by contrast, has
continuously suffered from an enormous and ever-
growing deficit in its trade with Japan. The specific contents of North Korean-Japanese trade are also
worth noting. While importing from Japan chemicals,
steel products, machinery, and synthetic fiber yarns,
North Korea exported to Japan iron ore, pig iron,
zinc, lead, copper, nonmetallic minerals, and foodstuffs (mainly soybeans). North Korea's economic
value to Japan thus appears to lie chiefly in its
role as a supplier of mineral resources for Japanese
industry.[77]

Although people-to-people diplomacy between
Tokyo and P'yŏngyang increased in both vigor and
frequency, as measured by the number and prominence
of Japanese visitors to North Korea and by the
warmth with which they were greeted by their hosts,
North Korean-Japanese relations at the governmental
level showed no signs of improving. P'yŏngyang
continued its violent attack on the vestiges of
"Japanese imperialism and militarism." The peak
of its anti-Japanese diatribe was reached in 1965,
when negotiations for a normalization treaty between South Korea and Japan were in progress.
P'yŏngyang repeatedly charged that the proposed
treaty was part of a conspiracy to colonize South
Korea and eventually the whole of Korea. Such a
treaty, it said, "would open the door to Korea for
Japanese militarists and monopolists." It was
tantamount to a "guarantee of the realization of
the pernicious aggressive designs of the Japanese
militarists." Not only would North Korea "resolutely
oppose" the conclusion of such a treaty, but it
would consider any treaty concluded between Seoul
and Tokyo completely null and void.[78]

The treaty was finally signed on June 22, 1965,
in Tokyo and went into effect later in the year
after both the Japanese Diet and the R.O.K. National
Assembly ratified it amid widespread and vocal
opposition in both countries. As in the repatriation case, the Chōren played a leading role in
organizing and spreading the antitreaty movement

in Japan. Once again it found a potent ally in
Japan's left-wing political parties and organizations. It is worth noting that North Korea has
spent huge sums of money in underwriting the
activities of the Chōren. Aside from providing
financial assistance to the latter's political
activities, P'yŏngyang has taken an active interest
in the education of Korean residents in Japan.
With North Korean funds, the Chōren has established
and operates all sorts of schools ranging from
kindergartens to a university. As of August, 1965,
North Korea had supplied the Chōren with a total of
$11,681,320 (4,205,275,493 yen) for educational
purposes alone.[79]

        The conclusion of the R.O.K.-Japanese Normaliza-
tion Treaty appears to have placed the Japanese
Government in the ranks of North Korea's sworn
enemies, alongside the United States and South
Korea.[80] On the other hand, the treaty has visibly
improved relations between Seoul and Tokyo. The
most notable effect has been a sharp increase in
commercial transactions between the two countries.
As Soon Sung Cho notes:

> By September 9, 1966, plants
> exported and under negotiation
> totaled nearly $800 million.
> Exports to Korea during the
> first eight months of 1966
> reached $205 million, thus
> making South Korea second only
> to the United States as a cus-
> tomer for Japanese products.
> Furthermore, as of August
> 1966, Japanese private loans
> and credits to South Korea
> exceeded those of other foreign
> nations by far, totalling $127
> million.[81]

        If their growing commercial intercourse has
proved to be mutually profitable, it has also made
Japan more vulnerable to South Korean pressure.
Never was this more graphically demonstrated than
in the summer of 1966, when Japan was forced by
South Korea to reverse its decision to admit three
technicians from North Korea to negotiate for a
$12 million acrylic-fiber-making plant. After pro-
testing Tokyo's initial decision, Seoul retaliated

by (1) stopping the issuance of visas to Japanese
intending to visit South Korea for commercial or
tourist purposes, (2) banning contacts between
Japanese businessmen and Korean government officials, (3) beginning investigations of the activity
and tax status of Japanese businessmen in South
Korea, (4) suspending negotiations by South Koreans
in Japan with Japanese firms, and (5) restricting
South Koreans from traveling to Japan for commercial
reasons.[82] The Japanese Government finally capit-
ulated. Additionally, many Japanese firms were
compelled by South Korea to cancel contracts with
North Korea.[83]

     Shortly after the preceding incident, the
Japanese Government announced that the repatriation agreement between the Japanese and North
Korean Red Cross Societies would be extended for
a year for the last time. Even this decision,
which had obviously been intended as a significant
concession to South Korea, immediately drew an
angry protest from Seoul.[84] Nor did it please
North Korea, which charged Tokyo with a breach of
both law and faith.[85] As the "final" expiration
date of the agreement approached, however, the Sato
Government appeared to have second thoughts on the
repatriation issue. It agreed to renegotiate with
North Korea in Moscow in August, 1967. Representatives of the Red Cross Societies of both countries
met in Moscow from August 25, to September 23, 1967,
but failed to produce any agreement.[86]

     In November, however, Japan proposed another
conference, to which North Korea promptly agreed.
The new conference, which opened in Colombo, Ceylon,
on November 27, proved to be more productive than
the Moscow talks. Within a few days, both sides
agreed that 16,000 more Korean residents in Japan,
who had already applied for repatriation to North
Korea, would be allowed to repatriate themselves.[87]
While negotiations were in progress, the Japanese
Government permitted the departure of 250 Koreans
for North Korea. They left the Japanese port of
Nigata aboard a Soviet vessel for the port of
Ch'ŏngjin on December 22. Thus the formal expiration of the Calcutta Agreement on November 12,
appeared to be meaningless in actual practice.
Angered by these developments, South Korea announced
that it would send three members of its National
Assembly to Tokyo and Geneva to lodge a "strong

protest" with the Japanese Red Cross and the International Red Cross, respectively. Dong-A Ilbo,
South Korea's largest newspaper, editorially criticized Tokyo for its "stunning duplicity" and voiced
a grave concern for the future of R.O.K.-Japanese
relations.[88] On January 13, 1968, the Colombo talks
reportedly reached a settlement, under the terms of
which repatriation would continue until July, 1968.[89]

     North Korea's desire to continue the repatria-
tion process as long as possible was eminently
justifiable in terms of its perceived national self-
interest. Apart from the obvious propaganda effect,
the transaction provided P'yŏngyang with a golden
opportunity to infiltrate both Japan and South
Korea. In November, 1967, for example, the Japanese
police arrested an official of the Japanese Foreign
Ministry on charges of handing over secret documents
to North Korean agents.[90] Moreover, according to
South Korean charges, huge quantities of strategic
materials were regularly smuggled into North Korea
by the repatriates.[91] On the other hand, Japan's
willingness to strain its ties with South Korea
over the repatriation issue reflected not only the
mounting pressure from its left-wing elements but
also its increasing uneasiness over the Korean
minority problem. Another factor, no doubt, was
the growing economic dependence of South Korea on
Japan. As Soon Sung Cho argues, Sough Korea was
by no means vital to Japan's economic interests,
whereas Japan was becoming more and more valuable
to the South Korean economy.[92]

     Nevertheless, the fact remained that Japan's
over-all posture was unmistakably pro-Seoul. At
the United Nations, it went out of its way to make
its support of South Korea fully known. Although
it would have sufficed merely to vote for pro-Seoul
resolutions, the Japanese delegation made speeches
in support of South Korea's position in 1966 and
1967.[93] In July, 1967, Prime Minister Sato attended
the inauguration of President Chung Hee Park in
Seoul, thus becoming the first Japanese chief
executive to enter Korea since 1945. Meanwhile,
North Korea stepped up its anti-Japanese propaganda. It accused the Japanese Government of
illegally attempting to suppress and harass the
Chōren-run educational establishments in Japan,
and contemptuously labeled Prime Minister Sato as
"Washington's agent in Tokyo"--that is, an American
puppet.[94]

As already noted, P'yŏngyang's animosity
toward Tokyo had absolutely no effect on its attitude toward individual Japanese citizens. Thus the
KWP has developed a singularly warm friendship with
the Japanese Communist Party. In February, 1959,
a JCP delegation headed by Miyamoto Kenji, General
Secretary of the JCP Central Committee, visited
P'yŏngyang on its way home from Moscow, where it
had attended the Twenty-first Congress of the CPSU,
and conferred with the leadership of the KWP. In
a joint communiqué issued after the conference, the
leaders of the two parties voiced complete agreement on major issues and declared their common
determination to struggle against American imperialism and for world peace.[95] In the summer of
1964, when the JCP came under attack from Moscow
for supporting Peking in the Sino-Soviet dispute,
the KWP, which was then openly identified with
the CCP, lost no time in coming to its defense.[96]
A top-level JCP delegation, also led by Miyamoto
Kenji, visited P'yŏngyang again in March, 1966.[97]
Another JCP delegation, led by Sunama Ichiro, a
member of the JCP Central Committee, was in North
Korea in May, 1967, indicating the continuance of
warm JCP-KWP ties.[98] Aside from their common
hatred of American imperialism, the two parties
share the conviction that interparty relations
within the Communist camp must be marked by independence and noninterference in the affairs of
fraternal parties. Both parties thus have dis-
sociated themselves from the "dogmatism" of the
CCP and have visibly improved their standing in
Moscow.[99]

In brief, North Korea has managed to maintain
informal relations with Japan in the form of trade,
formally nongovernmental but actually governmental
negotiations, and people-to-people diplomacy.
Tokyo's pro-American posture has been a perennial
source of conflict between the two countries, and,
more recently, the conclusion of the R.O.K.-Japanese
Normalization Treaty has virtually foreclosed any
possibility of reconciliation between P'yŏngyang
and Tokyo in the near future. Nevertheless, mutual
interests--particularly the value to North Korea of
continued ties, no matter how tenuous, with Japan--
ensure that trade and other "nongovernmental"
relations will remain intact for many years to
come.

NORTH KOREA AND THE WEST

North Korea's declared policy of separating economics from politics has enabled it to trade with capitalist nations with no apparent embarrassment. The list of P'yŏngyang's capitalist trading partners includes Japan, Austria, France, Great Britain, West Germany, and Holland. Furthermore, it has also made plain its desire to establish relations with "nations which have different social systems" in the spirit of peaceful coexistence. However, it has yet to establish diplomatic relations with any of the Western nations.

The available evidence indicates that individual visitors from Western nations began to arrive in North Korea shortly after the Korean Armistice. From August 14, to August 25, 1954, members of the Danish and British delegations to a world conference of the International Democratic Women's League joined their Romanian colleagues in visiting P'yŏngyang. A delegation of the World Democratic Youth League visiting the North Korean capital at about the same time (August 15-30, 1954) was led by an American woman.[100] In August, 1957, a group of French artists made a four-day visit to North Korea.[101]

In 1959, North Korea announced the establishment of Swedish-North Korean and Norwegian-North Korean Friendship Societies in Sweden and Norway, respectively. It claimed that such moves reflected the rising interest in North Korea on the part of "progressive social elements in capitalist countries."[102] In November, 1960, a North Korean trade delegation visited Austria at the invitation of the Austrian Chamber of Commerce and signed a two-year trade agreement with the Austrian Joint Economic Council. Under the agreement, trade missions would be set up in both Vienna and P'yŏngyang. North Korea, it was agreed, would export to Austria iron, lumber, textile, foodstuffs, handicrafts, and other materials, and Austria would export to North Korea aluminum, electric cables, chemicals, and other products. Representatives of the Austrian Joint Economic Council made a return visit to P'yŏngyang in April, 1960.[103]

In May, 1963, a West German industrial firm approached North Korea with an offer to help install thermal power plants. West Germany, through private sources, also indicated an interest in training North Korean technicians. It was additionally proposed that North Korea open a trade exhibit in West Germany. Generous terms for deferred payment were reportedly offered to the P'yŏngyang authorities by West Germany. In October of the same year, representatives of the British Association for the Promotion of International Trade visited P'yŏngyang to work out an agreement with their North Korean counterparts for bilateral trade. Under the agreement, North Korea would export to Great Britain iron ore and other minerals, chemical products, agricultural products, and other commodities, and would import from Great Britain special machines, ships, synthetic fibers, and other materials. A month later, an export manager of a Dutch industrial concern came to North Korea to explore trade opportunities. In February, 1964, a trade delegation from Holland conferred at length in P'yŏngyang with North Korean trade officials.[104] That substantial agreements were reached in those negotiations was indicated by the arrival of the 11,000-ton Paektusan Ho, the first Dutch ship ever to be purchased by North Korea, in the port of Ch'ŏngjin in January, 1965. Meanwhile, in October, 1964, a French businessman visited P'yŏngyang on a private trade mission. British businessmen were in North Korea in March, 1965, on a similar mission.[105]

British and French businessmen were also reported in North Korea in early 1966. In an interview with The P'yŏngyang Times, Ronald James Gatehouse of the Entores, Ltd., in England said that he had concluded a number of trade agreements on behalf of his company with North Korean trading corporations. Praising the high quality of North Korean machine tools and metal products, Gatehouse stated that a mutually profitable trade could develop between North Korea and Great Britain. He added that he saw no obstacles to such a trade.[106] The same newspaper also interviewed a visiting French businessman, Maurice V. Bracka of Getraco Finmetal in France. Bracka revealed that "many French trading corporations have long had trade relations with North Korean trade corporations." He said that he had concluded, during his North Korean visit, "long-term contracts for the purchase of large quantities of non-ferrous metals, ferrous metal products and cement." Echoing the high praise for North Korean products voiced by Gatehouse, the Frenchman predicted that North Korea would become "one of the outstanding machine-selling nations in the world."[107]

It is, then, apparent that North Korea is not totally isolated from the West. Nor has it closed its doors completely to capitalist nations of the West. However, it is equally clear that, as far as political and diplomatic intercourse is concerned, P'yŏngyang has all but written off the Western nations. It has sworn to continue its struggle to eradicate all "Western imperialists and their lackeys" from the face of earth. Heading the list of its archenemies, of course, is the United States. Great Britain is frequently lumped together with the United States as objects of P'yŏngyang's anti-Western diatribe. Its attitude toward France is mixed: Although French colonialism has been condemned on several occasions, President de Gaulle's criticisms of American policies and actions have invariably drawn loud applause from Nodong Sinmun.

That North Korea has played host to journalists and scholars from such Western nations as Australia, Canada, Britain, and France can be ascertained from a number of sources. Thus the names of a French journalist and a "Canadian public figure"--Jean-Emil Vidal and Nora Rodd, respectively--appear in a North Korean publication, along with their favorable impressions of the P'yŏngyang regime.[108] Joan Robinson, the noted Cambridge economist, also reported having visited North Korea twice, in 1954 and 1964.[109] Most recently, Wilfred Burchett, an Australian writer, visited P'yŏngyang and had an interview with Kim Il-sŏng. His dispatch from the North Korean capital, written for the Associated Press, appeared in The New York Times on May 15, 1967.

There is no need to recapitulate the reasons for North Korea's wholehearted opposition to the United States. A careful reading of Nodong Sinmun for the entire post-Korean War period reveals that North Korea's militantly anti-American posture has become so entrenched that the chances for a reconciliation between the two countries are practically nonexistent. P'yŏngyang has consistently depicted

the United States as the most despicable of all
possible enemies. A root cause of all the difficulties and frustrations with which the Korean
people are now faced, American imperialism must be
mercilessly annihilated, it insists. As Kim Il-sŏng
puts it:

> Central to the American imperialists'
> policy of colonizing and subjugating
> South Korea is the transformation of
> South Korea into a base of American
> military aggression, a military
> appendage. Hardly had the American
> imperialists set their feet in South
> Korea when they began to pursue
> their sinister objectives of making
> an American colony out of South
> Korea and then of using it as a
> stepping stone for the conquest of
> all of Korea and of Asia. In order
> to accomplish these objectives,
> they are endeavoring to retain their
> colonial domination of South Korea
> at all costs.
> ....
>   No imperialist power can subju-
> gate the Korean people and the peo-
> ples of Asia.
>
>   The imperialist aggressors are
> bound to perish, and our people are
> bound to triumph. Our great tasks
> of liberating the South Korean
> people and unifying our fatherland
> shall be accomplished.[110]

Significantly, however, North Korea has been careful
not to say that it will attack and crush without
provocation the "American imperialists" who are
occupying South Korea. Its Foreign Ministry statement of April 7, 1967, said:

> If the American imperialist aggres-
> sors should start a new war in
> Korea, the Korean People's Army
> and the entire Korean people who
> are armed would deal a crushing
> blow to them, thus eliminating
> each and every one of them.

> The American imperialists
> shall never be forgiven for all
> the crimes they have committed
> in Korea; they shall pay for
> their crimes with their own
> blood....[111]

In short, P'yŏngyang's intense hatred of American imperialism is tempered by its realistic appraisal of America's formidable military capacity.

Of some relevance for North Korea's anti-Western posture is its attitude toward international law. Some general, and necessarily superficial, observations can be made here. As might be expected, P'yŏngyang has repeatedly paid lip service to the sanctity of international law principles. Thus the Foreign Ministry of the D.P.R.K. declared on April 5, 1965, that Korean residents in Japan were entitled to the protection of their rights "as resident aliens commonly recognized by international law." It called on the Japanese Government to safeguard the life, property, and other rights of these residents "in accordance with all the principles of international law and international customs."[112] International law was also invoked on May 17, 1967, when North Korea condemned the alleged suppression by the Japanese Government of the rights of Korean residents in Japan. "The Government of the D.P.R.K.," it said, "strongly condemns the repeated suppression of, and atrocities against, Korean citizens in Japan being perpetrated by the Japanese Government in wanton disregard of the principles of both international law and humanitarianism."[113]

It is worth noting that North Korea has officially embraced the principles of international law embodied in the Charter of the United Nations. Although it has consistently denounced the United Nations as a tool of Anglo-American imperialism, P'yŏngyang has carefully refrained from attacking the principles for which it stands. In the preamble to the Treaty of Friendship, Cooperation, and Mutual Assistance between the D.P.R.K. and the U.S.S.R., signed in Moscow on July 6, 1961, is found the following expression: "aspiring to maintain and solidify the peace and security in the Far East and in the whole world on the basis of the purposes and principles of the United Nations." This phrase is conspicuously absent from a similar treaty concluded

five days later between the D.P.R.K. and the P.R.C.[11]
North Korea's attitude toward the United Nations has
been markedly influenced by the world body's participation in the Korean War. As noted, P'yŏngyang
has argued that the world organization has degenerated into a mere tool of imperialism as a result of
its participation as a belligerent in the three-
year conflict. Prior to that experience, North
Korea was just as eager as its southern rival to
gain admission to the United Nations. It applied
for U.N. membership at least on two occasions--in
October, 1948, and again in February, 1949--only to
be rebuked.[115] Moreover, it has indicated its
willingness to send its representatives to the world
organization by strenuously insisting on its right
to be heard during the annual U.N. debate on the
Korean question.

    To sum up, North Korea's uncompromising hos-
tility toward the Western nations in general and
the United States in particular is tempered by its
awareness of the potentially profitable commercial
intercourse with them. It has thus established
trade relations of a nominal scale with a number
of Western nations. P'yŏngyang has hosted scores
of Western visitors--mostly journalists, public
figures, and scholars--who have typically reciprocated North Korean hospitality by singing high
praises for the Communist regime before Western
audiences.

NOTES TO CHAPTER 4

    1. On the definition, traits, and problems
of the Third World, see J.D.B. Miller, The Politics
of the Third World (New York: Oxford University
Press, 1966).

    2. Chŏson chungang yŏn'gam, 1965, pp. 123-24;
Nodong Sinmun, July 26, 1966, and March 14, 1967;
Minju Chosŏn, May 19, 1967.

    3. Chŏson chungang yŏn'gam, 1958, pp. 93-94;
Tōitsu Chōsen nenkan, 1965-66, pp. 74-77.

    4. Chŏson chungang yŏn'gam, 1959, pp. 151-52.

    5. Ibid., p. 151.

6. Chŏson chungang yŏn'gam, 1960, p. 172.

7. Chŏson chungang yŏn'gam, 1961, pp. 141-42.

8. Ibid., pp. 142-43.

9. Ibid., pp. 143-44.

10. See Nodong Sinmun, October 24 and 26, 1960; December 1 and 7, 1960.

11. Chŏson chungang yŏn'gam, 1961, p. 144.

12. Chŏson chungang yŏn'gam, 1962, pp. 214-15.

13. Ibid., pp. 215-16.

14. Tōitsu Chōsen nenkan, 1965-66, pp. 82, 84.

15. Chŏson chungang yŏn'gam, 1962, pp. 214, 216-17.

16. Tōitsu Chōsen nenkan, 1965-66, p. 84.

17. Nodong Sinmun, April 18, 1961.

18. Chŏson chungang yŏn'gam, 1962, pp. 213-14.

19. Chŏson chungang yŏn'gam, 1963, pp. 189-91; Tōitsu Chōsen nenkan, 1965-66, pp. 85-87.

20. Chŏson chungang yŏn'gam, 1964, pp. 158-65.

21. See supra, pp. 97-100. For the text of the P'yŏngyang Declaration see Nodong Sinmun, June 24, 1964; for the significance North Korea attached to the event, see the Nodong Sinmun editorial of the same date, "The Demonstration of Friendship and Solidarity Among the Peoples Struggling Against Colonialism, Both Old and New, and For a New Way of Life."

22. Nodong Sinmun, October 29, 1964.

23. Ibid., November 5, 1964.

24. Ibid., January 17, 1965.

25. Chŏson chungang yŏn'gam, 1965, pp. 122-23.

26. Nodong Sinmun, April 16, 1965. For editorial reaction, see ibid., April 23, 1965.

27. Tōitsu Chōsen nenkan, 1965-66, p. 94.

28. Nodong Sinmun, March 22, 1966.

29. Ibid., April 26, 1966.

30. Ibid., July 26, 1966.

31. Ibid., October 13, 1966.

32. It visited the U.A.R., Iraq, and Syria. Ibid., August 18, 1966.

33. Ibid., October 5, 1966.

34. Ibid., October 19 and 21, 1966; November 14, 1966.

35. Ibid., December 29, 1966.

36. Soon Sung Cho, "Japan's Two Koreas Policy and the Problems of Korean Unification," Asian Survey, VII, 10 (October, 1967), 711.

37. Nodong Sinmun, October 28, 1966.

38. For his report, see Minju Chosŏn, May 19, 1967.

39. Ibid., June 7 and 8, 1967.

40. Ibid., June 11, 1967.

41. See Dong-A Ilbo, October 12-17, 20, 23, 1967. The South Vietnamese delegation was similarly humiliated by Algeria.

42. Ibid., October 13-16, 1967.

43. Ibid., October 31 and November 3, 1967.

44. The Chicago Daily News, November 10, 1967.

45. Dong-A Ilbo, October 20, 1967.

46. Ibid., November 11, 1967.

47. The Washington Evening Star, July 14, 1965; Nodong Sinmun, July 19, 1966; Kŭlloja, October, 1966, pp. 87-88.

48. Chŏson chungang yŏn'gam, 1958-1965, "Foreign Relations--Vietnam," and Tōitsu Chōsen nenkan, 1965-66, pp. 52-94. See also recent issues of Nodong Sinmun or Minju Chosŏn.

49. Nodong Sinmun, January 10, 1965.

50. The Washington Evening Star, July 14, 1965.

51. For Ho's letter, see Nodong Sinmun, January 31, 1966; for Ch'oe's reply, see ibid., February 2, 1966.

52. Ibid., April 2, 1966.

53. Ibid.

54. Ibid., July 19, 1966.

55. Ibid., September 1 and 4, 1966.

56. Kŭlloja, October, 1966, pp. 7-9.

57. See November and December, 1966, issues of Nodong Sinmun.

58. Ibid., December 2, 1966.

59. The New York Times, December 22 and 23, 1966; Dong-A Ilbo, September 18, 1967; NBC News (Huntley-Brinkley Report), September 19, 1967.

60. Nodong Sinmun, February 12, 1967.

61. For a recent statement, see Minju Chosŏn, May 23, 1967.

62. One Korea, October, 1967, p. 21. This is published monthly by Tōitsu Chōsen Shimbun-sha in Tokyo, Japan--an organization dedicated to the goal of Korean unification but with marked pro-P'yŏngyang orientation.

63. For the meaning of explicit and implicit recognition and relations officieuses, see Herbert W. Briggs (ed.), The Law of Nations: Cases, Documents, and Notes (2d ed.; New York: Appleton-Century-Crofts, Inc., 1952), pp. 125-27.

64. Tōitsu Chōsen nenkan, 1965-66, p. 69; ibid.,
1964, p. 345.

65. Ibid., 1965-66, pp. 71-73; Kiwon Chung,
"Japanese-North Korean Relations Today," Asian Survey, IV, 4 (April, 1964), 791-93.

66. Tōitsu Chōsen nenkan, 1965-66, pp. 73-74.
For the list of Japanese visitors, see Chosŏn
chungang yŏn'gam, 1958-65, and also Nodong Sinmun.

67. Chosŏn chungang yŏn'gam, 1958, p. 36.

68. Ibid., 1959, p. 151.

69. Nodong Sinmun, September 26, 1958.

70. There were an estimated 600,000 Koreans
in Japan when the repatriation campaign began. The
rival organization to Chōren is the Association of
Republic of Korea Residents in Japan (Mindan).
For the organization and rivalry of the two groups,
see Tōitsu Chōsen nenkan, 1965-66, pp. 577-86 and
861-72.

71. On the status of the Korean residents in
Japan, consult Edward W. Wagner, The Korean Minority
in Japan (New York: Institute of Pacific Relations,
1951); Soon Sung Cho, "Japan's Two Koreas Policy
and the Problem of Korean Unification," pp. 708-9
and works cited in footnotes 21 and 22 of the article

72. Tōitsu Chōsen nenkan, 1964, pp. 344-45;
ibid., 1965-66, p. 79; Chung, "Japanese-North Korean
Relations Today," pp. 795-800.

73. Dong-A Ilbo, November 14, 1967. More on
the repatriation issue shortly.

74. Chung, op. cit., p. 794.

75. Tōitsu Chōsen nenkan, 1964, p. 435; Cho,
"Japan's Two Koreas Policy...," pp. 712-13.

76. Ibid.

77. Ibid., pp. 713-16.

78. Nodong Sinmun, February 26, April 8, June
10, 1965.

79. Tōitsu Chōsen nenkan, 1965-66, pp. 584-85.

80. For a typical expression of North Korea's anti-Japanese feelings, see the editorial of The P'yŏngyang Times on January 13, 1966, "Let Us Fight Against Japanese Militarism."

81. Cho, "Japan's Two Koreas Policy...," p. 719.

82. The Washington Post, July 22, 1966.

83. Cho, "Japan's Two Koreas Policy...," p. 719.

84. The New York Times, August 21, 1966.

85. Nodong Sinmun, August 26, 1966; April 28, 1967.

86. Dong-A Ilbo, September 25, 1967.

87. Ibid., November 27 and 28, 1967; December 1, 4, 25, 26, and 27, 1967.

88. Ibid., December 22, 25, 26, and 27, 1967.

89. Ibid., January 15, 1968.

90. Ibid., November 30, 1967.

91. Ibid., December 7, 1967.

92. Cho, "Japan's Two Koreas Policy...," p. 717.

93. Dong-A Ilbo, October 31, 1967.

94. Nodong Sinmun, March 18 and 20, 1967; Minju Chosŏn, May 18, 1967. North Korea's charge pertained to the prolonged review of the status of Chōsen University in Tokyo by an accreditation board. No decision had been handed down as of December, 1967.

95. Nodong Sinmun, February 28, 1959.

96. Ibid., July 27, 1964.

97. Ibid., March 12, 1966. For an editorial underscoring the significance of the visit and reaffirming KWP-JCP solidarity, see ibid., March 22, 1966.

98. Minju Chosŏn, May 2 and 14, 1967.

99. The continuing deterioration of JCP-CCP relations was underlined by the former's recent decision to withdraw its permanent representatives from Peking. See The Washington Post, July 19, 1967.

100. She was identified as Gloria Sekhon (a transliteration from Japanese). See Tōitsu Chōsen nenkan, 1965-66, p. 71.

101. Ibid., p. 76.

102. Chosŏn chungang yŏn'gam, 1960, p. 172.

103. Ibid., 1961, p. 144.

104. Tōitsu Chōsen nenkan, 1964, p. 348.

105. Ibid., 1965-66, p. 688.

106. The P'yŏngyang Times, March 17, 1966.

107. Ibid., March 31, 1966.

108. Democratic People's Republic of Korea (P'yŏngyang: Foreign Languages Publishing House, 1964), pp. 21-22, 28-29.

109. Robinson, op. cit.

110. Kim Il-song, "Hyŏn chŏngse wa uri tang ŭi kwaŏp" ("The Present Political Situation and the Tasks of Our Party"), Kŭlloja, October, 1966, pp. 43, 54.

111. Nodong Sinmun, April 8, 1967. (Emphasis added.)

112. Ibid., April 6, 1965.

113. Minju Chosŏn, May 18, 1967.

114. Nodong Sinmun, July 7 and 12, 1961. For North Korea's attitude toward the United Nations, see ibid., January 8, 1965 (editorial), and The P'yŏngyang Times, February 17, 1966.

115.   See Key P. Yang, "The North Korean Regime, 1945-1955," unpublished Master's thesis, The American University, Washington, D.C., 1958, p. 149.

CHAPTER **5** SUMMARY AND CONCLUSION

   In the space of two decades North Korea has
evolved from a fragile Soviet satellite into a
nation vigorously pursuing and asserting politico-
economic independence. The most striking fact
about the North Korean experience is the amazing
durability of its political leadership: Kim Il-
sŏng, the chief of both its governmental and Party
apparatus, has not only survived all the turbulent
crises, internal and external, that have plagued
his regime, but he has so firmly consolidated his
power as to be indomitable.

   A former anti-Japanese partisan leader in
Manchuria, Kim won the favor and confidence of
the Kremlin and was finally installed as the
leader of North Korea under Soviet auspices. If
his rise to the position of prominence and power
was aided by the Soviets, however, his consolidation of political power was largely his own doing.
Applying Stalinist tactics, he ruthlessly eliminated
all political rivals, both actual and potential.
By the end of 1956, he had succeeded in subduing
all opposition elements. Practically all stragetic
positions in the Party and the Government were
safely in the hands of his own faction, the partisan
group.

   One of the most consistent themes in Kim's
rhetoric has been his militant nationalism--his
unquenchable desire to turn Korea into a strong,
proud, and independent nation. He has steadfastly
insisted that political independence is but an
empty slogan unless and until it is underpinned by
economic independence. He has thus vigorously
pursued the twin goals of economic self-reliance
and political autonomy for North Korea. However,

if Kim is a nationalist, he is also a power-hungry
and supremely egocentric politician. Practicing
the Machiavellian dictum that the end justifies
the means, he has sought personal power and glory
at any expense. The cult of Kim Il-sŏng in North
Korea today is matched only by the deification of
Mao Tse-tung in contemporary China.

As North Korea slowly but steadily recovered
from the shattering impact of the Korean War--a
gravely miscalculated venture on the part of both
Kim Il-sŏng and Stalin--Kim also began to assert
the self-identity of the P'yŏngyang regime. The
introduction of the now fashionable slogan, chuch'e
("self-identity" or "autonomy"), in his famous 1955
speech marked a significant milestone in North
Korea's path to independence. Arguing that North
Korea should emulate neither the Soviet Union nor
Communist China but should search for Korean solutions to Korean problems, Kim set the stage for
increasingly autonomous North Korean behavior in
the arena of international Communist politics.

The ever-widening schism between Moscow and
Peking must have presented P'yŏngyang with a serious
dilemma. The two giants of the Communist camp had
equally formidable claims for the loyalty of North
Korea, for although the Soviet Union created North
Korea, the People's Republic of China saved it from
annihilation. With which should the KWP side?
Fortunately for P'yŏngyang, there was an escape
route, the policy of nonalignment. And that was
precisely the path that North Korea chose in the
formative stage of the Sino-Soviet conflict. By
1962, however, North Korea found itself unmistakably
in the Chinese camp.

The single most important element in P'yŏngyang's
behavior was probably the coup d'état of May 16,
1961, that changed political leadership in Seoul.
The new military regime in South Korea was militantly
anti-Communist and appeared immensely menacing to
North Korea. Kim Il-sŏng's hurried trip to Moscow
and Peking in July, 1961, to conclude mutual-defense
treaties with both was symptomatic of his heightened
sense of alarm over the developments in South Korea.
At a time when North Korea's anti-imperialist feelings were reaching a new high, the Soviet Union
was busily pursuing the "revisionist" policy of
peaceful coexistence and detente with the West.

Furthermore, Kim Il-song was increasingly uneasy over Khrushchev's de-Stalinization and antipersonality cult campaigns. Having followed the footsteps of Stalin, Kim was acutely conscious of the implications of the campaigns. Whatever the reasons, North Korea began not only to echo Peking's views on major international and intrabloc issues, but also to defend openly the CCP against attacks from "revisionist parties" in the Communist bloc. The price P'yŏngyang had to pay for siding with Peking was a dear one: It was cold-shouldered, scorned, and ridiculed by practically all members of the socialist orbit save Communist China and Albania, another staunch Chinese ally. At the peak of P'yŏngyang-Moscow hostility in late 1964, North Korea went so far as to criticize openly the Soviet Union.

In early 1965, however, North Korea and the Soviet Union achieved a rapprochement. The initiative apparently came from Moscow, for P'yŏngyang's changed mood became apparent on the heels of a visit by Premier Aleksei N. Kosygin to the North Korean capital in February, 1965. The dominant factor in P'yŏngyang's shift of posture was probably economic. Its overly ambitious Seven-Year Economic Plan was lagging behind schedule. Renewed economic and technical assistance from the Soviet Union could not have been more welcome. Equally valuable was Soviet military assistance, which was vitally needed to modernize North Korea's defense machinery. Moreover, Moscow's stiff opposition to "the U.S. aggression in Vietnam" and its assistance to Hanoi had expelled Kim Il-song's fear that the Soviets were on the verge of selling out to the imperialists. No doubt, Kim's nationalism must have played its part in reappraising his ideological posture. His close alliance with Mao Tse-tung's China had helped to create the impression that North Korea was a Chinese satellite. Nothing could be more annoying to the independent-minded North Korean dictator. P'yŏngyang's increasing alienation in the Communist camp must also have been a source of discomfort. Another probable factor was the capacity of the Soviet Union to advertise North Korea's unification formula during the annual U.N. debate over Korea--a capacity which Peking sadly lacked. Finally, there was the convenient power shift in the Kremlin. The revisionist Khrushchev had been ousted from the Soviet

hierarchy, and the new Brezhnev-Kosygin team was
at the helm. Although the new Soviet leaders were
no less revisionist than their predecessor, they
were apparently offering Kim Il-sŏng an olive
branch. In short, the time was ripe for a reconciliation.

A renewal of friendly Soviet-North Korean
relations was marked by a sudden increase in the
number of Soviet visitors to North Korea. A new
agreement on Soviet economic, technical, and
military assistance to North Korea quickly followed.
Sino-North Korean intercourse began to taper off.
However, North Korea made it clear that its
rapprochement with the Soviet Union did not mean
that it had once again become an obedient satellite
of the Kremlin. P'yŏngyang insisted that it was
its own master and would allow itself to be pushed
around by no one. The most explicit statement of
its position was made in the Nodong Sinmun editorial
of August 12, 1966, entitled "Let Us Defend Our
Independence." Echoing Kim Il-sŏng's themes on
the importance of having a national pride and of
following an independent policy, the editorial
declared that the KWP recognized no superior party
which has authority to meddle in the affairs of
other fraternal parties. It also ridiculed the
dogmatism of the CCP, deploring the failure of the
Communist camp to form a united front against imperialism in Vietnam.

Ever since he assumed leadership in North
Korea, Kim Il-sŏng has had one towering wish: to
be the ruler of a unified and independent Korea.
Having failed to achieve his goal by military means,
Kim has tenaciously explored the so-called peaceful
approach. He has made repeated proposals to establish postal, cultural, and economic relations between the two halves of Korea; to hold negotiations
for the solution of the unification problem; and
to form a "confederation" of the North and South
Korean governments. Simultaneously, he has stepped
up propaganda and subversive campaigns toward South
Korea. His transparent motive, coupled with his
insistent demand for the withdrawal of U.S. troops
from South Korea, however, has discouraged the
Seoul regime from taking any of the proposals
seriously. More recently, North Korea has been
resorting increasingly to guerrilla-type techniques
designed to undermine the political and economic

stability of South Korea. There has been a sharp
increase in the use of political violence by North
Korean agents both in the DMZ and in the South Korea
proper. The latest and boldest manifestations of
P'yŏngyang's intransigence came in January, 1968,
with the abortive commando raid on the Presidential
mansion and the seizure of the U.S.S. Pueblo in
the Wŏnsan Bay. Barring revolutionary upheavals
in either or both of the two regimes, which would
radically alter its or their ideological complexions, a negotiated settlement of the unification
question remains only a remote possibility.

As North Korea inched toward the goal of
politico-economic independence, it expanded its
diplomatic activities in the world arena. It found
a fertile ground for making new friends in the
Third World--the conglomeration of newly independent
and developing nations in Asia, Africa, and Latin
America. Not only do these nations share with
North Korea their distaste for Western colonialism
and imperialism, they instinctively lend a sympathetic ear to North Korea's incessant apotheosis
of national independence and a self-reliant economy.
What makes P'yŏngyang's rhetoric doubly convincing
is its ability to produce substantial evidence of
actual accomplishments. P'yŏngyang has thus far
collected an impressive number of friends, allies,
and trading partners in all corners of the globe.
Its debut in the world arena has produced not only
material gains, but also psychic satisfaction.
It has repeatedly boasted that its international
prestige is steadily rising.

North Korea has developed singularly warm ties
with Fidel Castro's Cuba. Their common hatred of
"American imperialism" must have cemented their
mutual admiration and friendship. P'yŏngyang's
uncompromising opposition to the United States has
also made it one of the staunchest allies of North
Vietnam and the National Liberation Front of South
Vietnam. Its verbal support of the Vietnamese
"war of national liberation" and "anti-imperialist
struggle" has been unsurpassed. Its material
assistance to Hanoi has been considerable. It has
offered time and again to send its "volunteers" to
help repel the "American imperialist aggressors and
their running dogs" from the Vietnamese soil. As
noted, it has also been an outspoken proponent of
a united Communist front in Vietnam.

Kim Il-sŏng, however, refuses to allow Communist
ideology to subsume national self-interest completely. Even though he is totally opposed to the
capitalists, he is more than willing to establish
relations, in particular trade relations, with
"nations which have different social systems." North
Korea thus trades, through ostensibly nongovernmental channels, with such capitalist nations as Japan,
Austria, France, Great Britain, West Germany, and
Holland. Its opposition to the United States, however, is so strong and deep-rooted that there is
little or no chance of rapprochement between the
two. It continually depicts South Korea as a living
hell, making it abundantly clear that the root cause
of the South Korean misery is "the sinister aggressive designs of the American imperialists." The
vehemence and tenacity of its "hate-America" campaigns are truly staggering.

How do these disparate elements of North
Korea's foreign policy add up? In different words,
just what is North Korea's foreign policy? Jan
Triska's analytical scheme helps us to draw a composite picture of P'yŏngyang's over-all posture in
the world arena. First of all, what is the ideological component of its foreign policy? It seems
clear that North Korea is inextricably wedded to
the ideology of Marxism-Leninism. Although the
specific content of that ideology has never been
spelled out in clear and precise terms, it nevertheless provides P'yŏngyang with a frame of reference and basis for action. Its commitment to
socialist construction and revolution, its belief
in the eventual demise of capitalism, its opposition to imperialism, and its confidence in the
ultimate victory of Communism--all of these strongly
delimit the range of its international behavior.
Without acknowledging it publicly, North Korea has
co-opted a part of the "thought of Mao Tse-tung":
Mao's ideas on both guerrilla warfare and wars of
national liberation have become an integral part
of North Korea's official ideology. Supplementing
and sometimes supplanting Communist ideology is
North Korea's modernizing nationalism. To be more
accurate, Kim Il-sŏng's perceived self-interest,
which he equates with North Korea's national self-
interest, has been a powerful determinant of North
Korea's rhetoric and behavior. Kim is a firm
believer not only in the utility of the symbols of
nationalism in mobilizing the masses for rigorous

tasks of nation building, but also in the intrinsic virtues of nationalism as an end in itself. To build a strong and proud nation which can stand on its own feet has been one of his strongest desires.

The strategic objectives of North Korea's foreign policy may be summed up in two words: Communization and modernization. The two are inseparable. On the one hand, North Korea is intent on Communizing the entire Korean peninsula. This means, in effect, the political subjugation of South Korea. It also means the security of the present North Korean regime from both internal and external challenges. On the other hand, North Korea doggedly pursues the goal of economic modernization. Industrialization will not only increase its economic power and international prestige, but it will also appreciably enhance its ability to pursue the goal of Communization. By raising the living standard of the North Korean people, economic growth can make North Korea both more tolerable to its own people and more attractive to the South Korean people. That these twin goals emanate from and are guided by the ideologies of Communism and nationalism is quite obvious.

The major operational directions of North Korea's foreign policy have included the following: (1) neutrality in the Sino-Soviet dispute, (2) alliance with Peking, (3) rapprochement with Moscow, (4) military conquest of South Korea, (5) psychological warfare against South Korea, (6) guerrilla warfare in South Korea, (7) establishment and promotion of friendly relations with all nations professing opposition to imperialism and colonialism, (8) establishment of economic and cultural relations with all nations regardless of their ideological complexions, with the exception of the United States, and (9) vilification of the United States whenever and wherever possible.

The numerous tactical moves subordinate to these operational directions have already been described in the book. It has also been shown that propaganda plays an important part in North Korea's foreign policy. It serves as an indispensable tool of the ideological, strategic, operational, and tactical components of P'yŏngyang's international behavior. It is used not only to explain, justify, and defend

its actions, but also to confuse, deceive, and
denounce its enemy. Although it conceals more than
it reveals, it nonetheless yields valuable insights
into North Korea's problems and programs.

The preceding components are clearly inter-
dependent and interrelated. Any aspect of North
Korea's foreign policy is more clearly understandable in terms of its relation to the over-all
posture of the regime. North Korea's policy toward
the Moscow-Peking rift thus becomes more readily
comprehensible against the backdrop of the former's
obsessive dreams of Communizing South Korea and
building a self-reliant and prosperous economy.
Its diplomatic and economic offensive in the Third
World is also unmistakably related to its strategic
objectives, as is its posture toward the capitalist
Japan. To the extent that relations with other
nations, regardless of their ideology, promote
North Korea's long-term and short-term goals, P'yŏngyang avidly seeks them.

Although the ideology and strategy of North
Korea's foreign policy have remained remarkably
constant over the years, its operational directions
and tactics have been notably responsive to the
constantly changing internal and external situa-
tions. P'yŏngyang's oscillating posture toward
the Peking-Moscow quarrel has been influenced not
merely by its desire for autonomy and economic
growth, but also by the political and economic
climate of South Korea and the Vietnam War. In
addition, the results, be they fruitful or frus-
trating, of each operational direction as well as
the moods and attitudes of Peking and Moscow must
have entered into North Korean calculations. Similarly, P'yŏngyang's unification policies have been
a function of its own politico-economic-military
capabilities, its relations with Moscow and Peking,
its perception of South Korea's strengths and
vulnerabilities, and a host of other factors. The
sources of North Korean conduct in the Third World,
in Vietnam, in Japan, and vis-à-vis the capitalist
West are also to be found in the complex web of
its perceived interests, capabilities, and defi-
ciencies.

When measured against the yardstick of its
strategic objectives, North Korea's foreign policy
cannot be rated as a success. Its goal of

Communizing all of Korea remains as elusive as ever,
and its modernization program has apparently reached
a stalemate. Given the suffocating setting in
which the P'yŏngyang regime has had to operate,
however, its accomplishments in the international
arena are by no means unimpressive. Despite formidable obstacles, North Korea has managed not only
to survive as a viable politico-economic entity,
but also to grow in power and prestige. Driven by
an insatiable appetite for power and glory, Kim
Il-sŏng has succeeded in launching his regime on
the path of autonomy. Having consolidated his
political leadership beyond challenge, he has
applied his virtually unlimited power to the task
of mobilizing the North Korean people for the
industrialization of the country. Simultaneously,
he has asserted a growing measure of operational
autonomy in the fragmented Communist camp. His
Stalinist tactics, although abominable, have been
thoroughly consistent with his perceived self-
interest--the preservation and enhancement not only
of his personal power, but of the national power
of the regime he so firmly controls.

The real test of the viability of the North
Korean political system has yet to come, when it
has to face its first succession crisis. The
relative youth (born in 1912) and apparent health
of Kim Il-sŏng, together with his firm political
control, however, suggest that such a test will be
long in coming. Even in the unlikely event of
Kim's sudden death, it does not appear likely that
his successor or successors would radically alter
North Korea's posture in the world arena. When
Kim does pass from the North Korean scene, political control will most probably remain in the
hands of the partisan group, whose members share
with its present leader, Kim Il-sŏng, a predominantly military background, relative youth and vigor,
and a low level of educational attainment.[1] Regardless of who among the group will assume power, the
ideology and strategy of North Korea's foreign
policy are likely to remain intact, at least for
the time being. North Korea will tirelessly pursue
its goal of building an economically powerful
nation at home and of enhancing its international
prestige abroad. It will not relax its efforts
to downgrade and harass South Korea and the United
States in the hope of unifying the Korean peninsula
under its Red banners. In doing all this, it will

loudly and proudly proclaim its independence of all external influences. Its unflagging quest for autonomy will become more vigorous than ever before.

NOTE TO CHAPTER 5

1. See Dae-Sook Suh, "The Elite Group of North Korea," paper read at the annual conference of the Association for Asian Studies, Chicago, Ill., March 20-22, 1967.

BIBLIOGRAPHY

BIBLIOGRAPHY

GOVERNMENT DOCUMENTS AND PUBLICATIONS

Chosŏn Chungang T'ongsinsa. Chosŏn chungang yŏn' gam (/North/ Korean Central Yearbook), 1949, 1950, 1951-52, 1954-55, 1956, 1958, 1959 (Domestic Affairs), 1959 (Foreign Affairs), 1960, 1961, 1962, 1963, 1964, 1965. P'yŏngyang: Chosŏn Chungang T'ongsinsa, 1949-65.

Chosŏn Minjujuŭi Inmin Konghwaguk Kwahagwŏn, Kyŏnje Pŏphak Yŏn'guso. Haebang hu uri nara ŭi inmin kyŏngje palchŏn (The Development of Our People's Economy in the Post-Liberation Period). P'yŏngyang: Kwahagwŏn Ch'ulp'ansa, 1960.

_____. P'al iro haebang sibo chunyŏn kinyŏm kyŏngje nonmumjip (Collected Economic Essays Commemorating the 15th Anniversary of the Korean Liberation). P'yŏngyang: Kwahagwŏn Ch'ulp'ansa, 1960.

Chosŏn Minjujuŭi Inmin Konghwaguk Kwahagwŏn, Yŏksa Yŏn'guso. Chosŏn t'ongsa (A General History of Korea). 3 vols. P'yŏngyang: Kwahagwŏn Ch'ulp'ansa, 1962.

Democratic People's Republic of Korea. 2 editions. P'yŏngyang: Foreign Languages Publishing House, 1958, 1964.

Democratic People's Republic of Korea, State Planning Commission, Central Statistical Board. Statistical Returns of National Economy of the Democratic People's Republic of Korea, 1946-1960. P'yŏngyang: Foreign Languages Publishing House, 1961.

Facts About Korea. P'yŏngyang: Foreign Languages Publishing House, 1961.

Facts Tell. P'yŏngyang: Foreign Languages Pub-
    lishing House, 1960.

Korean Handbook. P'yŏngyang: Foreign Languages
    Publishing House, 1959.

Postwar Rehabilitation and Development of the
    National Economy in the Democratic People's
    Republic of Korea. P'yŏngyang: Foreign
    Languages Publishing House, 1957.

U.S. Air Force, Human Resources Research Institute,
    Air University. A Preliminary Study of the
    Impact of Communism Upon Korea. Maxwell Air
    Force Base, Ala.: Human Resources Research
    Institute, Air University, USAF, 1951.

U.S. Army Command Reconnaissance Activities, Paci-
    fic (Field). North Korean Administrative
    Divisions: A Research Aid. 1959.

U.S. Congress, House, Committee on Foreign Affairs.
    Sino-Soviet Conflict: Report on Its Implica-
    tions. 89th Cong., 1st Sess. House Doc. No.
    237. Washington, D.C.: Government Printing
    Office, 1965.

U.S. Congress, Senate. Military Situation in the
    Far East. Hearings before the Committee on
    Armed Services and the Committee on Foreign
    Relations, U.S. Senate. 82nd Cong., 1st Sess.,
    1951.

U.S. Department of the Army. U.S. Army Area Hand-
    book for Korea. Department of the Army Pamphlet
    No. 550-41. Washington, D.C.: Government
    Printing Office, 1964.

U.S. Department of Commerce, Clearinghouse for
    Federal Scientific and Technical Information,
    Joint Publications Research Service. Economic
    Report on North Korea. 1964-1966.

_____. Political Report on North Korea. 1958-1959

_____. Translations of Political and Sociological
    Information on North Korea. 1964-1966.

_____. Translations on North Korea. 1966-1967.

U.S. Department of State, Historical Office. A
    Historical Summary of United States-Korean
    Relations, with a Chronology of Important
    Developments, 1834-1962. Department of State
    Publication No. 7446, Far Eastern Series No.
    115.

_____. North Korea: A Case Study in the Tech-
    niques of Takeover. Department of State
    Publication No. 7118, Far Eastern Series No.
    103. Washington, D.C.: Government Printing
    Office, 1961.

_____. The Record of Korean Unification, 1943-
    1960: Narrative Summary with Principal Docu-
    ments. Department of State Publication No.
    7084, Far Eastern Series No. 101. Washington,
    D.C.: Government Printing Office, 1960.

               PARTY DOCUMENTS AND PUBLICATIONS

Chŏngch'i kyŏngje hak (Political Economy). P'yŏng-
    yang: Chosŏn Nodongdang Ch'ulp'ansa, 1960.

Chosŏn Nodongdang chesamch'a taehoe chuyo munhŏnjip
    (Principal Documents of the Third Congress
    of the Korean Workers' Party). P'yŏngyang:
    Chosŏn Nodongdang Ch'ulp'ansa, 1956.

Chosŏn Nodongdang chesamch'a taehoe chuyo munhŏnjip
    (Principal Documents of the Fourth Congress
    of the Korean Workers' Party). P'yŏngyang:
    Chosŏn Nodongdang Ch'ulp'ansa, 1961.

Chosŏn Nodongdang kyuyak haesŏl (An Interpretation
    of the Regulations of the Korean Workers'
    Party). Tokyo: Hagu Sŏbang, 1960.

Documents of the Fourth Congress of the Workers'
    Party of Korea. P'yŏngyang: Foreign Languages
    Publishing House, 1961.

Han Im-kyŏk. Kim Il-sŏng tongji e ŭihan Chosŏn
    kongsangdang ch'anggŏn (The Establishment of
    the Korean Communist Party by Comrade Kim
    Il-sŏng). P'yŏngyang: Chosŏn Nodongdang Ch'-
    ulp'ansa, 1961.

Joint Statement of Chairman Liu Shao-chi and President Choi Yong Kun. Peking: Foreign Language Press, 1963.

Kim Il-sŏng. All for the Postwar Rehabilitation and Development of the National Economy. P'yŏngyang: North Korea Press, 1954.

_____. Kim Il-sŏng sŏnjip (Selected Works of Kim Il-sŏng). 6 vols. Vol. I (Original Title: Choguk ŭi t'ongil tongnip kwa minjuhwa rŭl wihayŏ /For the Unification, Independence, and Democratization of My Fatherland7) was published in 1949 by Kungnip Inmin Ch'ulp'ansa, P'yŏngyang. The remainder were published by Chosŏn Nodongdang Ch'ulp'ansa, P'yŏngyang. Their publication dates are as follows: Vol. II: 1964; Vol. III: 1954; Vol. IV: 1954 and 1960; Vol. V: 1960; Vol. VI: 1960.

_____. On Eliminating Dogmatism and Formalism and Establishing Jooche /chuch'e7 in Ideological Work. P'yŏngyang: Foreign Languages Publishing House, 1964.

_____. On Some Problems Concerning Party and State Affairs in the Present Stage of the Socialist Revolution. P'yŏngyang: Foreign Languages Publishing House, 1964.

_____. On the Tasks of the Socialist Working Youth League. P'yŏngyang: Foreign Languages Publishing House, 1964.

_____. Selected Works. 2 vols. P'yŏngyang: Foreign Languages Publishing House, 1965.

_____. Theses on the Socialist Agrarian Question in Our Country. P'yŏngyang: Foreign Languages Publishing House, 1964.

Kyŏngje kŏnsŏl (Economic Construction). P'yŏngyang: Chosŏn Nodongdang Ch'ulp'ansa, 1954.

Kyŏngje sangsik (Economic Common Sense). P'yŏngyang: Choson Nodongdang Ch'ulp'ansa, 1960.

Taejung chŏngch'i yongŏ sajŏn (Everyone's Dictionary of Political Terms). P'yŏngyang: Chosŏn Nodongdang Ch'ulp'ansa, 1959.

Third Congress of the Workers' Party of Korea,
    Documents and Materials: April 23-29, 1956.
    P'yŏngyang: Foreign Languages Publishing
    House, 1956.

Yun Sŭng-ho. Hangil t'ujaeng ki (The Record of Anti-
    Japanese Struggle). P'yŏngyang: Kungnip
    Ch'ulp'ansa, 1963.

                        BOOKS

Barnett, A. Doak (ed.). Communist Strategies in
    Asia. New York: Frederick A. Praeger, 1963.

Berger, Carl. The Korean Knot: A Military-Political
    History. Philadelphia: University of Penn-
    sylvania Press, 1957.

Black, Cyril E., and Thornton, Thomas P. Communism
    and Revolution: The Strategic Use of Political
    Violence. Princeton, N.J.: Princeton Univer-
    sity Press, 1964.

Brzezinski, Zbigniew. The Soviet Bloc. 2d ed.
    New York: Frederick A. Praeger, 1961.

Cho, Soon Sung. Korea in World Politics, 1940-
    1950: An Evaluation of American Responsi-
    bility. Berkeley: University of California
    Press, 1967.

Chung, Joseph S. (ed.). Patterns of Economic
    Development: Korea. Kalamazoo, Mich.:
    Korea Research and Publication, Inc., 1966.

Farley, Miriam S., and Dean, Vera M. Korea and
    World Politics. Toronto: Canadian Institute
    of International Affairs, 1950.

Floyd, David. Mao Against Khrushchev. New York:
    Frederick A. Praeger, 1964.

George, Alexander L. Propaganda Analysis: A
    Study of Inferences Made from Nazi Propaganda
    in World War II. Evanston, Ill.: Row, Peter-
    son & Co., 1959.

Gordenker, Leon. The United Nations and the Peace-
    ful Unification of Korea: The Politics of
    Field Operations, 1947-1950. Hague, The
    Netherlands: Martinus Nijhoff, 1959.

Griffith, William E. Albania and the Sino-Soviet
    Rift. Cambridge, Mass.: The M.I.T. Press,
    1963.

Gross, Feliks. Foreign Policy Analysis. New York:
    Philosophical Library, 1954.

Hōchō Kishadan. Kita Chōsen no kiroku (The Record
    of North Korea). Tokyo: Shintoku Shōsha,
    1960.

Hudson, G. F., Lowenthal, R., and MacFarquhar, R.
    (eds.). The Sino-Soviet Dispute. New York:
    Frederick A. Praeger, 1961.

Joy, Charles T. How Communists Negotiate. New
    York: The Macmillan Company, 1955.

Kim Ch'ang-sun. Pukhan sibonyŏn sa (Fifteen-Year
    History of North Korea). Seoul: Chimungak,
    1961.

_____. Yŏksa ŭi chŭngin (A Witness to History).
    Seoul: Han'guk Asea pan'gong Yŏnmaeng, 1956.

Kim Chŏng-myŏng /Kim Sho Mei/. Chōsen shinmin-
    shushugi kakumeishi (A History of the New
    Democratic Revolution in Korea). Tokyo:
    Gogatsu Shobo, 1953.

Kim Sam-gyu. Chōsen no shinjitsu (The Truth About
    Korea). Tokyo: Shiseido, 1960.

_____. Konnichi no Chōsen (Korea Today). Tokyo:
    Kawade Shobo, 1956.

Kolarz, Walter. The Peoples of the Soviet Far East.
    New York: Frederick A. Praeger, 1954.

Lee Chong-Sik. The Politics of Korean Nationalism.
    Berkeley: University of California Press, 1963.

Levi, Werner. Modern China's Foreign Policy.
    Minneapolis: University of Minnesota Press,
    1953.

London, Kurt (ed.). Unity and Contradiction. New
    York: Frederick A. Praeger, 1962.

McCune, George M., and Grey, Arthur L., Jr. Korea
    Today. Cambridge, Mass.: Harvard University
    Press, 1950.

Meade, Edward Grant. American Military Government
    in Korea. New York: King's Crown Press, 1951.

Naeoe Munje Yŏn'guso. Onŭl ŭi pukhan: pukkoe
    tokchae kucho ŭi haebu (North Korea Today: A
    Structural Analysis of the North Korean Puppet
    Regime's Dictatorship). Seoul: Naeoe Munje
    Yŏn'guso, 1962.

_____. Pukkoe ŭi p'abŏl t'ujaeng sa: pukkoe
    sipch'ilnyŏn choeak ŭi palchach'wi (A History
    of Factional Struggle in the North Korean
    Puppet Regime: The Footprints of Its Seventeen
    Years of Crime). Seoul: Naeoe Munje Yŏn'guso,
    1962.

_____. Chungsso nonjaeng munhŏnjip (Collected
    Documents of the Sino-Soviet Dispute). Seoul:
    Naeoe Munje Yŏn'guso, 1963.

Paige, Glenn D. The Korean People's Democratic
    Republic. Stanford, Calif.: The Hoover Insti-
    tution on War, Revolution, and Peace, 1966.

Pak Tong-un. Pukhan t'ongch'i kiguron (A Study of
    the Government Structure in North Korea).
    Seoul: Koryo Taehakkyo Ch'ulp'anbu, 1964.

_____. T'ongil munje yŏn'gu: kongsan chŏllyak
    non'go (A Study of the Unification Problem:
    Communist Tactics). Seoul: Taeoe Munje
    Yŏn'guso, 1960.

Rudolph, Philip. North Korea's Political and Eco-
    nomic Structure. New York: Institute of
    Pacific Relations, 1959.

Ryu, Hun. Study of North Korea. Seoul: Research
    Institute of Internal and External Affairs,
    1966.

Scalapino, Robert A. (ed.). The Communist Revolu-
    tion in Asia: Tactics, Goals, and Achieve-
    ments. Englewood Cliffs, N.J.: Prentice-
    Hall, Inc., 1965.

_____. North Korea Today. New York: Frederick A. Praeger, 1963.

Sekai Seikei Chōsokai (ed.). Kankoku kita Chōsen jinmei jiten (Who's Who in South and North Korea). Tokyo: Sekai Seikei Chōsokai, 1966.

Sigmund, Paul E., Jr. (ed.). The Ideologies of the Developing Nations. New York: Frederick A. Praeger, 1963.

Suh, Dae-Sook. The Korean Communist Movement, 1918-1948. Princeton, N.J.: Princeton University Press, 1967.

Tsuboe Senji. Hokusen no kaihō junen (Ten Years of Liberated North Korea). Tokyo: Nikkan Rodo Tsushinsha, 1956.

Vatcher, William H. Panmunjom: The Story of the Korean Military Armistice Negotiations. New York: Frederick A. Praeger, 1958.

Wagner, Edward W. The Korean Minority in Japan. New York: Institute of Pacific Relations, 1951.

Whiting, Allen S. China Crosses the Yalu: The Decision to Enter the Korean War. New York: The Macmillan Company, 1960.

Yi Nayŏng. Chosŏn minjok haebang t'ujaeng sa (A History of the Korean People's Struggle for National Liberation). Tokyo: Hagu Sŏbang, 1960.

Yi Tong-jun (Lee Dong Jun). Hwansang kwa hyŏnsil: na ŭi kongsan chuŭi kwan (Fantasy and Fact: My Observations of Communism). Seoul: Tongbang T'ongsinsa, 1961.

Zagoria, Donald S. The Sino-Soviet Conflict. Princeton, N.J.: Princeton University Press, 1962.

ARTICLES AND PERIODICALS

Bradbury, John. "Sino-Soviet Competition in North
    Korea," The China Quarterly, No. 6 (April-
    June, 1961), 15-28.

Brzezinski, Zbigniew. "Patterns and Limits of the
    Sino-Soviet Dispute," Problems of Communism,
    IX (September-October, 1960), 1-7.

"Chajusŏng ŭl ongho haja" ("Let Us Defend Our Inde-
    pendence"), Kŭlloja (The Worker, P'yŏngyang),
    August, 1966, pp. 2-20.

"Ch'ŏngsan-li kyosi nŭn sahoe chuŭi nongch'on
    kyŏngni unyŏng ŭi chich'im ita" ("Ch'ongsan-li
    Instructions Provide Guidelines for Socialist
    Farm Management"), Kŭlloja, February, 1966,
    pp. 2-7.

Cho Soon Sung. "The Politics of North Korea's
    Unification Policies, 1950-1965," World Poli-
    tics, XIX (January, 1967), 218-41.

Chung, Joseph S. "Industrial Development of North
    Korea, 1945-1964: Some Strategic Quantitative
    Indicators," in Joseph S. Chung (ed.), Patterns
    of Economic Development: Korea (Kalamazoo,
    Mich.: Korea Research and Publication, Inc.,
    1966).

Chung Kiwon. "Japanese-North Korean Relations,"
    Asian Survey, IV (April, 1964), 788-803.

Cromley, Ray. "North Korea Sovietized," The Wall
    Street Journal, May 5, 1947.

Daniels, Robert V. "The Chinese Revolution in
    Russian Perspective," World Politics, XIII
    (January, 1961), 210-30.

Dean, Arthur H. "What It's Like to Negotiate with
    the Chinese," The New York Times Magazine,
    October 30, 1966, pp. 44ff.

Dubin, Wilbert B. "The Political Evolution of the
    P'yongyang Government," Pacific Affairs, XXIII
    (1950), 381-92.

Fisher, Charles A. "The Role of Korea in the Far
    East," Geographical Journal, 120 (1954), 282-98.

Gelman, Harry. "The Conflict: A Survey," Problems
    of Communism, XIII (March-April, 1964).

George, Alexander L. "American Policy-Making and
    the North Korean Aggression," World Politics,
    VII (January, 1955), 210-32.

Grajdanzev, Andrew J. "Korea Divided," Far Eastern
    Survey, October 10, 1945, pp. 281-83.

Haggard, M. T. "North Korea's International Posi-
    tion," Asian Survey, V (August, 1965), 375-88.

Johnson, Chalmers. "Building a Communist Nation
    in China," in Robert A. Scalapino (ed.),
    The Communist Revolution in Asia (Englewood
    Cliffs, N.J.: Prentice-Hall, Inc., 1965).

Kim Ilpyong J. "The Judicial and Administrative
    Structure in North Korea," in Robert A.
    Scalapino (ed.), North Korea Today (New York:
    Frederick A. Praeger, 1963), pp. 94-104.

Kim Il-sŏng. "Hyŏn chŏngse wa uri tang ŭi kwaŏp"
    ("The Present Political Situation and the Tasks
    of Our Party"), Kŭlloja, October, 1966.

Kim Joungwon A. "The 'Peak of Socialism' in North
    Korea: The Five and Seven Year Plans," Asian
    Survey, V (May, 1965), 255-69.

Koh, B. C. "North Korea and Its Quest for Autonomy,"
    Pacific Affairs, XXXVIII (Fall, Winter, 1965-
    66), 294-306.

Kuark, Yoon T. "Economic Development Contrast
    Between South and North Korea," in Joseph S.
    Chung (ed.), Patterns of Economic Develop-
    ment: Korea (Kalamazoo, Mich.: Korea Re-
    search and Publication, Inc., 1966).

Kŭlloja (The Worker, P'yŏngyang), 1952-67.

Lee Chong-Sik. "Kim Il-sŏng of North Korea,"
    Asian Survey, VII (June, 1967), 374-82.

_____. "Korean Communists and Yenan," The China
    Quarterly, No. 9 (January-March, 1962),
    182-92.

_____. "Korean Partition and Reunification," Journal of International Affairs, XVIII (1964), 221-33.

_____. "Land Reform, Collectivisation, and the Peasants in North Korea," in Robert A. Scalapino (ed.), North Korea Today (New York: Frederick A. Praeger, 1963), pp. 65-81.

_____. "Politics in North Korea: Pre-Korean War Stage," in Robert A. Scalapino (ed.), North Korea Today (New York: Frederick A. Praeger, 1963), pp. 3-16.

Lowenthal, Richard. "Schism Among the Faithful," Problems of Communism, XI (January-February, 1962), 1-14.

McCune, Shannon. "The Thirty-eighth Parallel in Korea," World Politics, I (1949), 223-32.

Minju Chosŏn (Democratic Korea, P'yŏngyang), 1960-67.

Nam Il. "The Foreign Policy of the Korean People's Democratic Republic," International Affairs (Moscow), IX (1958), 24-29.

New York Times, The, 1960-67.

Nodong Sinmun (Labor News, P'yŏngyang), 1952-67.

"North Korea," Far Eastern Economic Review (Hong Kong), 1965 Yearbook, pp. 231-34.

Paige, Glenn D. "Korea and the Comintern, 1919-35," Bulletin of the Korean Research Center, No. 13 (December, 1960), 1-25.

_____. "Korea," in Cyril E. Black and Thomas P. Thornton (eds.), Communism and Revolution (Princeton, N.J.: Princeton University Press, 1964), pp. 215-42.

_____. "North Korea and the Emulation of Russian and Chinese Behavior," in A. Doak Barnett (ed.), Communist Strategies in Asia (New York: Frederick A. Praeger, 1963), pp. 228-61.

P'yŏngyang Times, 1965-67.

Robinson, Joan. "Korean Miracle," Monthly Review,
     January, 1965, pp. 541-49.

Rudolph, Philip. "North Korea and the Path to
     Socialism," Pacific Affairs, XXXIII (June,
     1959), 131-43.

Rush, Myron. "Esoteric Communication in Soviet
     Politics," World Politics, XI (July, 1959),
     614-20.

Scalapino, Robert A., and Lee, Chong-Sik. "The
     Origins of the Korean Communist Movement,"
     Journal of Asian Studies, XX, No. 1 (November,
     1960), 9-31, and XX, No. 2 (February, 1961),
     149-67.

Scalapino, Robert A. "Moscow, Peking and the
     Communist Parties of Asia," Foreign Affairs,
     January, 1963, pp. 323-43.

_____. "The Foreign Policy of North Korea,"
     in Robert A. Scalapino (ed.), North Korea
     Today (New York: Frederick A. Praeger, 1963),
     pp. 30-50.

Schram, Wilbur, and Riley, John W., Jr. "Commu-
     nication in the Sovietized State, as Demon-
     strated in Korea," American Sociological
     Review, XVI (1951), 757-66.

Schram, Wilbur, et al. "Flight from Communism: A
     Report on Korean Refugees," Public Opinion
     Quarterly, (Summer, 1951), pp. 274-86.

Shabad, Theodore. "North Korea's Postwar Recovery,"
     Far Eastern Survey, XXV (June, 1956), 81-91.

"Soviet Economic Aid to North Korea," Bulletin of
     the Institute for the Study of the USSR
     (Munich), January, 1957, pp. 16-23.

Thomas, S.B. "Chinese Communists' Economic and
     Cultural Agreement with North Korea," Pacific
     Affairs, XXVII (1954), 61-65.

Tonga Ilbo /Dong-A Ilbo/ (East Asian Daily, Seoul),
     1966, 1967.

Triska, Jan F. "A Model for Study of Soviet For-
      eign Policy," American Political Science
      Review, LII (March, 1958), 64-83.

Washburn, John N. "Russia Looks at North Korea,"
      Pacific Affairs, (June, 1947), pp. 152-60.

_____. "The Soviet Press Views North Korea,"
      Pacific Affairs, (March, 1949), pp. 53-59.

_____. "Soviet Russia and the Korean Communist
      Party," Pacific Affairs, (March, 1950).

Washington Evening Star, 1964-67.

Washington Post, 1964-67.

Zagoria, Donald S. "Sino-Soviet Friction in Under-
      developed Areas," Problems of Communism, X
      (March-April, 1961), 1-12.

YEARBOOKS

Tōitsu Chōsen Shimbunsha. Tōitsu Chōsen nenkan
      (One Korea Yearbook), 1964 and 1965-66. Tokyo:
      Tōitsu Chōsen Shimbunsha, 1964 and 1966.

UNPUBLISHED MATERIAL

Suh, Dae-Sook. "The Elite Group of North Korea."
      Paper read at the annual conference of the
      Association for Asian Studies, Chicago, Ill.,
      March 20-22, 1967.

Yang, Key P. "A Guide to North Korean Periodicals
      and Newspapers." Unpublished manuscript,
      Korean section, Orientalia Division, Library
      of Congress, Washington, D.C., 1967.

_____. "The North Korean Regime, 1945-55."
      Unpublished Master's thesis, The American
      University, Washington, D.C., 1958.

ABOUT THE AUTHOR

Byung Chul Koh is an Associate Professor of Political Science at the University of Illinois at Chicago Circle. From 1963 to 1965, he was an Assistant Professor of Government at Louisiana State University.

A close observer of North Korea for several years, Dr. Koh is a native of Seoul and was in Korea during the Korean War. He has served as an officer in the Republic of Korea Air Force and has worked as a reporter for The Korean Republic, an English-language newspaper in Seoul.

Dr. Koh holds an LL.B. from Seoul National University, a master's degree in political science from Miami University (Oxford, Ohio), and an M.P.A. and a doctorate in public administration from Cornell University. He is author of The United Nations Administrative Tribunal and editor of Aspects of Administrative Development in South Korea. Dr. Koh has also contributed to many scholarly journals, including International Review of Administrative Sciences, Pacific Affairs, Western Political Quarterly, and Journal of Politics.

DATE DUE